WSU Military Veterans

The Washington State University Alumni Association (WSUAA) salutes the contributions and sacrifices made by WSU alumni who have served our country. The WSUAA is honored to endorse this book and proud of the extraordinary Cougars it profiles.

Tim Pavish
Alumni Executive Director

WSU Military Veterans

Heroes and Legends

C. James Quann

TORNADO CREEK
PUBLICATIONS

Spokane, Washington 2005

Published in 2005
Printed in the United States of America.
by
Walsworth Publishing Company
Marceline, Missouri 64658

Library of Congress Catalog Card Number: 2005926877
ISBN-13: 978-0-9740881-5-0
ISBN-10: 0-9740881-5-3

Front cover photo:
Capt. Asa Clark Jr. and his crew with a B-26 named *Los Lobos Grandes* in England in 1944,
courtesy Catherine "Kaye" (Mrs. Ace) Clark.

Back cover photo:
Lt. James Baker at the front in Korea, courtesy the James Baker family.

Tornado Creek Publications
Tony and Suzanne Bamonte
P.O. Box 8625
Spokane, Washington 99203-8625
(509) 838-7114

 **Dedicated to our military nurses, the unsung heroes caring for the men and women of our armed forces**

The Author

**C. James Quann,
Registrar Emeritus**

C. James Quann served higher education for more than 40 years, with faculty and administrative positions at four universities in three states (Eastern New Mexico University, Central Washington University, Washington State University and the University of California, Santa Cruz). In retirement, he holds the titles of WSU Registrar Emeritus and Coordinator, Veterans' Research. He served for more than 25 years as University Registrar (including four years as Associate Registrar) at Washington State, hence the title, Registrar Emeritus.

He is a Korean veteran (34th Infantry Regiment 24th Division) and founder of the WSU Veterans Memorial, initially built and dedicated in 1993, and competed in 2000. The memorial honors all WSU veterans, especially those 350-plus who were killed or missing in action in World War II, Korea, Vietnam, and the 1991 Persian Gulf War.

Quann and his wife, Barbara, have three children and six grandchildren. He is the author of four books and over 60 articles published in professional journals. His writings have also been published by the Spokane Corral of the Westerners in their publication *The Pacific Northwesterner.* These publications are: "Blazes of Glory: Biographies of Spokane Military Heroes;" Vol. 48, issue 1, 2004; "Mary B. Packingham: WSC's Own Florence Nightingale" (coauthored by Randall Johnson), Vol. 41, issue 4, 1997; and "Kate Williams Roberts, 1867-1947, Washington Territory Pioneer: Teacher, Preacher, Philosopher and Medical Care Giver," Vol. 44, issue 1, 2000.

This book is a massive achievement. The cumulative effect of all those stories is almost overwhelming, certainly moving and inspiring. Quann's writing is so good and the narratives so compelling that the book becomes a "page turner." I am struck not only with the heroism of these people, but with their level of achievement, both within the military and in their subsequent careers. It is hard to imagine any university having its veterans so well documented.

Laura Arksey, retired Librarian/Archivist, Eastern Washington State Historical Society and Assistant Editor, *The Pacific Northwesterner.*

Jim Quann has researched and written with great skill of the military service and the war experiences of Washington State University veterans. This book honors all of those who served in World War II, Korea, Vietnam, and the first Persian Gulf War. It is a book that must be read and remembered. They are stories of great heroism and courage in the face of extreme danger and stories of surviving impossible odds. This book is an epic achievement and because of it, these men and women will be long remembered.

Maj. Gen. Robert Goldsworthy (Ret.)

WSU Military Veterans is a passionate tribute and reflection of Jim Quann's ten-year journey to research and document the military experiences of many of our former Cougars. His admiration and respect for our valiant veterans is evident and was seasoned by his administrative responsibility for Veterans Programs as WSU Registrar. The book serves as testimony to our veterans' courage, sacrifice, and loyal service to our country. This book is a significant and lasting contribution to the Quann legacy.

Bob Smawley, WSU 1952

Table of Contents

Photo Index

Foreword

According to a recent newspaper report, the battleship *Arizona*, which was sunk by Japanese planes on December 7, 1941, still contains 500,000 gallons of fuel oil that is leaking a quart a day. At this rate, there will be an oil slick on the surface waters near the Pearl Harbor memorial for the next 500 years as a constant reminder of that tragic event and of the sacrifices made in World War II.

In fact, the far-flung conflict that followed Pearl Harbor provided the defining influence, the one indelible memory that altered forever the world view of an entire generation of Americans. As television newscaster and author Tom Brokaw has observed: "There was never a time in American life when so many people were involved in so many ways in a shared cause. It was impossible not to be affected in some fashion by the war effort, however far you may have been from the front lines." [1]

Undoubtedly the most important and enduring monuments of this war – and all the other wars fought by the United States – are the participants' own experiences of blood, sweat, and tears. That is the task C. James "Jim" Quann has shouldered in this volume – to compile a sampling of the shared wartime adventures and misadventures of Washington State College/University (in Pullman, Washington) alumni and others who have been associated with the institution, not only in World War II, but in other twentieth century American foreign conflicts as well.

A Korean veteran himself, Quann adds a keen understanding to these accounts of battlefield drama and heroism. Because World War II was the greatest foreign war in American history, and of relatively recent vintage, vignettes based largely on personal interviews with the "Greatest Generation" who fought in that conflict are more numerous. But there is a rich variety and an individual texture in each case. For example, the contribution of several women, all of whom volunteered, are recognized, including Jeanne Lewellen Norbeck, who became a Women's Air Force Service Pilot (WASP) in World War II when her husband entered the Army soon after Pearl Harbor. As a flight-test engineer, Jeanne Norbeck was killed while on a checkout flight of a repaired military plane.

Earlier, during World War I, nurse Mary Packingham served tirelessly in Pullman, at then Washington State College, in the great Spanish influenza pandemic, losing her own life to the dreaded disease.

Also included is the heart-wrenching story of Edith Munro, who, distressed by her son's heroic death on Guadalcanal, joined the Women's Reserve of the Coast Guard (SPARS) and served until the end of World War II. As the author points out, the names of those valiant women omitted from previous campus memorials, such as civilian nurse Packingham, have been inscribed on the modern Veterans Memorial at WSU.

Other notable features have equal appeal. The experiences of brothers – three in the case of the Fabian and two in the Goldsworthy families – as well as the heroism of Congressional Medal of Honor recipient James P. Fleming, are graphically depicted. Several accounts bear the well known, much dreaded label KIA (Killed in Action), while others stand out because of the slightly less appalling designation POW (Prisoner of War).

Familiar names in WSU history, such as President Glenn Terrell, who participated in the momentous D-Day invasion of World War II, and Veterinary Medicine Dean Leo Bustad, who spent many months as a POW in German stalags, also appear in these pages.

One after another, the intriguing biographies unfold, often in the person's own words – Doolittle air raid pilot (and later a German POW), Ross Greening, Air Force General Harry Goldsworthy Jr., who flew combat missions in World War II, Korea, and Vietnam, and Toll Seike, who died in Europe while serving with the most decorated unit of World War II, the 442nd Regimental Combat Team, one comprised of Americans of Japanese descent. From enlisted personnel to generals, in World War II to the Gulf War, they all get their due.

Likewise, the "big picture" of historical mainstream events helps provide the setting for individual case studies. For instance, at home in America, the worldwide Spanish influenza pandemic of 1918-19 that took the life of nurse Mary Packingham also killed a minimum of 550,000 Americans, at least 10 times more than the number of U.S. soldiers who died in action during World War I.

Unlike some other catastrophic disease onslaughts, which targeted children and the aged, the Spanish flu was especially deadly among the young from the late teens into the thirties. At Washington State College, as the author relates, 41 young servicemen quickly died; ten others in Pullman, including Packingham herself, suffered the same fate. Altogether, 825 individuals showed severe symptoms of the disease, making the five percent death rate at WSC and Pullman one of the lowest recorded.

Later, as part of the World War II framework, the overall military strategy of the Allied Powers against the Axis Powers involved two parts of the world, more specifically the European Theatre of Operations (ETO), which received top priority, and the Pacific

Theatre of Operations, which got less attention until Hitler's Germany was defeated.

In the popular culture, as exemplified by Hollywood films, this preferred status of the ETO persists today. Obviously cognizant of the imbalance, the author does an admirable job of giving representation to the Pacific Theatre as well as the ETO. The same can be said for the attention paid to the various other twentieth century conflicts, although understandable details about the campaigns, battles, and veterans of World War II most often appear.

Quite logically, the questions might arise as to why those closely associated with WSU deserve special consideration, why so many of them entered military service relatively soon after completing their degrees, and, also, why so many became officers immediately. Like other land grant schools, Washington State University can trace its origins back to the Morrill Act of 1862. U.S. Representative Justin S. Morrill of Vermont was the son of a village blacksmith who firmly believed that education was the gateway of opportunity for the average American. The congressional measure that bore his name allotted thirty thousand acres of public land for each senator and representative to the states for the founding of colleges in which "the leading object shall be, without excluding other scientific and classical studies, *and including military tactics* [italics added], to teach such branches of learning as are related to agriculture and the

mechanic arts . . . ." [2] The states themselves could decide how to fulfill these provisions. In short, the land-grant institutions not only had the responsibility of educating the nation's citizenry but of producing military officers as well.

The Washington Legislature, in implementing the Morrill Act's brief, imprecise reference to military training, made such instruction mandatory for male students. Other states did not write this specific obligation into law, but land-grant colleges generally emphasized the importance of what became the Army's Reserve Officers Training Corps (ROTC).

Over the years, the mistaken belief arose that congressional legislation required compulsory military training in those schools identified with the Morrill Act. In fact, Washington State College (now WSU) made this assertion in its 1925 catalog and for several years thereafter. As a result of the federal law's vagaries and the Washington legislation specifying compulsory military training, the ROTC flourished at WSC, probably more so than at many similar institutions. ROTC also became one of the most important organizations on campus, with its prestigious student officers' corps, its own band, and its special calendar of social events and military balls. Famed radio and television newscaster Edward R. Murrow (WSC speech major, class of 1930) always counted his selection as ROTC cadet colonel, or commanding officer, as one of the greatest honors and achievements of his college career.[3]

As early as 1917, the ROTC requirement at WSC had been altered to obligate all male freshmen and sophomores to enroll for only two years of basic training. Those who aspired to become either active duty or reserve commissioned officers had to sign up for the next two years of advanced military training, which included off-campus summer camps. Despite the change of policy, which mandated only two years of enrollment, advance ROTC leading to an officer's commission remained popular among young men, if for no other reason, because of the Army paychecks that helped pay college bills. Not until after World War II and the Korean War did another major shift come in military training requirements at land-grant institutions.

In 1957, the Department of Defense decided that it would no longer fund basic training for everyone but was interested only in the select group of students who would complete the advanced phase and who were, therefore, potential active duty officers. A few years later, in 1961, the WSU Board of Regents reluctantly asked the state legislature to abolish required ROTC, which was done. In another major adjustment, Congress passed the Reserve Officers Training Corps Vitalization Act of 1964, which created two-year and four-year scholarships and increased the monthly stipend substantially.

Still, the various military branches, including Army and Air Force contingents as well as a coordinate Navy program shared with the University of Idaho, usually had full components, even during turbulent times of antiwar protests such as the Vietnam era. In fact, from 1931 to 1969, even when not including the World War II period of the 1940s, WSU produced 1,411 Regular and Reserve Army officers, and from 1951 to 1969, the Air Force (established as a separate branch in 1947) commissioned 742 on the Pullman campus. The first female was commissioned from the WSU Army ROTC program in 1980. Significantly, the requirement for compulsory military training had remained in place during three great twentieth century wars – World Wars I and II and the Korean War – and personnel trained at WSU had served the nation in considerable numbers in each conflict, as well as in subsequent military emergencies.

As special attractions, the author explains his research procedures and documents the sources he has used in each account. In long appendices, he also lists those from WSC/WSU who died in major U.S. foreign conflicts and adds biographical information about them. The impressive contents of the book clearly reflect the countless hours of tedious, painstaking research, extensive travel, and thoughtful analysis that Jim Quann has devoted to what can only be termed a labor of love.

David H. Stratton, Professor Emeritus
WSU Department of History

Preface

The concept for this book first came to mind as I conducted the preliminary investigation and research that led to the founding and eventual construction in 1993 of the Washington State University Veterans Memorial in Pullman, Washington. My initial research uncovered dozens of documents listing inspirational accounts of gallantry and heroism on the part of WSC/WSU* men and women in the armed forces. At the time, those stories were simply filed away in my memory bank for future consideration.

The week of June 4, 1994, the 50th anniversary of D-Day, brought these initial discoveries back into focus. During that time, I took the opportunity to talk personally to a number of students, and I asked them what they thought of the D-Day invasion as recounted on nearly all of the television stations that week. Their answers were uniformly astounding; they didn't seem to know anything about it, didn't care, and expressed hope that their favorite television channels would soon return to regular fare. Thus, it dawned on me that there is a lot of our military history, especially

*Washington State College became Washington State University on July 1, 1959.

information pertaining to those whom historian Stephen Ambrose classified as "citizen soldiers," buried in military files in St. Louis, Missouri, and on military reservations; but few, outside of individual families, know or remember those heroic deeds. Because of this awareness, in June 1995, just prior to retirement, I accepted a WSU courtesy appointment (title but no pay) as University Registrar Emeritus and Coordinator, Veterans' Research. My appointment was made official by Provost Geoff Gamble (now the president of Montana State University) and the task I gladly accepted was to research the lives, heroism, and gallantry of selected veterans – students, faculty, and staff. Some gave their lives, or are still missing in action (MIA). Others, while serving in uniform, honored themselves, their state and the University. Many of their names are inscribed on the WSU Veterans Memorial.

I began the research with a population of about 600 veterans who served during World War II, Korea, Vietnam, and the first Persian Gulf War. My rationale for such an extensive project was that current public school curricula cover little about these wars, and contemporary and future students need to have some knowledge and understanding of the sacrifices made that allow Americans to enjoy the freedoms we all too often take for granted. The late WSC President Holland put it more succinctly in letters he wrote in 1944-45 to the families of students killed in World War II. An excerpt from one such letter read:

. . . Young people of future generations should know of John's sacrifice for he clearly exemplified the splendid spirit with which our young Americans are facing this tragic time. If Americans of the future can meet the demands of good citizens in days of peace with the same gallantry as John did in the days of war, such sacrifices as his may never again be necessary.

I had two major concerns in taking on this project. First, a very high percentage of the GIs I was researching were officers rather than enlisted personnel. This bothered me a great deal until I realized that a high percentage of our WSC/WSU students were Reserve Officer Training Corps (ROTC) cadets, later becoming commissioned officers.

My other concern was that I might not do justice to the memories of our gallant veterans, or worse yet, that I might not uncover records of heroism that ought to be in this volume. In either case, I apologize. While I found fairly reliable records for World War II, this was not true for the other conflicts. In addition, most military records are archived at the National Personnel Records Center in St. Louis. Due to a disastrous fire at the Missouri center in 1973, many of those records were destroyed. **Thus, I fully acknowledge that the research contained herein is incomplete, and I ask my readers to notify the Veterans Affairs section of the WSU Registrar's Office of case studies that ought to be included in any future volume.**

Are all of the veterans in this study heroes? Maybe yes, maybe no. I believe most are, but some, like Randall Johnson, the designer of the famous Cougar logo, Bob Smawley, Cougar historian and conscience of the university, and Edward R. Murrow, the fabled broadcaster, are legendary Cougars – hence, as in the title of this book, "Cougar Legends." The case studies that follow may be only the "tip of the iceberg," as I know there are many more yet to be discovered.

C. James Quann
Spokane, Washington
July 2005

Acknowledgments

I am deeply indebted to many people and agencies that had a profound influence on this project. First, I want to acknowledge and thank the many WSU veteran work-study students, led by Ms. Heather Reed, a Gulf War Navy veteran who spent countless hours researching and developing the list of veterans for this project. Most of their time was spent comparing, by hand, records received from the Department of Defense, via Marine Lt. General Keith A. Smith (WSC class of 1952), of those killed or missing in action, trying to match names from those lists with names in the WSU Registrar files.

I am also indebted to the WSU Registrar's staff, chiefly David Guzman and Marsha Sandall, for their conscientious help and advice, and to then Provost Geoff Gamble, who supported the project. Thanks, too, to Bob Smawley of the WSU Lewis Alumni Centre for constant encouragement and sharing of alumni files.

I am also deeply indebted to several of my colleagues at the Washington State University Spokane campus, notably Bart Brazier, our computer guru; Phyllis Hornbeck, Finance and Operations; Helen Bolen for secretarial assistance; and Dean William Gray for providing office accommodations.

Within the military, I am indebted to Msgt. William A. Tooles of the Records Procedures Branch of the Air Force; William G. Swarens, head of Personnel Management Support Branch for the Marine Corps; Bob Browning, Coast Guard Historian Commandant; and B. B. Herman, Director, Personnel Records Systems Division, Department of the Navy. I am also grateful for the continued help and guidance of personnel in the National Personnel Records Center in St. Louis, particularly Ms. Barbara Bauman, management analyst, who arranged and hosted my visits to the Records Center, and Ms. Ange F. Blair, Freedom of Information and Privacy Act Officer, Department of the Army.

I also acknowledge the many contributions of Pat Caraher, senior editor of the *Washington State Magazine*, for his tremendous help along the way, for sharing photographs from his files, and for authoring the Edward R. Murrow story in this book. I also wish to spotlight and thank Randall Johnson, pioneer designer of the famous Cougar logo, for his thoughtful help and advice on my journey. Many additional obligations have been incurred during the research phase of this book; some are as impossible to identify as they are to repay.

I also wish to acknowledge and thank the PEMCO Insurance Company, through board member Edward K. Erickson (WSC class of 1946) for the grant that helped underwrite the research phase of this project. In addition, I thank, with sincere gratitude, my wife Barbara (Barbara Heathman, WSC class of 1954) for the unending support and forbearance that allowed this project to be completed. My thanks and appreciation to Laura Arksey for her encouraging words and editing contributions, to Nancy Compau for a final proofreading, and to Doris Woodward for preparing the index. And my grateful thanks and gratitude to my publishers, Tony and Suzanne Bamonte, whose patience, skill and dedication to accuracy helped shape this book.

Finally, I owe a debt of gratitude to the dozens and dozens of men and women veterans who volunteered to sit with me for taped oral-history interviews. Although I used only small portions of the interview data for this manuscript, each interview was transcribed, photos and supporting documentation added, and the documents were printed, bound, and filed with the Archives Section of the WSU Library. Moreover, to the 18 or so who passed away before my scheduled interviews could take place, I salute and say goodbye with a few lines from "Taps," that sad and melancholy tune that has become a soldier's final farewell and tribute:

Day is done, gone the sun,
From the lake, from the hills,
From the sky.
All is well, safely rest,
God is nigh.

WORLD WAR II

Lieutenant (JG) I. Katherine Achre (Chew)
Navy WAVES

Ida Katherine "Kay" Achre was born April 14, 1917 to Mr. and Mrs. J. A. Achre of Spokane, Washington. She graduated from Spokane's North Central High School in 1935. She enrolled at Washington State College that fall, majoring in business administration with emphasis on accounting. A member of Pi Beta Phi sorority, Kay dropped out of college in 1937 due to Depression-related financial woes.[1]

Engaged to a fellow Spokane resident and experienced pilot, Kay took flying lessons and earned her private license. Her fiancé, Robert L. Little, enlisted in the Army Air Corps and volunteered for duty, becoming a fighter pilot with the "Flying Tigers" in Burma. Robert Little was killed in action May 22 1942. His death prompted Kay to want to do her part for the war effort.

The newly formed women's Navy, Women Accepted for Volunteer Emergency Service (WAVES) appealed to Kay, so she

Lt. (JG) Katherine Achre. *(Photo courtesy Katherine Chew.)*

Battalion Commander Lt. (JG) Katherine Achre's unit marching in the funeral procession for President Franklin D. Roosevelt, April 14, 1945. *(Photo courtesy U. S. Navy.)*

immediately volunteered. She was assigned to Midshipmen's School in Northampton, Massachusetts, and classified as seaman.

After training, she became an ensign assigned to the Shipbuilding Division of the Navy Bureau of Ships. The offices were situated across the reflection pool from the Lincoln Memorial in Washington, D.C.[2] Kay was responsible for coordinating clerical personnel activities of approximately 300 military and civilian personnel. Assigned various other responsibilities, she was eventually promoted to lieutenant (JG) and made battalion commander

of the First WAVE Battalion. Her work with the Shipbuilding Division seemed inspired, and she received accolades from many high-ranking officers, including a rather difficult and opinionated young Captain Hyman Rickover, who much later gained fame as the "father" of the U.S. nuclear submarine fleet.[3]

Lieutenant Achre was discharged from the Navy two months after the war's end and returned to WSC to complete her studies. After receiving her degree, this former Navy officer and mother of two children taught accounting for the Extension Division of WSC in Spokane, and later managed her own accounting firm. She earned a master's degree from Whitworth College in 1970 and taught for 14 years at Spokane Falls Community College before retiring. She married Firth J. Chew in 1984 and presently resides in Spokane.

Sergeant Dale W. Aldrich
B-17 Belly Gunner and
Stalag 17 Prisoner of War

Dale Wilfred Aldrich was born February 23, 1921 in Coulee City, Washington, to Mr. and Mrs. C. H. Aldrich. He graduated from Coulee City High School in June 1939 and enrolled at Washington State College that fall, majoring in business administration. Money was short, so after completing his first semester, he needed to drop out to work for the Bonneville Power Administration, helping to survey for the new power lines that were to transmit power from Grand Coulee Dam to the Puget Sound area. He returned to WSC for the 1940-41 academic year, but dropped out again to join the war effort.[1]

In July 1942, Aldrich received his draft notice and reported to Fort Lewis, near Tacoma, Washington, for induction. After initial training at Fort Lewis, he was reassigned to continue basic training at Jefferson Barracks, Missouri. While there, he was selected to attend the "Air College," a training base for aircraft mechanics. Buck Private Dale Aldrich finished Air College training on New Year's Eve, 1942 and reported to the AFB near San Antonio, Texas, for duty as an aircraft mechanic.[2] Serving as a mechanic seemed like a rather dull assignment to Aldrich, so when he learned the Army Air Force was seeking gunners, he volunteered for gunnery school at Laredo, Texas, to learn how to operate 50-caliber machine guns. At the end of gunnery training, he was promoted to sergeant to fly in combat.[3]

Aldrich was sent for further training to an air base near Moses Lake, Washington, just 30 from his home in Coulee City. There he was assigned as a member of a B-17 crew and met his fellow crew members with whom he would serve from then on. The B-17, nicknamed the "Flying Fortress," was armed with thirteen 50-caliber machine guns: two in the nose of the aircraft, two above, one in the midsection, two in the ship's waist area, two in the tail, two in the chin turret, and two in the ball turret manned by the belly gunner.[4] Aldrich was initially assigned to be a waist gunner, but his colleague, the belly gunner, was a big man who didn't fit properly into the ball turret. Aldrich, being slight in stature, traded places with the larger man to become the official belly gunner of the crew. This move undoubtedly saved his life later on when his plane was shot down. He was quoted as saying that the inside of the ball (belly) turret felt almost like sitting in a recliner chair, except the arms were connected to two machine guns. When he needed to fire the guns, all he had to do was press the buttons with his thumbs. Two foot pedals were located at such a position that he could aim the guns with his feet. It took some practice but he soon found that he could turn the whole ball turret in a full circle and shoot both guns in any direction (except straight up).[5]

In August 1943, Sergeant Aldrich and his crew were transferred for further training to Walla Walla, Washington. In September, he and his crew were sent by train to St. Louis, Missouri, and then on to Camp Kilmer in New Jersey. In October, he was ordered overseas, traveling by ship to England. He arrived in Liverpool and went by train to Horham, assigned to the 95th Bomber Group. He expected to fly a maximum of 25 bombing missions, and then be sent home.[6]

Each crew had a plane, and all the bombers had distinctive names. Aldrich's plane was christened the *Princess Pat*, perhaps after Aldrich's younger sister, Patsy, or the pilot's wife, Pat. He flew his first two missions over Europe in mid-November. His third mission was destined for Enden, Germany, a seaport where the Germans had sub pens in place (ports used for rearming, repairing, and refueling Nazi submarines). His next mission was to Munster, a port city in western Germany, and a key railroad center. It was December 22, 1943 and Aldrich's fourth and final mission. Luck had been with him on the first three missions, but on his fourth, luck ran out.

Sergeant Dale Aldrich's B-17 experienced engine troubles and had to drop out of the formation and head home. Once away from the protection provided by the larger formation, the *Princess Pat* became a "sitting duck" under attack by numerous German fighters. His plane received several direct hits, killing both waist gunners, and the pilot and copilot went down with the plane. The survivors were ordered to bail out. Aldrich's parachute opened properly and while descending he was subjected to withering ground fire. He watched as his plane exploded in air. He and two fellow soldiers landed near a grove of trees, and hid out there until discovered. Captured, they were placed in the back of a truck and driven to a prison in a small town near Amsterdam.

On December 26, 1943, Sergeant Aldrich and his two friends were taken by train to a prison near Frankfurt am Main, Germany, where they were placed in solitary confinement. Daily rations per prisoner were one slice of bread, some water, and occasionally some ersatz tea. Sometime in January 1944, the three were placed aboard another train headed for a prison camp, Stalag 17, near a little town called Krems in Austria. Each day at Stalag 17 began with a whistle calling the prisoners to Appell, or roll call. They had two roll calls each day, at 7:00 a.m. and 6:00 p.m. The barracks were cold with no heat, and the supply of food was minimal except for an occasional Red Cross parcel. Prisoners were always cold, hungry, and bored, but the boredom was somewhat relieved by planning various escape attempts. Stalag 17 became a household word after the war when a famous World War II movie by the same name detailed the various escape attempts as well as the German stoolie who passed himself off as an American and kept the Nazi officials informed of the escape plans.

On April 1, 1945, the German guards ordered Sergeant Aldrich and his fellow prisoners to leave the camp for a march westward, away from the advancing Russian Army. The Americans were divided into eight groups of 500 men each, and the march began. They marched south from Krems to the Danube River and then turned west. They walked all day every day without provisions by the Germans for food or water. Thus, the prisoners scrounged for whatever they could find in fields along the way. After days of this treatment, Aldrich came down with a severe case of dysentery. On May 2, an American Army officer approached them, shouting that they were no longer prisoners.

On May 8, after several days of eating and sleeping, the now-liberated prisoners were flown out to Camp Lucky Strike, just outside of Le Havre, France. Sergeant Aldrich spent a week in the hospital before boarding a ship headed for home. He arrived in New York later that month and finally made it home to Coulee City in June only to discover that his hometown sweetheart had married another while he was in prison.

Aldrich was formally discharged on November 19, 1945. He was awarded the Purple Heart with Bronze Oak Leaf Cluster, the Prisoner of War Medal, Good Conduct Medal, American Campaign Medal, Europe-Africa-Middle Eastern Campaign Medal with Silver Service Star, and the World War II Victory Medal.[7]

Elizabeth L. Anderson
Physical Therapist to the Troops
in North Africa

Elizabeth Lee Anderson was born on July 15, 1913 in Tacoma, Washington. She graduated from Lincoln High School in June 1932 and enrolled at Washington State College that fall. She majored in physical education and was an active leader on campus. Elizabeth was a member of Spurs, Women's Athletic Association Council, Intercollegiate Play Day Chairman, and member of Pi Lambda Theta. She served as secretary to Gamma Phi Epsilon, the women's hockey team, and served as president of Crimson "W" her senior year. She graduated from WSC in June 1937 with honors and a bachelor's degree in physical education.[1] She became a licensed physical therapist.

Elizabeth was assigned to an Army hospital in Egypt. An article with her photograph read:

> *Carrying her share of the burden of war in the sand-swept battlefront in Egypt, Miss Elizabeth Anderson, daughter of Mr. and Mrs. Albert Anderson, of 3584 Spokane Avenue [Tacoma], arrived safely in the land of the Pharaohs on October 31st [1943]. She hinted however, that the trip across the Atlantic and through the Mediterranean with a convoy of army troop ships was not altogether uneventful. Miss Anderson, chief physical therapist in an army hospital . . . is now settled in her permanent station somewhere in the mountains behind the lines. She is a graduate of Lincoln High School, Washington State College, and Walter Reed Hospital in Washington, D.C. Her first post was at the army-navy hospital in Hot Springs, Arkansas. She went from there to LaGarde General Hospital in New Orleans, La., where she was chief physical therapist, and later accepted her present civilian position with the army.[2]*

Army Captain Emil S. Bitar
Killed In Action - Sicily
Distinguished Service Cross

Emil S. Bitar was born March 27, 1913, the son of Mr. and Mrs. Saleem Anthony Bitar of Raymond, Washington. He graduated from Raymond High School in June 1931 and enrolled at WSC that fall as a political science major. He received a bachelor's degree in political science in June 1935 and an Army Reserve commission on the same day. He was promoted to first lieutenant in the Infantry Reserve on August 3, 1938.[1] He later earned a law degree from the University of Washington and practiced law, serving as city attorney in his hometown.[2] Lieutenant Bitar went on active duty on June 16, 1941. He left for his overseas assignment in May 1942 and received his captain's bars. He was awarded the Distinguished Service Cross posthumously with the following citation:

Emil S. Bitar . . . Captain, Company 'E,' 15th Infantry, for extraordinary heroism in action on 4 August 1943, near San Fratello, Sicily. Captain Bitar personally led his company in the attack against strong enemy positions atop a hill 566 feet high, held by an estimate of one battalion of enemy infantry, reinforced by automatic weapons, mortars, and artillery. When 350 yards from the enemy machine guns and riflemen, the company came under an intense artillery barrage which lasted for two hours and inflicted approximately 30 percent casualties. At the time of this barrage, the company was in the midst of an enemy mine field, from which more than 70 antipersonnel mines were later removed. His first sergeant was killed by shellfire, and Captain Bitar was seriously wounded in the side by the same burst, rendering his left arm useless. In spite of his wounds, Captain Bitar rallied his company and led them forward through the minefield to within 150 yards of the enemy positions, where he was mortally wounded by a mortar shell. Captain Bitar's leadership and bravery under intense enemy fire while seriously wounded was an inspiration to the men of his command, and reflects the finest traditions of the military service. By command of Lieutenant General Patton.[3]

Captain Bitar was also awarded the Purple Heart, and one of the main streets on the Fort Lewis Reservation in Washington was named in his honor. The captain was survived by his wife Frances and two daughters.

Colonel Robert V. Bowler
Guerrilla Warfare Commander, Philippines

Robert Verne Bowler, a lad from Bellingham, Washington, entered Washington State College in September 1929 and graduated with a bachelor's degree in business administration in February 1933. He enrolled in advanced Reserve Officer Training Corps (ROTC) at the beginning of his junior year, serving as a battalion commander during his senior year.[1] He went on active duty before Pearl Harbor and was dispatched to the Philippine Islands. He was reported missing in action in May 1942 shortly after the fall of Mindanao. His name was engraved on the WSU Veterans Memorial along with other Cougar war dead. However, it should not have been because, unbeknown to the military, Bowler escaped into the jungle and spent the rest of the war heading up various guerrilla activities. This is his story.

His first assignment after Pearl Harbor was to command the defenses of the Malabang Airfield at Malabang, Lanao, on the island of Mindanao. In early January 1942, he was transferred to Digos, Davao, where he commanded a battalion of USAFFE troops that were in continuous combat until the first week of March. He was then made commanding officer of the 3rd Battalion, 103rd Infantry Regiment to defend against the Japanese landings on Mindanao. Although driven off the beach on May 4, 1942, he kept his battalion intact, fighting a delaying action, and, although taking heavy losses, he and his dwindling number

Colonel Robert V. Bowler viewing his World War II medals.
(Photo courtesy Washington State University.)

of men fought through multiple enemy ambushes as they fled to higher ground. On May 10, he learned of the surrender of Mindanao. Rather than surrender, he sent his few remaining Filipino troops to their homes, and he and several of his fellow Americans escaped into the jungle. With assistance from friendly civilians, they were able to stay hidden and avoid capture. The following January, using a homemade radio and scrounged parts, he made contact with General Douglas MacArthur's headquarters in Australia. Word came back for him to continue to recruit and train guerrilla forces to oppose and harass the Japanese invaders. In November 1943, MacArthur made Bowler chief of staff for the Tenth Military District, and in January 1944, he became commanding officer of "A" Corps, which included four divisions of USFIP soldiers and garrisoned six of the nine provinces on Mindanao. By this time he was commanding more than 28,000 troops. The guerrillas set up watch stations on the seacoast to watch for enemy shipping. When sighted, the information was relayed to U.S. submarines operating in Philippine waters. Lieutenant Colonel Bowler and his men plotted enemy planes, troop movements by land and sea, identified targets for air raids, and continually harassed the enemy from ambush and hit-and-run attacks.

In March 1945, Bowler was promoted to full colonel and ordered to report to 8th Army Headquarters on Leyte as liaison officer in support of the American occupation of Mindanao.

By midsummer, he was in command of a regiment of American troops and a division of Philippine troops with the mission of mopping up various pockets of resistance. His guerrilla activities were at an end. He was officially missing in action from early May 1942 to July 11, 1945, had been wounded twice, and suffered with reoccurring bouts of malaria and dysentery. Nevertheless, he had survived.

In late July 1945, Bowler left the Philippines with orders to report to the Command and General Staff School at Fort Leavenworth, Kansas.[2] For his long and heroic service, he was awarded the Distinguished Service Cross, Purple Heart with the Oak Leaf Cluster, two Legion of Merit medals, Bronze Star, Silver Star, Air Medal, Combat Infantryman's Badge, and several Campaign Medals. The citations accompanying Colonel Bowler's Distinguished Service Cross and Silver Star awards covered the same battle. The following is the citation for the Distinguished Service Cross:

Colonel Robert V. Bowler . . . For extraordinary heroism in action near Cagayan, Misamis Oriental, Mindanao, Philippine Islands on 3 and 4 May 1942. When the enemy, after a terrific naval bombardment of the beach defenses attempted on 3 May 1942, to establish a beachhead in his sector, Colonel Bowler as an Infantry Battalion Commander, heroically repulsed several attempted landings and continued the gallant fight until his beach defenses were overwhelmed. Cut off from other American forces he skillfully withdrew the remnants of his forces and fought a delaying action. Heroically and at great risk to personal safety and under heavy enemy naval and ground fire, he remained in the front lines encouraging and leading his small force in a losing battle. Although other United States Forces surrendered, Colonel Bowler withdrew with the remnants of his battalion to the hills from which he continued the fight as a guerrilla leader. Colonel Bowler's leadership, courage, and complete disregard for his own safety, during these trying days, were an inspiration to his troops and bring the highest honor and prestige to the fighting spirit of the American soldier, and reflect great credit on himself and the military services.

The following is the citation for the Award of the Legion of Merit:

Colonel Robert V. Bowler . . . For exceptionally meritorious conduct in the performance of outstanding service on the island of Mindanao, Philippines, during the period from 15 October 1942 to 1 November 1943. In the early days of the resistance movement, Colonel Bowler, by outstanding leadership, was responsible for the organization of the home defense group in the vicinity of Talakag, Bukidnon. Using initiative of the highest degree, he organized the training of troops, formed a civil government, maintained transportation facilities, established hospitals, recruited voluntary labor, and formulated and executed plans for harassing the enemy. Because of his untiring efforts and zealous devotion to duty, the 109th Division, Tenth Military District was formed and activated. Colonel Bowler's achievement at this time contributed greatly to the successful guerrilla operations on Mindanao and the reestablishment of the prestige of American leadership after the defeat of the American Forces by the Japanese in the Philippines. His actions are in keeping with the highest tradition of the Armed Forces of the United States.

Although essentially an infantry commander during the reoccupation, because of his familiarity with the terrain and enemy emplacements, Colonel Bowler made many flights as an aerial observer, helping to locate attack routes and enemy troop movements. He was awarded the Air Medal for this valor and the citation read:

For meritorious achievement while participating in aerial flights in the combat zone during the period 17 April to 30 June 1945. Colonel Bowler made frequent flights in liaison and combat aircraft, over dangerous terrain in order to better coordinate the efforts of the Philippine units under his command. Many of these flights were reconnaissance missions over enemy territory to gain information of road and bridge conditions, and to gain information of enemy movements, necessary for contemplated operations. Through his many flights under dangerous combat conditions, he was able to furnish valuable enemy information for planning.

The following is the citation for his Bronze Star:

Colonel Robert V. Bowler . . . with military operations against the enemy in Mindanao, Philippine Islands, during the period 6 May to 30 June 1945. As Commanding Officer of a guerilla division, he relieved the attacking U.S. troops of guarding lines of communications and bridges in captured areas. From troops under his command, he established roadblocks, patrolled large areas, and furnished guides for American patrols. His intimate knowledge of the terrain, trails, and possible locations of enemy strong points assisted U.S. ground force commanders in planning operations and reduced casualties through previous knowledge and cautious approach to dangerous areas. His wide experience in handling of the island's people of many creeds and races assisted the commander and civil affairs officers in establishing suitable civil government in the different areas. His leadership, wide experience, administrative ability, and loyalty were of great benefit to U.S. force commanders, relieved them of the difficult task of policing and guarding wide areas and contributed greatly to the rapid and successful conclusion of the campaign.[3]

Colonel Bowler retired with the rank of colonel in 1948, after 20 years in the Reserves and Regular Army. He and his wife Lillian now reside in the Seattle area.

Author's note: For a more detailed account of guerrilla warfare in the Philippines, read *American Guerrilla in the Philippines* by Ira Wolfert, published by Simon and Schuster, New York, 1945.

Lieutenant George B. Brain
Superintendent of Schools
WSU College of Education Dean

George Brain was born in Thorp, Washington, on April 25, 1919. He graduated from Thorp High School and attended the University of Washington from autumn 1939 through spring 1942. He majored in education with a minor in Japanese, but did not complete his degree until after the war. He enlisted in the Navy in 1942, and then transferred to the Marines with a commission as an intelligence officer. After the war, he returned to Central Washington College of Education and under the GI Bill completed both a bachelor's and master's degree. He earned his doctoral degree from the Teachers College of Columbia University.

After his Naval and Marine training at San Diego, California, Boulder, Colorado, and Quantico, Virginia, Lieutenant Brain was assigned to Hawaii then shipped out to the Fourth Marine Division

Lieutenant George B. Brain, Dean, WSU College of Education 1965-1983, at the George B. Brain Library in Cleveland Hall.
(Photo courtesy Washington State University.)

on Tarawa. Using his Japanese language skills, he was to capture and translate Japanese documents, attempt to convince enemy soldiers to surrender, and capture and interrogate prisoners. His duties included serving as an interpreter aboard the USS *Sheridan* en route to the Marianas Islands in June 1944, and as a combat interpreter on Tinian of the Marianas Island in July 1944. He was in combat in the battle of Iwo Jima from February through March of 1945, and in May and June in Okinawa, followed by service as an intelligence officer during the initial occupation of Japan.[1]

On Iwo Jima, Lieutenant Brain was in the thick of the battle with the Fourth Marine Division. As before, his role was to work, sometimes behind enemy lines, attempting to capture and interrogate enemy prisoners, and to translate enemy maps, records, and other captured documents that might help substantiate what the Japanese were attempting or were using as battle plans. After a harrowing experience, he wrote the following account of his experience:

> *After a couple of rough and trying days, I am back where the only thing that can bother me is my own conscience. Yesterday, six of us went on patrol; we had a war dog with us and we went into a Jap cave looking for prisoners and documents and anything else that we might find of value. The dog and his handler went first, then an MP rifleman, then myself followed by one Jap we had taken*

prisoner the day before and who had consented to lead us through the cave on our search for gear, and then another interpreter and two more riflemen brought up the rear. If you have ever looked at the inside of an ant hill you have a very definite and clear picture of this cave . . . It consisted of one main tunnel, which was about four feet high with a series of smaller tunnels branching off from the main one. There were eight separate entrances to the main tunnel and another that went clear through under the hill and came out behind Jap lines . . . It was quite a terrifying experience . . . We were underground going through this thing for about five and one-half hours and our search was very fruitful. The Nip we had with us led us to the HQ of a Jap unit and we picked up some good documents . . . It [the cave] was littered with literally hundreds of Jap dead and stunk like a tomb, and every three or four feet there would be a mine or booby-trap so you can see that we had to proceed with caution. I've been in many of these caves before but I have never seen anything that would compare with this. We got out eight prisoners, most of them wounded. We only lost one man and I guess considering everything, we were very fortunate . . .[2]

In another skirmish on Iwo Jima, Brain was sent to scout enemy positions on the northern corner of the island. The enemy, hidden in deep caves, had held up the advancing Marines for eight days, and something had to be done. Lieutenant Brain was sent with a squad of men to investigate and, if possible, to take prisoners. He was told that Navy pilots would be filming in the area, trying to locate enemy positions. They advanced over 300 yards into enemy territory without drawing fire, only to see a Navy plane flying low overhead, presumably filming the area. On a second pass, within 200 yards of Brain's position, the plane was hit and subsequently crashed. Later, Brain was informed that the dead pilot was his Thorp High School schoolmate Leon Ellsworth. On a previous mission, Ellsworth had taken exceptionally clear photos of enemy emplacements, and his efforts were recognized with posthumous awards of the Air Medal, the Distinguished Flying Cross, and two Gold Stars in lieu of a second and third Air Medal.[3]

Shortly after the war ended in late August 1945, Lieutenant Brain was sent into Japan, as part of the occupying forces, to conduct intelligence work. He and supporting personnel gathered intelligence information in the Hiroshima and Nagasaki areas while the ground was still "hot" with radiation from the atomic blasts.

Brain separated from active duty in late February 1946 and was awarded the Navy and Marine Corps Achievement Medals, the Joint Meritorious Unit Award, Meritorious Unit Citation, the Occupation (of Japan) Medal, and the Armed Forces Service Medal. He felt very fortunate that a Purple Heart was not included in his awards.

Captain Brain reunited with his wife Harriet and son George Jr., born in 1942 in Ellensburg. He enrolled at Central Washington College of Education to complete bachelor's and master's degrees in education. After working as both a teacher and principal in Ellensburg and Bellevue, Washington, he became assistant superintendent, followed by superintendent of schools in Bellevue in 1953. In 1959, and after an outstanding career at Bellevue, he was appointed superintendent of schools in

George B. Brain (L) and a seaman buddy at boot camp. *(Photo courtesy the George Brain family.)*

Baltimore, Maryland. In 1965, following a splendid career in public schools, and after facing off the well-known atheist, Madelyn O'Hare, in the U.S. Supreme Court decision on school prayer, Brain replaced Dr. Zeno Katterle as dean of the College of Education at Washington State University. Dr. Brain ended his distinguished career in education with retirement in 1983.

In 1986, Dean Brain was honored with the official naming of the WSU Education Library, located in Cleveland Hall, as the "George B. Brain Education Library."

Captain Arthur Brunstad
Office of Strategic Services Operative, China/Burma Theatre

Arthur Brunstad was born on February 24, 1908 on a small farm in southern Norway near the town of Orandahl. He came to the United States with his parents and two brothers at age 12. The family settled near Port Orchard, Washington. Speaking only Norwegian, he was taught English in grade school.[1] He graduated from South Kitsap High School in June 1926 and enrolled at Washington State College that fall, majoring in chemistry. He joined the Phi Sigma Kappa fraternity in his sophomore year, and graduated in June 1931. While in college, he played football until injured, and later became the intramural light-heavyweight champion boxer.[2] After earning a master's degree in chemistry in 1933, he accepted a position first with a firm in Wenatchee, then with the U.S. Bureau of Reclamation, working on the Grand Coulee Dam Project.

After the Japanese attack on Pearl Harbor, Brunstad volunteered for the Army and went on active duty in early 1942 as a second lieutenant in the Army Chemical Warfare Service. He earned his first lieutenant's bars in 1942 and was promoted to captain in 1943. Captain Brunstad was then recruited by the Office of Strategic Services (OSS) for a covert airdrop into Norway. The OSS selected him because he was fluent in Norwegian and still had family residing in Norway. Eventually the Norway operation was scrapped and Brunstad was trained for a behind-the-lines clandestine operations in Japanese-held territory in China and Burma. His role with the OSS was to train native soldiers to fight, collect and analyze strategic information, and to conduct sabotage operations. Captain Brunstad was successful in all three roles. Although he experienced many narrow escapes, he managed to survive unharmed through the end of the war. The Army unit he led, the OSS Detachment 101, received a Presidential Citation for disrupting Japanese activities in China and Burma, and for furnishing strategic information in support of U.S. air operations in that theatre.[3] He was discharged in the fall of 1945. Brunstad returned to his family, wife Helen and sons Harold and George, as well as to his former job at Grand Coulee Dam. Later he worked for the Atomic Energy Commission at Hanford as chief of Nuclear Safety. Mr. Brunstad died in January 2002.

Lieutenant Archie M. Buckley*
WSC Cougar Quarterback
Navy Hero Killed in Action at Iwo Jima

Archie Myrl Buckley was born July 16, 1906 in Colville, Washington. After graduation from Colville High School, Archie blazed a brilliant 1926-1930 path through WSC athletics starring as a forward in basketball, third baseman on the Cougar baseball team, and sensational quarterback. He graduated in June

1930, coached football for a year at Centralia High School and, in the fall of 1931, joined the staff at North Central High School in Spokane as teacher and head football coach. He coached his team to the Spokane city football championship in 1933 and his teams were a force to contend with from that point on. At age 36 in 1943, Archie volunteered for naval duty and was assigned to the aircraft carrier USS *Saratoga*.

On February 21, 1945, the *Saratoga* was in action off the shores of Iwo Jima. Lieutenant Buckley, at his post as catapult officer, saw a Japanese kamikaze plane zeroing in on the launch area of his ship. Buckley died a hero's death in a frantic effort to protect his men while saving several crew members and pilots from instant death. He was awarded the Bronze Star for his heroism. The citation, signed by the Secretary of the Navy on behalf of President Roosevelt, read:

For heroic achievement as Catapult Officer on board the USS Saratoga in action against enemy Japanese forces near Iwo Jima, Volcano Islands, on February 21, 1945. First to observe the Japanese plane headed in on lightning course for his carrier, Lieutenant Buckley remained in the line of enemy strafing, desperately striving to attract the attention of his crews and the pilots of two aircraft secured to the catapults. Refusing to seek cover for himself, he directed all his men to positions of comparative safety, and was still at his post when the

Lieutenant Archie M. Buckley. *(Photo courtesy James Buckley.)*

attacker crashed into the forward end of the flight deck on the starboard side. Through his alert warning and gallant consideration of others in the face of imminent peril to himself, the lives of several men were saved. His courageous conduct was in keeping with the highest traditions of the United States Naval Service. [1]

Lieutenant Buckley was also awarded the Navy Cross and Purple Heart, posthumously. Ensign Leo Andrecht, one of the pilots Archie saved, gave the following account of the kamikaze attack:

A plane director had just completed hooking my plane to the starboard catapult, when I suddenly saw Lieutenant Buckley frantically waving his arms to attract my attention. Upon getting it, he then pointed starboard aft. As I turned to look aft, I saw him trying to attract Ensign Powell's attention on the port catapult. I saw two enemy planes, one on starboard beam, coming in very fast and strafing with an obvious intent of flying into the starboard side, the other, further aft of which, I soon lost sight of. I unbuckled my shoulder straps and made the starboard life nets as the first bomb hit the port catapult. I sincerely believe that Lieutenant Buckley's courage to stay and warn us of the impending danger, before seeking safety himself, kept me from possible death or serious burns. [2]

Cougar Three-Sport Star

Longtime Cougar sports reporter, Dick Fry, noted that Buckley was an all-around athlete, earning three varsity letters in football as quarterback in 1927-1930, lettering three years in basketball, and winning two awards in baseball during his WSC athletic career.[3] In 1929 his teammates voted that he be awarded the prestigious J. Fred Bohler Medal, WSC's greatest athletic honor. The following passage from the 1930 college yearbook, *Chinook*, describes Buckley's athletic career:

That blonde Cougar flash was known all along the coast for his brilliant football work. No game was ever drab or dull as long as Buckley was on the field, for his specialty was to uncork a sensational play any place and any time. One of the best field generals in the Northwest, he was placed on the Northern division all-star team as quarterback. The pint-sized signal barker was a hard man to down despite his lack of weight. He shone mostly in returning punts, but was also good for yardage on quarterback sneaks and quick-opening line plays. He possessed one of the best-educated toes in the conference and more than one ball game was broken up by his well-aimed place kicks. Remember the little substitute who raced onto the field to reorganize the tottering Cougars in their Homecoming clash with Washington last fall? Washington had swept through the Cougars for two touchdowns, but the peppery signal caller brought them out of their lethargy and led the drive that sent the Huskies back on their haunches to a 20-13 trimming. That dash and fire that was not to be denied was typical of "Buck's" gridiron career.[4]

Coach Buckley also had a great record at North Central High. Robert "Bob" Carey, who played left end on Buckley's city championship team, described his coach as probably one of the most versatile athletes that ever attended WSC. Bob said Archie was good enough in baseball to have played in the major leagues, and was one of the best infielders ever to attend WSC. Bob thought Archie was an excellent coach and a real fireball, highly disciplined, and demanding discipline on his ball teams. The coach insisted that all players be on hand, and on time, for every practice, and the coach was always excitable and exciting. He was a perfectionist, demanding the players give to the best of their abilities at all times, or perhaps even better. Bob also said that Coach Buckley was an outstanding motivator who led by example, a trait that was most evident during his naval career.[5]

Lieutenant Archie Buckley was survived by his wife Mary Maude, son James, and daughter Betty Moe. During his life and after his premature death, Archie received many honors including induction into the WSU Athletic Hall of Fame. Archie's memory is honored with the following citation engraved on the Veterans Wall at North Central High in Spokane:

A TRIBUTE TO ARCHIE M. BUCKLEY – Teacher and Coach, 1931-1943. A native of Colville.

Archie Buckley excelled in athletics at Washington State College. He began his teaching career at North Central in 1931 and coached football, basketball, and baseball. He became one of the areas best known and most popular coaches. In March 1943, he volunteered for active duty in the navy and was assigned to the Aircraft Carrier Saratoga. Lieutenant Buckley was killed in a kamikaze attack on his ship during the battle of Iwo Jima, February 21, 1945. In his memory, the Archie Buckley Inspirational Award is annually awarded to a member of the North Central football team.

*This Buckley story previously appeared in the May 2001 issue of **Nostalgia Magazine**, and the April 2004 issue of **The Pacific Northwesterner**.*

Captain Leo K. Bustad
Prisoner of War and Humanitarian
Dean, WSU College of Veterinary Medicine

Dr. Leo Bustad was born January 20, 1920 and raised near Stanwood, Washington. He entered Washington State College in the fall of 1937 and graduated with honors with a bachelor's degree in agriculture in June 1941. He was commissioned as a second lieutenant on graduation day and

Leo K. Bustad at the dedication of the Bustad Veterinary Science Building, 1985. *(Photo courtesy Washington State University.)*

reported for duty the next day.[1] He was initially assigned to Fort George Wright in Spokane then transferred to Fort Lewis near Tacoma, joining the 3rd Infantry Division. Bustad was home on leave December 7, 1941, but was immediately called back and transferred to Fort Ord, California. Following additional training, including beach landings, the 3rd Division was dispatched to the North African campaign, coming ashore near Fedala, Morocco, just a few miles from their objective, Casablanca.

Leo's outfit endured several furious firefights that included being fired on by a French vessel. His men also admired but were somewhat terrified by the Ghurkas, allied members of a Nepalese commando unit assigned to help clean up the area and capture Germans. Apparently the Ghurkas were night fighters who battled only with steel, no guns. Their favorite tactic was to slip into a front line foxhole or bunker at night, feel for a certain insignia that most German soldiers wore on their collars, and if they found the insignia in place, "off would come the enemy heads."[2]

Following the North African Campaign, the 3rd Division took part in the invasion of Sicily, a massive operation that involved more than 2,000 ships and landing craft. By this time, Leo had been promoted from platoon leader to company commander of the Regimental Headquarters Company with the title regimental communications officer.

On the way to Sicily, the landing craft encountered a terrible storm with 30- to 40-foot sea swells and 50- to 60-mph winds.

A huge swell washed over the deck of Leo's landing craft infantry (LCI) and he was washed overboard. Leo was a very devout man and this was not the first of several incidents that convinced him of the power of divine providence. The last LCI in the flotilla defied orders not to turn around but did so anyway and managed, on the second try, to pluck Leo from the sea. Later, the LCI from which he was washed overboard took a direct hit from shore batteries, and many of the men aboard were either killed or wounded. Sicily was overtaken in prompt order, and soon First Lieutenant Bustad was sent to the beachhead at Salerno on the southwest coast of Italy. There he was hospitalized with hepatitis. Six weeks later, he was able to rejoin his outfit in time for the beach landing and assault at Anzio. With the Assault Battalion, he served as commanding officer of the Regimental Headquarters Company. The landing was successful, experiencing only light opposition, but then the troops were bogged down waiting for supplies and the fight was on.

In preparation for a night attack, Bustad and some of his men were sent on a reconnoitering mission behind enemy lines. They were soon cut off, surrounded, and captured. The capture is detailed here in Captain Bustad's own words:

The 1st Battalion 7th Infantry made a night movement on 30 January, 1944 . . . I was at the head of my company with the command post group following . . . advance was slow, for our progress was impeded by lateral ditches, canals and fences . . .

Just before dawn, the battalion halted momentarily to reorganize. The enemy immediately shot up flares and then opened up with machine gun and rifle fire . . . Hoping to bypass the resistance and gain the objective . . . I moved out urging my men along the shallow ditches to move forward . . . By this time, perhaps six o'clock, it was quite light and visibility was good. We knocked out a strong point and took a few prisoners . . . On surveying the terrain more closely, I saw numerous enemy, perhaps a company . . . to my immediate front . . . They were apparently very surprised, but shortly began dropping mortar shells into every group of our men. I discussed the situation very briefly with Lieutenant Busby and Lieutenant Van Scoyac (both KIA shortly thereafter) and then ordered a defense to be set up about 500 yards to our rear by a house and a ditch . . . I had approximately 60 men of all units of the battalion . . . I knew I was surrounded at this time for I could hear enemy machine gun fire to my rear and around my flanks . . . During the course of the morning, one enemy squad came right up to our rear and shouted for our surrender. I made a show of strength and shouted for them to surrender. After much hollering they opened fire at about 50 yards . . . All morning we were subjected to small arms and automatic fire, and we stemmed many small attacks, suffering numerous casualties in our own ranks . . . We killed numerous enemy . . . I told Lieutenant Melgard and the men with me we might get away to a ditch half-full of water to our right rear . . . On reaching the canal we began moving back with our heads above water. . . We made fairly good progress although sporadic fire was going over our heads . . . We could see about a squad of men approaching led by an enemy paratrooper . . . Very shortly thereafter they closed in on us. Lieutenant Melgard who was to my immediate front opened up and was promptly shot . . . My carbine was inoperative. A grenade then landed on the bank above my head. I looked back and saw two enemy soldiers ready to throw two more grenades. I looked up and saw standing right above me an enemy with bayonet fixed, rifle ready to deliver the final blow, so I promptly threw my carbine in the water, and he didn't shoot . . . Another enemy said, "Kom" and getting behind me with a bayonet made it very plain to me that he wanted me to hurry. Beside myself there were three others, two I believe, were wounded. I was promptly taken to a Regimental Command Post and then a Division Command Post . . .[3]

To Bustad, his capture without being shot was another example of "divine providence" at work. Apparently the Germans were well fortified and ready to counter any American advance. They had captured most of Captain Bustad's unit and many of the British troops operating on the left flank. The captives were interrogated, strip searched, and after their clothes were returned, sent on a forced march through Rome, and then imprisoned in a POW camp at Laterina, Italy. They were then loaded into boxcars bound for POW camps in and near Germany, including Mooseberg, Germany, Offizierslager (Oflag) #64 in Poland, Oflag XIIIB in Bavaria, Luft III near Nuremberg, Germany, and then Stalag VIIB, again at Mooseberg. Of his 15 months in confinement, Bustad's longest stay was nine-plus months at Oflag #64, a camp near Szubin in the Polish Corridor. The winter of 1944-45 was very cold and the prisoners were not well fed or clothed.[4] Captain Bustad was hospitalized, suffering from malnutrition. In later years, Dr. Bustad said that the cold and hunger left their mark on him and so he swore that he would never be cold again, overdressing each day, sometimes even wearing long johns in June, and he was never without a food supply close at hand.[5]

While a prisoner, Captain Bustad performed various duties, including as camp shower officer, barracks adjutant, and operations officer, and while at Mooseberg, liaison officer with the Underground. In early 1945, the Germans realized that the Russian Army was advancing rapidly towards them and began to panic. The worst rumor of the time was that all POWs would be shot to prevent their liberation by the Russians. Fortunately that did not happen, but movement became a reality when the German guards force-marched the prisoners deeper into Germany and away from the Russian front.

The prisoners were forced to hide out in the woods at night or take refuge in barns and other farm buildings. The forced march turned into many miles of misery, but Bustad, having been a farm boy, knew how to glean food from the countryside, and he and his men subsisted on greens and vegetables left in gardens and on purloined eggs and milk. All prisoners were warned that to kill a chicken or pig meant instant death. Bustad knew that eggs discovered in hidden nests and the loss of milk pilfered from a friendly cow would not be detected.

The forced march began on March 29, 1945 at Hammelburg, Germany. The POWs were loaded into boxcars for the first part of the trip, and American fighter-bombers attacked the train. The POWs signaled the aircraft to get them to stop shooting. The train eventually arrived at Nuremberg, and the prisoners were encamped outside the city. Nuremberg came under siege by allied planes. On April 4, the prisoners were marched out, destination Mooseberg. Captain Bustad recorded the following details of the March:[6]

April
4: Nuremberg, left early in the morning on foot. Pfeiffenhutte, 12km. We slept in a pine grove. Were bombed and strafed by American aircraft at Feucht (a hamlet and rail center) while on the march.
5: Neumark, 14km. Received 1/9th of a loaf of bread (about 4oz.) each. Soup at 0100 hours. Marched all night in rain.
6: Bershin, 23km. Received 1/9th of a loaf of bread each, one English Red Cross parcel for four men.

8: Samsdorf, 23km. Layover. Received three raw potatoes. Lots of air activity.

9: Neustadt-A Donau, 19km. Crossed the Danube River. Received 1/4 loaf of bread each (about 9oz.), four potatoes and one #10 Red Cross parcel for two men.

12: Niederrumelsdorf, 14km. Bombed again by American planes. Some POWs injured. Received 1/2 loaf of bread (about 18oz.) per man. Incendiary bombs dropped near us. Many houses on fire.

15: Stopped at large farm, 4km. Farm was former baronial estate. Made soup from greens we found in field. Turned out to be mustard greens. Tasted awful. Received 2/9 of a loaf of bread per man, then 1/9 loaf, two potatoes, and four carrots.

16: Holzhausen, 11km. Received 1/9 loaf of bread, three potatoes per man, one French Red Cross parcel per four men, and one #10 American Red Cross parcel for four men.

17: Obermunchen, 6km. Received one #10 American Red Cross parcel for two men. Marched at 16:30 hours. Received Scotch parcel, one for four men while marching.

19: Gammeldorf, 6km. Arrived in the night. Received 1/3 loaf of bread per man.

20: Mooseberg, 7km. Arrived at Stalag 7A having marched 139km. (about 87 miles). We were now back where we started! The Mooseberg Camp had about 40,000 Allied POWs, Scotch, English, New Zealand, French, and American.

On April 28, 1945, General Patton's 3rd Army entered Mooseberg, and the POWs were liberated. Back under U.S. control, Captain Bustad and his mates were transported to Camp Lucky Strike near Le Havre, France, until they were shipped home. Bustad was promoted to the rank of major in September 1945 and separated from service. He was awarded the Combat Infantryman's Badge, the European-African Middle Eastern Service Medal with seven Bronze Stars, the Bronze Arrowhead, the American Defense Service Medal, the American Theatre Service Medal, the World War II Victory Medal, and the Prisoner of War Medal.

Civilian Leo Bustad returned to Washington State College to earn a master's degree in 1948 and a doctorate in veterinary medicine in 1949. In 1960, he was awarded a Ph. D. in physiology and biophysics from the University of Washington School of Medicine. He held significant positions with General Electric, Hanford Laboratories, the University of Washington School of Medicine, and the College of Veterinary Medicine at the University of California, Davis. Dr. Bustad returned to his alma mater, WSU, as dean of the College of Veterinary Medicine in 1973, where he spearheaded the establishment of the Washington, Oregon, Idaho (WOI) Regional Program in Veterinary Medical Education, the nation's first regional veterinary medical curriculum. During his tenure as dean, he raised more than $35 million in state and federal construction money for the WOI Regional Program. This and other funds resulted in the construction of the $11.3 million Veterinary Science

Building, the $9.5 million renovation and enlargement of Wegner Hall, the $1.1 million remodeling of McCoy Hall, and construction of the $240,000 Hitchcock Equine Research Track.[7] The new veterinary science building was named in his honor in 1985.

Dr. Bustad was the honored recipient of the WSU Regents Distinguished Alumnus Award in 1987. During his many years of dedication to higher education, he authored several books and over 300 articles in scientific journals. He was also known nationwide as the director of the People-Pet Partnership Program and the creator of a special academic course titled "Reverence for Life." Dr. Bustad died on September 19, 1998. He was preceded in death by his wife Signe and daughter Karen.

Colonel Robert H. Carey
P-38 Pilot
European Theatre of Operations

Then a First Lieutenant, Robert "Bob" Carey, a pilot in the 474th Fighter Group, was leading a dive bombing mission over enemy-occupied France when his squadron was attacked by more than 50 enemy aircraft. He led the attack on the enemy fighters, driving them off and downing several. On December 31, 1944, he was awarded the Distinguished Flying Cross for his leadership and courage on the mission and the following is from this citation:

Air Force Colonel Robert H. Carey, highly decorated P-38 fighter pilot. *(Photo courtesy the Carey family.)*

For heroism and extraordinary achievement while participating in aerial flight in the European Theatre of Operations on 18 July 1944. On a dive bombing mission over enemy occupied France, his squadron was attacked by more than fifty hostile planes. In a brilliant exhibition of aerial skill, Lieutenant Carey attacked the enemy aircraft and dispersed several formations of hostile planes which were in pursuit of friendly pilots. By the sustained vigor and forcefulness of his attacks, he was instrumental in saving the lives of three friendly pilots whose aircraft had sustained severe damage from hostile fire, thus reflecting great distinction upon himself and the Armed Forces of the United States. By direction of the President.[1]

The foregoing is just one example of Bob Carey's contribution to the war effort, and of his heroism and leadership. However, his story should start at the beginning.

Robert H. Carey was born in Spokane on May 11, 1916 and died in Spokane June 12, 2001. He attended North Central High School where he starred in baseball and football. He was one of the All City players coached by Archie Buckley (see the Archie Buckley Story in the April 2001 issue of *Nostalgia Magazine*) on the 1933 team that won the Spokane city high school football championship. Bob enrolled at Washington State College in September 1934, graduating in June 1938 with a bachelor's degree in metallurgy engineering, and a second lieutenant's commission in the Army Reserve. While at WSC, he lived in the Sigma Nu fraternity house and was active in Scabbard and Blade and Reserve Officer Training Corps (ROTC) activities. He was a member of Sigma Tau and Tau Beta Phi, and the National Scholastic Engineering Honor Society. In the summers, he earned college money working for the Morning Mine near Mullan, Idaho, and fighting forest fires. Between his junior and senior years, he worked in the gold fields of Alaska. During the school years, he labored as a houseboy at the Kappa Alpha Theta sorority, where he met his future wife, Bernadine. They married in 1940.[2]

In July 1941, Bob was called to active Army duty and assigned to Fort Leonard Wood in Missouri. He was later assigned to an aviation engineering outfit building airport landing fields in the Alaskan Aleutian Islands. He "cut his combat teeth" building a landing field only to see it destroyed by Japanese bombers. He and his crew would work all night to put the field back into service only to have it bombed again the next evening. This building and destroying continued until his superiors brought in P-40 fighters to defend the field and drive off attackers. At this point, Bob received orders to head for flight school and his P-38 adventures began.

After training at airfields near Santa Ana and Ontario, California, Carey and his fellow pilots were shipped to England in March 1944 aboard the *Ile d'France*, one of the largest ships afloat next to the *Queen Mary*. Stationed near Warmwell, England, he continued training, flying at ever-higher altitudes, and learning

P-38 pilot Lieutenant Robert "Bob" Carey, 1944. *(Photo courtesy Randall Johnson.)*

to fly in tight formations. On a mission before D-Day, Carey's squadron of P-38s was to hit a German airfield near Dijon, France. After several strafing runs, he spotted a large railroad marshaling yard just northeast of the airfield and attacked. He made 12 passes in his heavily armed P-38 named *Baby Shoes the 3rd*. In an interview in 1996, Carey recalled, "There must have been some flak somewhere, but I didn't see any and I didn't get hit. Each time I took a different locomotive to strafe . . . I could see my bullets hitting them and ripping them apart . . . that was a beautiful mission. We didn't lose anybody, and we must have done maximum damage."[3]

On June 6, Lieutenant Carey's squadron flew several strafing and bombing missions in support of D-Day, and on a run two days later over Omaha Beach, he saw the muzzle flash of a big gun that was pounding our troops and our ships just off the beach. Putting *Baby Shoes* into a sharp dive, he let a large bomb loose, securing a perfect hit and knocking the gun out of action permanently. On July 17, he was on a mission with targets between Dreaux and Evreux in northwest France when more than 70 German ME 109s and FW 190s attacked his squadron. The air battle lasted 30 minutes and Carey's outfit (the 474th Fighter Group) destroyed 27 enemy fighters, with another 19 probable hits, nine damaged, and suffering the loss of only three P-38s. As the dogfight ended, Carey spotted a colleague heading toward home on one engine. The cripple was about to be attacked by five ME 109s. Carey immediately joined the battle, attacking the enemy head on and dispersing them. For this undertaking, he was awarded the Distinguished Flying Cross.

During the Battle of the Bulge, Carey and his mates made history by knocking out an entire German headquarters position that was housed in a very large French chateau. That day, the P-38s were armed with two 165-gallon fuel tanks each, filled with napalm. "In the lead, Carey . . . dove to the deck and came right up to the massive double front doors of the chateau, and slammed both tanks right through the doors." On a reconnaissance mission a few days later, Carey found that the entire headquarters had been destroyed along with the military vehicles parked in an adjacent motor pool.

Victory in Europe (VE-Day) came on May 8, 1945, and Captain Carey rotated home shortly thereafter. He was then assigned to Wright Field with a regular Army Air Force commission. He spent the next 11 years of his Air Force career assigned to Wright, with corresponding duties in Baltimore, working in research and development. During that period, he had an opportunity to fly nearly every aircraft in the Air Force arsenal, including his first jet, a P-80. During the Korean War, he was deeply involved with the development of a new jet, the F-86H. He stayed in the continental U.S. even though he wanted to go to Korea and fly F-86 Sabres. In 1957-58, he served as the commanding officer of an Air Defense Fighter Base in King Salmon, Alaska. During the Vietnam War, Colonel Carey put his engineering expertise to work serving as the commander of the Red Horse Construction Battalion building airfields and other related facilities.

Colonel Carey's distinguished military career spanned more than three decades and three wars, from Alaska to combat in Europe, followed by stints in the Air Research and Defense Command, the Tactical Air Command, and extended service on the Nuclear Safety Board of the Air Force. He retired in 1969 and returned to Spokane with his wife Bernadine and daughters Robin, Coralie, and Colleen. Colonel Carey died in June 2001.

* *The Carey story previously appeared in the April 2004 issue of* **The Pacific Northwesterner**.

Major James R. Carter
P-47 Pilot
European Theatre of Operations

James Richard "Dick" Carter was born May 2, 1919, the son of Mr. and Mrs. Kenneth W. Carter of Palouse, Washington. He graduated from Pullman High School in 1937 and entered Washington State College that fall.[1] Although his military records were destroyed in the 1973 fire at the National Personnel Records Center in St. Louis, a search of area newspaper files revealed much important information about his heroism and gallantry as a P-47 Thunderbolt pilot.[2]

The following are from these articles:

> *The promotion of James R. Carter from the rank of first lieutenant to captain was announced recently somewhere in England. A veteran fighter pilot, Captain Carter has shot down one enemy aircraft, registered a probable, and damaged an additional Jerry. He chalked up his 'kill', a Messerschmitt 109, on a recent combat mission over continental Europe. The captain holds the Air Medal with three oak leaf clusters and the Distinguished Flying Cross. Enlisting in the Air Corps October 4, 1941, he received his primary training at Stamford, Texas, basic at Randolph Field, Texas, and advance at Kelly Field, also in Texas. He received his wings and commission as second lieutenant at the latter field.[3]*

Captain James R. Carter, of Palouse, now on leave in the states, is a fighter plane pilot of a P-47 Thunderbolt group that has been awarded the presidential citation for 'exceptional aggressiveness and extraordinary heroism in action.' Since beginning combat operations in April 1943, this fighter group has destroyed approximately 550 German planes in the air, plus 50 more on the ground. It is the highest-scoring P-47 outfit in the European Theatre. Capt. Carter . . . has destroyed six Hun planes, probably destroyed two others, and damaged still two more in aerial combat. [4]

Major James R. Carter, fighter pilot of Pullman, has been awarded the Silver Star for gallantry in action while leading a squadron of P-47 Thunderbolt planes on a strafing mission over Germany. The citation accompanying the award states the action took place last November 18, 1944. Arriving in the vicinity of the mission's objective after flying most of the way on instruments, Maj. Carter's squadron was the only one in the 56th fighter group successful in locating the target. Strafing the target, Maj. Carter set fire to six large oil storage tanks and destroyed a German fighter plane which attempted to frustrate the attack. A few minutes later 20 Focke Wulfe 190s attacked from above and during the fierce battle which followed, Maj. Carter's squadron destroyed six German planes, probably destroyed three others, and damaged four. [5]

A news release from the Eighth Air Force Fighter Station in England stated:

A crack fighter pilot from Pullman, Wash., Maj. James R. Carter, has been named commanding officer of one of the squadrons comprising the 56th Fighter Group, highest-scoring fighter outfit in Eighth Air Force. A veteran of more than 300 combat hours, Maj. Carter has shot down six German planes, probably destroyed three others, and damaged two more. He also has knocked out a number of Nazi locomotives, freight and oil cars, supply trucks, flak installations, and other ground targets. A much-decorated pilot, Maj. Carter holds the silver star, distinguished flying cross with two oak leaf clusters and the air medal with seven clusters. [6]

The Clark Family – Cougars All

Asa V. Clark Sr.
Rose Bowl Victor
State Representative and Senator

The Clark brothers and their father are Cougars through and through; so much so, one might speculate that had they been wounded in combat, the sons would have bled crimson and gray.

Asa "Ace" Jr. and D. Girard are both veterans, but this story begins with their father. Asa "Ace" Varnell Clark Sr. was born in 1889 and lived with his family on land homesteaded by his father, Girard Clark, near Albion, Washington. He graduated from the Washington State College Preparatory School in Pullman and entered WSC in fall 1914. Ace was an outstanding athlete, playing center then tackle on the football team with William "Lone Star" Dietz as coach. The team was undefeated in 1915 and went on to play in the Rose Bowl. Ace's team defeated Brown University 14-0 on January 1, 1916 and made history as the first winners of the modern Rose Bowl. Ace was named to the first All Conference team.

After graduating from WSC, Ace returned to the farm but remained active in WSC athletics and entered politics. With two sons sharing farm work and management, Ace was able to run for the Washington State House of Representatives in 1941 and won; in 1949, he was elected to the State Senate. He retired

The 1916 Rose Bowl team captain, Asa V. Clark Sr., is fourth from the right (standing). *(Photo courtesy Betty Clark.)*

from political life in 1956. While in the House, he served two terms as Chairman of the Ways and Means Committee, ensuring WSC received a fair share of state appropriations. During a meeting on November 19, 1971, the Regents of Washington State University honored Clark by naming the newest Agricultural Sciences building in his honor. The citation read:

> *Clark Hall reflects honor and appreciation to Asa V. "Ace" Clark – He was a prominent Whitman County farmer, state legislator, and friend and supporter of Washington State University.*

The previous year, WSU gave Ace the Alumni Achievement Award for providing inspirational leadership in the advancement of intercollegiate football, 15 years of service to the Washington State House of Representatives and Senate, and a lifetime of service to Washington State University. Ace Sr. died in 1972.

A pen-and-ink drawing by John Gulbransen of Asa V. Clark Sr., chairman of the Washington State Legislative Appropriations Committee. This sketch was published in one of the Seattle newspapers in 1947. *(Courtesy Betty Clark)*

Captain Asa V. "Ace" Clark Jr.
B-26 Bomber Pilot, 70 Missions

Ace Clark Jr. was born November 22, 1918 and raised on the Clark farm near Albion, Washington. He graduated from Albion High School in June 1937 and entered Washington State College in the fall. He joined the Kappa Sigma fraternity and, in his senior year, served as house president and was designated a "Distinguished WSC Senior." [1] Ace received his bachelor's degree in agriculture and was commissioned as a second lieutenant on June 9, 1941. He reported for active Army duty the following day. While in college, he took flying lessons and earned a private pilot's license.[2]

Originally assigned to the Quartermaster Corps, Ace later volunteered for pilot training and received his wings as a B-26 bomber pilot. The B-26 was a medium-size, two-motor bomber. He was shipped overseas in September 1943, joining the 9th Air Force at an Army Air Force base near Chelmsford, about 40 miles northeast of London. From there, Ace and his crew flew 70 missions over France, Holland, Belgium, and Germany.

Fortunately never wounded, on numerous occasions Ace brought his badly damaged bomber home on "a wing and a prayer." He flew his 45th mission on D-Day, June 6, 1944; his primary targets were the German gun emplacements overlooking Omaha Beach. Other targets of his many missions included enemy airfields, bridges, railroad marshaling yards, and enemy rocket launching pads. Ace described one of his more dangerous missions in an interview with this author:

Yes, we got shot at a lot and had a few pretty tough ones [missions], and some easy ones. Some were very, very, dangerous. I came home on one engine a few times. Probably my roughest mission was a bombing run into U-boat pens near Ijmuiden, Holland. Our squadron commander was Glen Grau, a fantastic man and a fantastic pilot . . . Glen was leading our mission and I was serving as deputy squadron commander. I saw this big explosion right in front of my aircraft and I knew it was Glen's plane. I said "good-bye Glen." He was really hit hard. I made my run, caught my share of ground fire, dropped my bombs, and made it back over the Channel. My plane was badly crippled, and flying on only one motor, so I landed at the first airfield I could find on the coast of England. Then, to my amazement after landing, I looked up and here came Glen Grau limping in over the trees. I don't know how in the world he got that plane back to England, but he did! [3]

When asked if on his missions his plane was most vulnerable to ground fire or attack by German fighters, Captain Clark replied emphatically:

Ground fire, but we called it flak. The fighters didn't bother us too much. We were too speedy for them. The

New pilot Asa "Ace" Clark Jr. in advanced flying school at Stockton, California, 1943. *(Photo courtesy Mrs. Kaye Clark)*

B-26, named the *Los Lobos Grandes,* and crew in England in 1944. Front, from left: S/Sgt. Earl E. Kennedy, radio and waist gunner; Pvt. Carl L. Sundland, tail gunner; S/Sgt. Robert J. Wrighton, engineer top turret gun. Standing: Thomas O. Rader, bombardier; Edward E. Agner, copilot; Capt. Asa V. Clark Jr., pilot. *(Photo courtesy Mrs. Kaye Clark)*

German fighters would rather attack the slower B-17s and B-24s. Flak was our big problem and we got lots of it. Oh, we were attacked once in a while by fighters – provided conditions were favorable for them such as a crippled U.S. plane that could not stay in formation.[4]

Captain Ace Clark completed his 70th mission in August 1944 and then rotated back to a base in the states. He was awarded the Air Medal with 11 Oak Leaf Clusters, and one source indicated that he had been awarded the Distinguished Flying Cross. He denies receiving the Cross, but a 1944 newspaper article noted that Clark had "... participated in supporting operations during the Normandy invasion. His plane would drop bombs and then fly low to strafe the enemy. He has been awarded the Distinguished Flying Cross and Air Medal with 11 Oak Leaf Clusters."[5] Awarding of the Cross cannot be proven or disproved. According to a letter dated April 7, 1997 received from the Air Force by this researcher, "Asa Varnell Clark Jr.'s military service records were completely destroyed by the 1973 fire at the National Personnel Records Center in St. Louis."

After the war, Ace returned to his wife Catherine and the family farm. Ace Clark Jr. died January 19, 2002. Until that time, he farmed with his two sons and brother Girard and his three sons, although admitting that the boys were doing most of the work.

Lieutenant D. Girard Clark
Air Force, Korean Era, and Wheat Rancher

Girard Clark was born September 5, 1925 to Asa V. "Ace" and Lillian Clark. He was raised on the Clark family farm homesteaded by his grandfather. He graduated from Pullman High School in the middle of World War II and farmed with his father on the home place. He was deferred from active duty to help feed the nation as his older brother, Ace Jr., was already serving overseas. He enrolled at Washington State College in fall 1946, majoring in agriculture. He received his bachelor of science degree on May 28, 1950 and a commission as a second lieutenant in the Air Force.[1]

Girard was called to active duty shortly after the start of the Korean War and received training at Lackland Air Force Base in Texas. Following training, he was assigned to the Air Materiel Command at Kelly AFB near San Antonio. Later, he was transferred to the Aircraft Engine Maintenance Section, with responsibility for the overhaul of aircraft engines. His role was of a strategic nature, supervising the hundreds of enlisted men and civilians doing the overhaul work. The main thrust of their activity was to get the aircraft repaired and back in service in support of the ground offensive in Korea.[2]

Girard was discharged in late September 1953 and returned to the family farm to work with his brother. Over the years, Girard

Girard Clark with his combine. *(Photo courtesy Betty Clark)*

became one of the acknowledged leaders in the area for dryland farming on the Palouse. He was also very civic minded, serving on many committees and commissions including the Pullman School Board and the Community Colleges of Spokane Board of Trustees. Girard and his wife Betty have three sons and a daughter.

Girard Sr., Girard Jr., Betty and Asa Webb Clark. Photo taken at San Antonio, Texas, in 1953. *(Photo courtesy Betty Clark)*

Lieutenant Alfred "Bud" Coppers
Captured 19 German Pillboxes
Awarded the Silver Star

Alfred B. "Bud" Coppers graduated from Fall City (Washington) High School in June 1939 and entered Washington State College that fall as an English major. He played on the varsity basketball team, and served as editor of the 1943 *Chinook* college yearbook his senior year. In college, he completed his first two years of mandatory Reserve Officer Training Corps (ROTC) training but did not sign up for Advanced ROTC until his senior year, a move that placed him with the juniors.[1] One week after graduating from WSC in 1943, his entire ROTC class was ordered to active duty for training at Camp Roberts, California. Bud was selected for Officer Candidate School the following spring, and in the interim, he was assigned to the Army Specialized Training Program (ASTP) at WSC in Pullman.

Bud was commissioned an Infantry second lieutenant in September 1944 and, after additional training, entered the Army replacement pipeline headed for the European front via Liverpool, England, and Bar le Duc, France (60 miles east of Paris). The day after Christmas 1944, Lieutenant Coppers reported to Company E, 319th Infantry Regiment as platoon leader of the Third Infantry Platoon. His unit occupied the high ground on the far side of the Sur River overlooking the German-held town of Bochholtz.[2]

His unit's first attempt to capture Bochholtz failed, with the loss of an entire squad of Coppers's platoon, including the medic. Their second attempt succeeded with minimal casualties. On February 4, 1945, Coppers's unit moved into a little town on the Luxembourg side of the Our River. Across the river and nearly invisible from his company observation point were a series of 300 or more German pillboxes aligned along the Siegfried Line. Coppers later discovered that each pillbox was approximately 20 by 20 feet and built with reinforced concrete walls four feet thick. The interiors were rooms with concrete wall dividers, with one room containing bunk beds, no closable doors, and concrete floors. Each pillbox had a rectangular firing aperture facing west and, inside, a mounted 30-caliber machine gun.

At daylight on February 5, units of Company E, in small boats supplied by Army engineers, attempted to cross the Our River. They came under heavy enemy artillery and the 15 men that survived (the others were killed or wounded) dug in behind protective cover on the Luxembourg side of the river. Lieutenant Coppers received word that his company commander had been wounded and he was to take command.

Leading the remnants of his company, Coppers approached the first pillbox from the blind side. In his own words, he relates what happened:

I went up a fairly steep incline and came to a trench which paralleled a ramp leading into the rear of the pillbox. I then returned to our confined company area and enlisted the help of Sgt. Sawyer who had been sent to us from the Battalion Pioneer and Ammunition Platoon, along with satchel charges [TNT packed in canvas cases about the size of a field telephone case]. With both of us back in the trench, I tried my best "kommen sie aus" German several times ...the answers to my invitations were Burp Gun bursts which ricocheted off the concrete wall of the entryway . . . I threw a succession of hand grenades down the entrance ramp to keep the Burp Gun quiet and allow Sgt. Sawyer to cross the ramp and access the top of the pillbox . . . The sergeant dropped a charge into the ventilation shaft and sprinted back to our trench. After two or three minutes we decided that the fuse was probably wet. The procedure was repeated and there was certainly nothing wrong with the second fuse. I believe both of the charges detonated and Sawyer and I were very lucky to not have been hit by the chunks of concrete which rained around us. After a dead silence of a moment or so, we heard a cry of "kamerad" from the pillbox, and ten or twelve occupants filed out with their hands in the air ... Those two satchel charges opened the flood gates, and as soon as we were able to get on the tops of three additional pillboxes, the invitations to come out were promptly accepted.[3]

For their heroic action, Coppers and Sawyer were awarded Silver Stars for gallantry. Coppers's citation read as follows,

Alfred B. Coppers, First Lieutenant, Inf., Army of the United States. For gallantry in action in connection with military operations against an enemy of the United States. During the crossing of the Our River into Germany, the Commanding Officer of Company E, 319th Infantry, became a casualty and Lieutenant Coppers assumed command. He quickly reorganized, dispelled the fears of the men and led the company with such bold aggressiveness as to capture nineteen pillboxes and quickly gain the battalion objective. Throughout the assault Lieutenant Coppers was foremost in the attack urging his men forward. His inspirational leadership, courage, and aggressiveness are commensurate with the highest traditions of the armed forces of the United States.[4]

On interview, Coppers acknowledges the four pillboxes he and Sawyer captured, but professes to know nothing about the other fifteen. However, he speculates that their success in eliminating the first four may have caused the German soldiers in the adjacent fifteen pillboxes to think they were surrounded by superior forces, about to be killed or wounded, and thus to surrender.[5]

Lieutenant Coppers continued to command Company E as it moved forward, capturing or occupying towns and villages along the way, including Hochheim and Kassel in Germany. Company E was then ordered south into Bavaria and Austria. When the war ended, Coppers and his men were near the resort cities of Gmunden and Ebensee.

Coppers' next assignment was to Headquarters Company of the 6th Tank Destroyer Group with administrative duties at the infamous Nazi Dachau Concentration Camp. The responsibility given Coppers and his men was to hold and guard a large number of officers and enlisted men awaiting war-crime trials as defendants or witnesses.

Later Lieutenant Coppers participated in a large interview session with General George S. Patton. General Patton, seeking information and recommendations that might aid the military in future battles, interviewed the officers attending in order by rank, starting with the highest. When given his opportunity to provide input, Coppers made a sincere plea for the soldiers to be provided better winter clothing and a fully automatic individual weapon, comparable to the German Schmeiser machine pistol.

Captain Coppers rotated home in the summer of 1945, but remained in active service for another year. After his discharge, he remained in inactive reserves with the rank of major. Bud was called up again in June 1951 for service in the Korean War and assigned as executive officer of 2nd Battalion, 27th Infantry Regiment. His unit was on the front lines through November 1952.

At the time of his second discharge, Bud Coppers had been awarded the Silver Star, Bronze Star with one Oak Leaf Cluster (ETO and Korea), the Korean Service Medal, United Nations Service Medal, and the Combat Infantry Badge twice (ETO and Korean War).

Major Edna L. Cox
Women's Army Corps,
European Theatre of Operations

Edna Leelia Cox was born March 12, 1909 in Monroe, Washington. She graduated from Union High School in June 1927 and entered Washington State College in the fall. Edna's mother, Mary Millard Cox, was a journalist and early supporter of women's suffrage. Her father, Edward W. Cox, was a medical doctor and graduate of Stanford University. Her brother Earl graduated from WSC ahead of Edna, then spent his entire career with the U.S. State Department, assuming many critical and dangerous assignments during World War II. Edna joined Kappa Delta sorority, majored in home economics (dietetics), and was an outstanding member of the 1931 graduating class.[1] Edna was an extremely active student, serving on the Associated Students State College of Washington (ASSCW) Board of Control and as president of the Associated Women Students. She was also active in the Women's Athletic Association and served as president of the Women's Council. In those days, women were

Lieutenant Edna L. Cox being sworn into the Women's Army Auxiliary Corps in 1942. *(Photo courtesy Edna L. Cox.)*

not allowed to participate in the Reserve Officer Training Corps (ROTC) program so she served as a sponsor of it instead.[2] She got to know most of the young Army men, becoming especially enamored with Cadet Edward R. Murrow. They became good friends and she was his favorite date for important events like the Senior Prom and the Military Ball. Over the years they remained friends and confidants until his death in 1965.[3]

After graduation, Edna accepted the position of clinic dietitian for the King County Hospital in Seattle. On June 21, 1942, a Japanese submarine attacked Fort Stevens near the mouth of the Columbia River, lobbing 17 high explosive shells at the fort. Although little damage was done, the attack was highly publicized, changing the attitude of many up and down the coast and prompting nearly everyone to get solidly behind the war effort. Edna resolved to do her part by immediately volunteering for the newly formed Women's Army Auxiliary Corps (WAAC). She was selected as one of 400 from more than 30,000 women volunteers. She reported for duty at Fort Des Moines in Iowa on July 17 and was commissioned as a second lieutenant on August 29, 1942, then sent to Fort Riley, Kansas, for technical training. Regarding her enlistment, a local newspaper quoted Lieutenant Cox as saying, "I'm going in because I know members of my profession are needed and I don't usually 'let George do it.' I feel this is the best way I can help."[4]

Lieutenant Cox held several important positions in the Quartermaster Corps, serving for five years in Chicago as chief of the Subsistence Division of the Quartermaster Purchasing Office, supervising over 500 soldiers and civilians, charged with procuring and distributing foodstuffs for the Army. Due to her training and experience, she was shipped to the European Theatre of Operations at war's end where she was put in charge of purchasing, shipping, and distribution of perishable foodstuffs (fresh fruit, vegetables, diary products, and meat) to feed the troops and displaced civilians in the occupied areas of Western Europe. She and her unit played a major role in executing the Marshall Plan.

In 1959, Major Cox retired from military service, but spent many more years serving her state and local community through volunteer work with the American Legion and the American Association of University Women. An active Legionnaire, Major Cox served for several years as post commander for the entire San Francisco area. In 1980, she was the honored recipient of the WSU Home Economics Alumni Association Distinguished Alumnus Award and, in 1981, the Washington State University Alumni Achievement Award for "continued patriotism and commitment to the improvement of life for the citizens of her community and country." Recently, the Halfmoon Bay, California branch of the American Association of University Women honored Citizen Cox by naming its scholarship program for her. The aim of the long-range "Edna L. Cox Scholarship" program is to award 500 scholarships of $5,000 each to qualified women from her community and surrounding areas. Major Cox died in January 2002.

Major David G. Davis
A-20 Bomber Pilot
180 Missions Over the Aleutians and Europe

David Gilbert Davis was born June 12, 1917 in Coulee City, Washington, to Mr. and Mrs. D. M. Davis. David, nicknamed "Dovie" by his family, graduated from Coulee City High School in 1936 and enrolled at Washington State College in the fall, majoring in forestry. He pledged Phi Sigma Kappa fraternity and lived in the house until graduation. He received a bachelor of science degree in February 1941 and joined the Army Air Corps.[1] Dovie successfully completed seven and one-half months of pilot training at Victorville, California. From May 1942 to May 1943, he flew 80 missions on submarine patrol duty in the Aleutian Islands. Lieutenant Davis then became a flight instructor at Will Rogers Field in Oklahoma before entering flight leader training in Louisiana. In February 1944, he joined the 640th Bomb Squadron, 409th Bomb Group flying from a base in England. He served as squadron operations officer and pilot of an A-20 Havoc bomber, leading from 36 to 54 aircraft per mission over various targets. During that period, Davis and his crew flew more than 100 bombing missions in less than four months, breaking the record for light bombers.[2]

In August 1944, Colonel Robert H. Parham, public relations officer for the Ninth Air Force, released the following news article praising the then Captain Davis:

Army Air Force Pilot Lieutenant David "Dovie" Davis. *(Photo courtesy the Davis family.)*

A cluster of tiny, black dots appears faintly in the sky and a jeep goes racing around the perimeter of the airdrome. The dots are larger by the time the jeep reaches the dispersal area, and the trim clean lines of the A-20 Havoc light bombers can be easily seen . . . The lead ship of the flight hits the strip, bounces gently as smoke bubbles up from the tires and rolls quickly into the dispersal area . . . Out of the jeep, maps in hand, hops and intelligence officer. He opens the hatch underneath the nose of the Havoc, and a tall, thin, pale bombardier drops, a bit warily, out of the plane. "Did you hit it, Gene?" "Yeah . . . Where?" asks the intelligence officer as he holds up a photo of the target – a German airfield in France. "Here . . ." indicating where the bomb pattern spread over the target. When the intelligence officer has checked the route with the bombardier . . . he moves around to the side of the bomber where the pilot is filling out a form for the crew chief. "How'd she go Dave?" "Okay, Bob." is the answer, and Captain David G. Davis of Coulee City, Washington, smiles as he looks at the photo of the target. "It was a good mission, Bob." This 26 year old pilot, a 1941 graduate of Washington State College, and a veteran of 11 months of sub patrol in the Aleutians, has teamed up with young Gene Salzmann to form one of the finest pilot-bombardier teams in this A-20 Havoc group that has recently broken all light bombardment records in the ETO by completing 100 missions in less than four months. They don't talk much, but their quiet manner gives a feeling of confidence and steadiness. Leading a bomber formation against targets in France, in close support of the ground forces, is a big job. They do it on every mission they fly. As the intelligence officer hurries off in the jeep to phone in the mission report . . . Staff Sergeant William Hicks . . . grabs his partner: "Did you ever see such flak, Vern?", he asks the tail gunner Staff Sergeant Vernon Mondl . . . a veteran of 41 missions, rolls a jagged fragment of German steel around the palm of his hand, a souvenir that had cut through the fuselage. "I don't see how he got through it, he's one of the best damn pilots in this outfit." [3]

After the war, Major Davis returned to civilian life having served the Army Air Corps with distinction from April 24, 1942 to April 7, 1946. He was awarded the Distinguished Flying Cross, Air Medal with ten Oak Leaf Clusters, European African Middle Eastern Campaign Medal with four Bronze Service Stars, Asiatic-Pacific Campaign Medal, American Campaign Medal, American Defense Service Medal, and World War II Victory Medal. [4]

In 1996, at a special ceremony at Fairchild Air Force Base near Spokane, Major Davis was awarded the Bronze Star for meritorious service. The medal, earned 51 years earlier, but not received, capped Davis' military career. [5] He and his wife Helen operated a wheat and cattle ranch west of Coulee City. They have two sons, David Gilbert Jr. (WSU '71) and Bill, and daughters, Carol (WSU '71) and Patty. Major Davis died in June 1997.

Lieutenant Leon W. Ellsworth
Marine Pilot Killed In Action – Iwo Jima

Leon Wheeler Ellsworth was born in Ellensburg, Washington, on May 24, 1923, the son of Mrs. Irene Ellsworth of Thorp, Washington. He graduated from Thorp High School in June 1941 and spent the fall 1941-42 semester taking class work at Washington State College.[1] He enlisted in the Marine Corps shortly after Pearl Harbor, and received pilot training at an air field near Pasco, Washington. While training, he parachuted safely after a midair collision of two training planes.[2] Following training, he was assigned to Marine Observation Squadron Five on Iwo Jima in the Pacific. His job was to fly low over enemy territory, allowing his observer passenger to take photographs of enemy positions. On March 13, during his 26th such flight, Ellsworth's plane was shot down and both he and the observer were killed. Fellow Marine and a Thorp High School schoolmate George Brain witnessed Ellsworth's daring flight and the subsequent crash (see the George Brain story). Lieutenant Ellsworth was awarded the Distinguished Flying Cross posthumously:

For heroism and extraordinary achievement in aerial flight as Pilot of an Observation Plane in Marine Observation Squadron Five, in action against enemy Japanese forces on Iwo Jima, Volcano Islands, from 28 February to 13 March 1945. Landing his unarmed and unarmored plane on a captured airstrip in enemy-held territory on 28 February, Second Lieutenant Ellsworth operated from this exposed base to complete twenty-six low-altitude missions over enemy territory despite intense antiaircraft fire, thereby enabling the observer to obtain valuable intelligence data. Shot down on 13 March, by Japanese antiaircraft fire which caused the loss of one wing and resulted in a crash that was fatal to both pilot and observer, Second Lieutenant Ellsworth had contributed essentially to the success of subsequent offensive operations on the island. His unceasing vigilance, dauntless initiative, and valiant devotion to duty in the face of tremendous odds sustained and enhanced the highest traditions of the United States Naval Service. He gallantly gave his life for his country.

Signed for the president, James Forrestal, Secretary of the Navy.

Lieutenant Ellsworth was awarded, also posthumously, the Air Medal with three Gold Stars and the Purple Heart. He was buried in the 5th Marine Division Cemetery on Iwo Jima, and after the war, his remains were removed to the International Order of Odd Fellows (IOOF) Cemetery in Ellensburg, Washington.[3]

The Goldsworthy Family:
Harry E. Goldsworthy Sr.
Lieutenant General Harry E. Goldsworthy Jr.
Major General Robert F. Goldsworthy

The Goldsworthy brothers, Harry and Robert, were raised on a farm near Rosalia, Washington. Their parents, Harry Sr. and Pearl, were successful farmers and Harry Sr. had attended Washington State College where he was student body president and editor of the college yearbook, *Chinook*. He was a starter on the Cougar football team for four years, serving as captain in 1906 and 1907. His 1906 team was undefeated, untied, and un-scored upon! Harry Sr. was elected to the state legislature in 1923. He served successive terms and was chair of the House Appropriations Committee during the 1925, 1927, and 1929 sessions. In 1934, he ran for the state senate but was defeated.

In 1942, Harry Sr. was appointed to the Board of Regents of Washington State College, serving until 1947. He was president of the board throughout the last year of his tenure. In 1962, WSC honored him by naming a residence hall in his honor.

The years of World War II were difficult for Harry Sr. and Pearl. Before the war, both sons joined the Army Air Corps and became pilots. The real trauma for the parents came in December 1944 when Bob was reported missing in action following a B-29 bombing raid over Tokyo. Based on military reports, there seemed to be little hope that he could have escaped from his severely damaged plane set on fire by Japanese fighters. No further word was received until the war ended and the POWs were evacuated, and Bob was found in bad shape but alive. Harry Jr. went to the Pacific soon after Bob was shot down. Consequently, their parents did not sleep well until both sons came home alive.[1]

Lieutenant General Harry E. Goldsworthy Jr.
Served in World War II, Korea and Vietnam

Harry Edgar "Ed" Goldsworthy was born April 3, 1914 on a farm near Rosalia, Washington. He attended elementary school in a one-room schoolhouse for grades one through eight. He graduated from Rosalia High School in 1931, then Washington State College in June 1936 with a bachelor of arts degree in education and a commission as a second lieutenant in the Infantry Reserves. While at WSC, he played football his first year, track all four years, was editor of the yearbook, *Chinook*, and student body president his senior year.[2]

In 1939, Harry was accepted for flight training with the Army Air Corps, receiving his "wings" in 1940. His choice to join the Air Corps was influenced by his close friend and bomber pilot C. Ross Greening, who had earned his wings in 1937.

In 1940, Lieutenant Goldsworthy was assigned to submarine patrol duty out of Puerto Rico and Trinidad, with a mission of protecting the Panama Canal. Twice on patrol, he spotted sailors in the water, and helped to rescue many who might otherwise have drowned because of German submarine attacks.

In June 1943, Captain Goldsworthy was assigned to an airbase near Columbia, South Carolina, commanding a replacement training unit flying B-25s. In early 1945, he was transferred to 42nd Bombardment Group in Biak, then Morotai, and then Palawan, a long slender

A young Goldsworthy as WSC student body president, 1936-37. *(Photo courtesy the United States Air Force and Washington State University.)*

island that is part of the Philippine Islands. His early missions, piloting a B-25 (twin motor-twin tails) were in support of attacking ground forces at Balikpapan in east Borneo, and various ground missions on Luzon. On one mission over Luzon, Goldsworthy had a harrowing time and a near-fatal experience. The following is his account of that mission:

I was vice commander of the group . . . when you do a strafing mission you try to go in line abreast with enough aircraft to cover so they can't shoot at you from the sides . . . I was piloting my B-25 . . . on the outside so they kind of scraped me off against a high point on a ridge – so I had to go down to the left of the ridge – and when I pulled back up I couldn't find the formation, but I could see where the Army had marked the target, so I decided I would go in and attack the target by myself – which was really stupid – and drop my napalm bombs, and then the rest of the formation wouldn't have any trouble identifying the target. So I went down by myself, strafing and dropped the napalm – and something hit us, and it was speculated that the Japanese, because we were strafers, had started the practice of putting land mines up in the tops of the tallest palm trees, which they detonated when we went over. We speculated that might be what happened to my aircraft. It didn't damage us too much but I had a napalm bomb under one wing that didn't release, and then our wheels came partially down and we couldn't get them back up – we were rapidly losing flying speed . . . so we got away from the target and bailed out. [3]

Fortunately, Major Goldsworthy and his six-member crew dodged several Japanese search parties. They were finally rescued by Philippine guerillas who helped them return to their base. (**Author's note:** Being shot down by a land mine cannot be proven, but Goldsworthy's crew and others were certain it is what actually happened.)

The war ended as Goldsworthy and his fellow flyers were preparing to depart their base on Palawan and relocate in Okinawa. He had completed seven missions when it ended. Lieutenant Colonel Goldsworthy was later assigned to Itami Air Base near Osaka in occupied Japan. From there, he was rotated back to the states, ending up at Davis-Monthan Field near Tucson, Arizona, with "regular" Air Force status. In the ensuing years, he flew B-25s, B-36s, and B-29s with the Strategic Air Command; in 1949, he was assigned duty at the Pentagon and shortly thereafter promoted to full colonel. He was there when the Korean conflict erupted, serving until the end of the war when he was sent to the Army War College at Carlisle Barracks, Pennsylvania, and became deputy chief of Staff Operations for the Air Proving Ground Command at Eglin AFB in Florida. In 1956, Col. Goldsworthy became chief of staff of the 17th Air Force in Morocco, North Africa, and then Libya. He attended the Industrial College of the Armed Forces in Washington, D.C., and in 1959 joined the Strategic Air Command as vice commander of the 4061st Air Refueling Wing at Malmstrom Air Force Base in Montana. In September 1960, he was transferred to the Ballistic Missiles Center of the Air Materiel Command and assigned as Site Activation Task Force Commander for the first Minuteman Intercontinental Ballistic Missile Wing. He had

a task force to excavate the holes, do the construction, install the missiles, and then turn the operation-ready missiles over to the Strategic Air Command. This task took three years and, when it was completed, he and his command had put in place 150 Minuteman missiles with 15 launch-control centers. In 1962, he was promoted to brigadier general and assigned to the Pentagon as director of production for the Air Force.

Flying Cadet Harry Goldsworthy at flight school in Santa Maria, California, 1939. *(Photo courtesy Harry Goldsworthy.)*

During the Vietnam War, General Goldsworthy, as director of production, had responsibility for production of all items used to conduct the air war, including airplanes, motors, bombs, fuses, and allied equipment. His command also had the responsibility of shipping the planes, bombs, and equipment, which meant arranging for shipping in the right place and at the right time.[4]

In June 1967, Major General Goldsworthy assumed command of the Aeronautical Systems Division, AFSC, at Wright-Patterson Air Force Base in Ohio. There he had direct contractual responsibility for building the airplanes, including writing the specifications, awarding contracts, and supervising construction to ensure the planes were built properly according to specifications. In this capacity, he and his command were directly responsible for designing and building the gunship with side-firing guns that turned out to be one of the most effective weapons used against truck convoys on the routes coming down from the north into South Vietnam. In addition to armament, the gunships were equipped with low-level lightweight televisions and infrared equipment that could detect the incoming convoys. In 1969, he was promoted to lieutenant general and sent back to the Pentagon as deputy chief of staff for Systems and Logistics.

Lieutenant General Goldsworthy retired from the Air Force in 1973. Over his career, he was awarded the Distinguished Service Medal, Legion of Merit with two Oak Leaf Clusters, American Defense Medal, American Campaign Medal, Asiatic-Pacific Campaign Medal, World War II Victory Medal, National Defense Service Medal, Philippine Liberation Medal, Philippine Independence Ribbon, Distinguished Unit Citation, Air Force Longevity Service Award with one Silver and one Bronze Oak Leaf Cluster, Air Medal with four Oak Leaf Clusters, Guided Missile Insignia, and the Armed Forces Reserve Medal. The citation for his first Distinguished Service Medal follows:

Lieutenant General Harry Goldsworthy. *(Photo courtesy the United States Air Force and Washington State University.)*

The President of the United States of America, authorized by Act of Congress July 9, 1918, awards the Distinguished Service Medal to Major General Harry E. Goldsworthy, for exceptionally meritorious service in a duty of great responsibility. General Goldsworthy distinguished himself as Commander, Aeronautical Systems Division, Air Force Systems Command, from 28 May 1967 to July 1969. In this important assignment, General Goldsworthy's expert guidance, exceptional leadership, outstanding management skill, and creative imagination, contributed immeasurably to the development and procurement of a broad variety of aeronautical systems and equipment programs, in addition to ancillary development and procurement projects in direct support of Southeast Asia operations. During this period, General Goldsworthy's outstanding achievements, accomplished through his unselfish devotion to duty and singleness of purpose, significantly improved the current and future operational capabilities of our military forces. General Goldsworthy reflects the highest credit upon himself and the United States Air Force.[5]

A second Distinguished Service Medal was awarded to Harry in December 1972. Harry has been married to Edith Lyons of Spokane since 1937. They have two sons, Harry E. III and James.

Major General Robert F. Goldsworthy
Command Pilot and Prisoner of War
Washington State Legislator

Robert Flood "Bob" Goldsworthy was born on September 26, 1917 and raised on the farm near Rosalia. He graduated high school in Rosalia and enrolled at Washington State College in September 1935. He was a member of the Sigma Nu fraternity, served on the Associated Students Board of Control, and was president of his senior class. He was active in the Radio Guild (working at the KWSC radio station), had starring roles in several college stage productions, and was manager of the Cougar football team. In June 1939, Bob graduated with a bachelor of arts degree in speech and went to work for radio station KFPY in Spokane. He volunteered for Army Air Corps duty, earning his wings and a commission as a second lieutenant in October 1940. He then served as a flight instructor for several years, and eventually qualified to attend four-engine school to prepare for an overseas assignment as a B-24 pilot. He was kept on as a flight instructor for another two years, and then in 1944 volunteered for B-29 training, as the new super forts were just rolling off the assembly lines. His B-29 training was at a base near Hays, Kansas. In October 1944, he and his squadron were sent to Saipan in the Marianas Islands where they flew the first B-29 missions over Japan.

Bob's first mission was the Japanese submarine pens on Truk Island and then it was on to Tokyo. On December 3 on his third

Major General Robert F. Goldsworthy. *(Photo courtesy the United Stated Air Force.)*

mission, Bob's plane named the *Rosalia Rocket* was heavily damaged over Tokyo, and he and his crew were forced to bail out. His hands were severely burned and he was captured immediately.[1] He was a major at the time of his capture. The following narrative is his own story:

On December 3, 1944 at 8:30 in the morning two groups of B-29s with 45 planes each left Saipan for a raid on Tokyo. The first group to take off was led by Major Gay of Spokane, Washington who lost his life on a later raid. I led the second group. With me in my plane were Colonel Brugge of the Wing Command, who was along as an observer; Colonel Richard King, our group commander who replaced Lieutenant Bob Sollock, my regular copilot; Lieutenant Edwards, navigator; Lieutenant "Pat" Patykula, bombardier; Lieutenant Warde, engineer; Sgt. Wright, radioman; Sgt. Coeffrey, CFC gunner; Sgt. Wells, radar; Cpl. Abel, ring gunner; Cpl. Schroeder, right gunner; and Sgt. Corrigan, tail gunner. On the 1,500 mile trek to Tokyo, Major Gay's navigator got just slightly of course, enough that instead of his proceeding us over the target, we arrived first . . .

It was a beautiful clear day. Our particular target, the Mitsubishi aircraft engine factory, was clearly outlined 30,000 feet below and Patykula hit it right on the button with all of our bombs . . . It was then, just as we got the "bombs away" signal that all hell seemed to break loose.

All fighter planes in the Tokyo-Yokohama area were up waiting for us that day, and being the lead plane we caught the brunt of the attack . . . "Tony's" were everywhere, mostly making head-on attacks. The guns of my plane were all open and firing to good effect. I saw one Japanese plane explode from direct hits, another went down trailing smoke and three, or four others were seen to be badly damaged. In the meantime, we were taking a terrific beating. Three of our four engines were shot out and the communication system, too. All control cables with the exception of one aileron were inoperative. One wing was burning and the front compartment was in flames . . . All my efforts were directed toward keeping the plane on an even keel as long as possible to allow the crew members a chance to bail out. With no power, one wing crumpling, and flames licking at the seat of my pants, this was no easy task . . . I turned and yelled at Pat to hurry it up. He seemed in a daze. He was slowly and methodically preparing to jump. Finally, I went back to him and dragged him to the escape hatch. Flames were everywhere. We dropped through the opening. Sometime later, I saw Pat's chute open, turn brown and burst into flame. A fine boy, a grand friend, and one of the best bombardiers in the Air Force, dropped to his death . . . Because of Japanese fighters all around, and because I had forgotten to connect my emergency oxygen cylinder, I chose to make a free fall of what I judged to be about 15,000 feet before pulling my ripcord. I guess that is always an anxious moment. It was doubly so for me, as I suspected fire might have gotten to my chute, too.

I landed safely in a rice paddy on the outskirts of Tokyo . . . Much had happened in a short time. I had lost my plane. I didn't know then how many of my crew had survived the battle. I had seen one drop to his death. And now, I discovered that practically all the skin was burned off the backs of both of my hands. I was one lone, badly scared flier in the midst of 80 million enemies.[2] My first thought was to hide . . . but there was no place to hide. Presently a Japanese woman came along the road that bordered the field where I had landed and for want of any thing better to do, I started following her . . . After about 30 minutes a crowd of angry civilians, armed with clubs began to gather. About the same time, the military, attracted by my parachute, arrived. They were armed with swords only . . . The soldiers, frightening looking men, making those frightening animal sounds, and the sullen, threatening civilian crowd closed in. I fully realized that this might be it . . . The soldiers took my .45, my only weapon, and then deliberately turned me over to the civilians . . . they worked me over. One wrinkled old woman, especially, irked me. Whereas others pounded me with their clubs, she used hers as a prod much as I used to help prod cattle and hogs up the loading chute at home on the farm, only no one was there to caution her against unnecessary roughness as Dad used to caution me. When my guard was up protecting my face, she would jab her club into my ribs, or when my arms were lowered I would catch it in my face . . . I was beginning to wonder if this was the end. Finally, the soldiers rescued me from my reception committee. They bound my hands tightly behind my back with ropes. This, at least, helped deaden the pain from my burns . . .

After walking for approximately three miles, we halted in a small opening among many houses. A small mat was placed on the ground and I, blindfolded by this time, was made to sit down. What we were waiting for I didn't know. I prayed that it wasn't my execution. After about a two-hour wait a truck drove up . . . My blindfold was removed and I was motioned into the truck . . . I sat in the back of the truck with several guards. After about an hour's drive over a very rough road, we came to a halt; then another hour or two of waiting. I have some scars today as a reminder of that wait – scars caused by guards holding lighted matches to my legs. In the truck was a rope with a knot in the end. This they used to pound me over the head.

At long last we stopped at what seemed to be a police station. We were taken inside the building, lined up, and an English-speaking Japanese officer asked us our names

It was then I learned that my two fellow prisoners were Cols. Brugge and King . . .

We finally arrived at what was called Kempei Tai Headquarters. Kempei is their word for military police. It was in reality a federal prison. The three of us were taken to separate rooms for interrogation. In the next room, I could hear someone shouting at Col. Brugge. What he was threatening was not a bit reassuring. I was then stripped of my wristwatch, dog tags, and everything in my pockets. It wasn't much. In trying to get the buckle off my flying suit, they ripped the suit from waist to neck. The cold this rip let in was to cause me much additional misery in the months to come. Next, one of the Japanese officers stepped up and without warning slapped me in the face. What I wanted to do to that little Nip must have shown in my eyes, so he kept slapping until his arm got tired. I knew that to resist would have been suicide so I took it. The guards then took me to the door of my little wooden cell where I was stripped of all my clothing and motioned to enter the door. Now these cell doors were about two feet high and one entered on hands and knees. No guard ever resisted the tempting target thus offered. We soon learned to enter crabwise. Once inside the cell, the guards completed that long eventful day by working me over with a club. A short time later my shorts, flying-suit, and four small blankets were thrown in to me. I rolled up on the floor but no sleep came to me that night . . .

In the morning, I was taken to another part of the prison known as the "stables," as it formerly housed the horses. Here were six cells in a row. Number 3 cell was to be my home . . . Underneath my blindfold I could see GI shoes lined up in front of the other cells. It was a comfort to know I was not alone. I soon learned that Cpl. Schroeder was in the first cell, Col. King to my right, Col. Brugge on my left and Sgt. Geoffery on the other side of Brugge.

Here began what was to be over four months of solitary confinement, with all the refinements of cruelty that diseased minds could conjure up. Only three of us were destined to survive. I was motioned into the cell . . . A guard came into the cell with me and showed me the place and the way I was to sit . . . at attention, cross-legged on the floor, eyes straight ahead. No movement was allowed, not even of the eyes, and guards paced the corridors continually to see that instructions were obeyed. At the end of 15 minutes, I thought my back would break. Japanese can sit that way for hours. I can't – but I did, sixteen hours a day for four long months . . . My new cell was eight by ten feet and absolutely bare. A hole in the floor in one corner was my latrine . . .

My clothing was a pair of shorts and my summer flying suit. We were not allowed to wear shoes or socks in the cell. The food consisted of about 90 grams of rice a day with occasionally a cup of thin soup . . . Now and then we would get a little fish. This would be cooked head, bones, and all. We ate the works. I'll say right here, fish heads are not bad. We would save the eyes for dessert. It was a starvation diet. In four months, I lost 85 pounds.[3] The days, weeks, and months of imprisonment continued, with daily beatings and interrogation. One interrogator asked, "What is your name, rank, serial number?" I told him. He asked, "What group and squadron are you from?" "Sir," I said, "under the rules of international law, the only information I am required to give is name, rank, and serial number." He looked at me for a moment, then said, "You realize of course that we will have this information. Now tell me what group you are from." I remained silent. He called a guard and suddenly I was given a terrific blow on the side of the head. The guard had swung his rifle butt. Now he said, "What is your group?" I was too dazed from the blow to answer at once, so he took his cigarette and stamped it out on my hand. When I flinched, the guard slapped me in the face.[4]

Major Goldsworthy described the cold and hunger he experienced:

My feet and hands were my greatest source of anxiety. We were not allowed to wear shoes or socks in the cell. The cell was without heat and the temperature dropped below zero during the winter. For many weeks, I had little use of my burned hands. That made it difficult for me to make the best use of my abbreviated blankets. It was especially difficult for me to keep my feet covered during the nights. They both nearly froze and turned black. When I could get them warmed enough to stimulate circulation, the pain was excruciating. The fear of losing my feet dogged me for months. It was many months after my release before feeling was completely restored. My hands . . . were burned in the plane before I bailed out. Strips of skin from the back of my hands hung below my fingertips. I was given no medical attention and they became badly infected. The odor got so bad that when I was taken before officers for interrogation they would cover my hands with paper. When they could no longer stand the odor, and I am sure for that reason only and not from any humanitarianism, they had a doctor apply some dressing and bandages. These were left on for a week. The doctor accompanied by a nurse came again. The nurse, without soaking the bandages, just yanked them off. Most of the flesh on my hands came away with them. Gradually they healed over. Time accomplishes wonders and I had lots of time.

I received many beatings . . . they were almost a daily occurrence. Guards would stand me at attention and start slapping with the open hand, then with a fist, winding up with the gun butt or club. A favorite pastime of the guards was to take me into a corridor blindfolded and chase me toward an open door at the end. The upper door jamb, not designed for a six-footer, would catch me above the eyes. If you ever walked into an open door in the dark, you can imagine the shock of running into an obstacle with the speed induced by a bayonet at your back. The torture of this was in regaining consciousness only to look up into the grinning faces of my tormentors. Similarly, they would chase me blindfolded toward steps. I had one stretch of three weeks with a bruised knee that wouldn't support me as a result of this pastime.

I developed bad sores on my posterior from sitting 16 hours a day. One day a guard caught me sitting slightly off center to ease the pressure on one such sore. He came in the cell and kicked me in the jaw. For many days thereafter, I had to shove my rice through jaws that would not open and swallow it unchewed. Luckily my fears of a fractured jaw proved false. Another day, a well-directed kick reopened a sore I had spent weeks getting healed over. It took more weeks to repeat the healing process. One learned patience. As bad as the beatings and mistreatment were, far worse was the cold and the hunger. You can get used to a club, and strangely enough, it sounds worse than it was. But no words can ever describe the torture suffered from cold and hunger.[5]

The beatings and horrible conditions continued until Bob was repatriated on September 2, 1945, about two weeks after VJ Day. When liberated, he weighed only 100 pounds, down from his healthy 180 pounds. He was taken aboard a hospital ship in Tokyo Bay for several weeks of treatment before being flown to a military hospital on Guam, then on to Letterman General in San Francisco. He was promoted to the rank of lieutenant colonel in October, and once sufficiently recovered to go back on active duty, he was stationed at March Field in California, then Davis-Monthan Field in Arizona. In 1947, Bob left the Air Force for the Reserves and returned to Washington to take over his father's farm.

When the Korean War broke out, Colonel Goldsworthy was recalled and sent to Japan with the bomber command stationed at Yakota AFB, and then transferred to a base in Okinawa. Once there, he was made deputy wing commander of a bomb wing flying B-29s. After his Korean tour of duty, he was reassigned to Fairchild AFB near Spokane. His flying skills over Korea earned him the Air Medal. The citation, presented under the direction of the President of the United States read as follows:

Colonel Robert F. Goldsworthy distinguished himself by meritorious achievement as a pilot while participating in aerial flight in the Korean conflict from 19 November 1951 to 6 March 1952. These flights were exceptionally hazardous because of long distances over water and the number of hours spent over enemy territory, during which time enemy contact was probable and expected.

Great damage was inflicted on enemy installations and equipment as a result of the bombing attacks made during this period, which undoubtedly restricted enemy operations. By his courage, fortitude, and his desire to aid the United Nations cause to the best of his ability, Colonel Goldsworthy brought great credit upon himself, the Far East Air Forces, and the United States Air Force.[6]

In April 1953, at his own request, Colonel Goldsworthy separated from the service and returned to his farm near Rosalia in time for harvest. However, he remained in the Air Force Reserves, putting in the required training and operations time each month at various Air Forces bases throughout the United States. Since the reserves were just a part-time activity, Goldsworthy threw his hat in the political ring. In 1956 he was elected to the Washington State House of Representatives, serving in the House until 1972 when redistricting placed him in Spokane County, away from his regular constituents. On May 19, 1967, while serving part-time in the Air Force and as a representative, in addition to farming, Bob was promoted to the rank of major general. During the Vietnam War, General Goldsworthy served with the Strategic Air Command (SAC) and the North American Air Defense Headquarters (NORAD) near Colorado Springs. The general retired from the Air Force in 1977. In addition to the Air Medal, he was awarded the Purple Heart, Air Force Commendation Medal, American Defense Service Medal, Asiatic-Pacific Campaign Medal, Korean Service Medal, Air Force Longevity Service Award with Oak Leaf Cluster, Armed Forces Reserve

Second Lieutenant Bob Goldsworthy in cockpit during his pilot training. *(Photo courtesy the Goldsworthy family.)*

Forces Medal, Presidential Unit Citation, and the United Nations Service Medal.[7]

In the Japanese prison, Bob was beaten, starved, and nearly frozen to the point his feet and extremities were numb throughout the winter months. Of his 12-man bomber crew, five parachuted safely, but only three survived their nine-month imprisonment as POWs. Over the years, Goldsworthy relived the experience in his mind and tried to seek peace, but it would not come. Then in 1997, while vacationing in Hawaii with his wife, Bob met Nori Nagasawa, a Japanese woman who lived through the bombing raids on Tokyo. They became friends. Later, working with a Japanese historian, Nagasawa located the *Rosalia Rocket's* crash site, as well as the widow of the Japanese pilot who shot down Goldsworthy's plane.

A visit to the site was organized for Goldsworthy, his wife Jean and about 150 others to attend a peace ceremony at the crash site. A white cross bearing the words "Going in Peace," in both languages, was erected on the now hallowed ground. Bob Goldsworthy said it was like coming to the end of a book and finishing the last chapter. He had finally found peace.[8]

Bob Goldsworthy on the farm. *(Photo courtesy the Goldsworthy family.)*

General Goldsworthy and his wife Jean have a son and daughter. Their son took over the farm in 1982. Now retired, this versatile farm boy from Washington has become a prolific artist with many fine oil paintings hanging in the homes and offices of friends and relatives.

Colonel C. Ross Greening
Doolittle Raider
German Prisoner of War
Consummate Artist

Charles Ross Greening was born November 12, 1914 in Carroll, Iowa, and raised in Miles City, Montana, and Tacoma, Washington. In 1932, he graduated from Lincoln High in Tacoma and enrolled at Washington State College. He threw the javelin for the Cougar track team, and was an active student leader. The 1936 WSC yearbook, the *Chinook,* is filled with Greening's endeavors, with each major section of the book highlighted by a full page of his artwork. He graduated in 1936 with a bachelor's degree in fine arts and a commission as a second lieutenant in the Army.[1] He was torn between two potential careers, one as a professional artist (portraits were his forte), or as a pilot in the Army Air Corps. He chose the Air Corps, but vowed to continue his painting.

In early 1942, Captain Greening and other flying colleagues volunteered for a secret and highly dangerous mission that later became known as the "Doolittle Raid" over Tokyo. The April 18, 1942 successful raid was made famous in the movie *Thirty Seconds Over Tokyo.* The plan was simple: Sixteen B-25 bombers would be transported into striking range of the Japanese mainland by a U.S. Naval task force and launched from the carrier USS *Hornet.* The rest is history.

Colonel C. Ross Greening
(Photo courtesy Dorothy Greening)

Fifteen of the sixteen B-25s ran out of gas over China and their crews were forced to bail out, but one plane landed safely near Vladivostok in Russia. Greening and his mates, with the help of friendly Chinese, made it to safety and returned to the States for more training. Greening was then assigned to the 17th Medium Bomb Group, eventually leading bombing runs over North Africa, Sardinia, and targets in Italy.

On July 17, 1943, Lt. Colonel Greening's plane was hit by antiaircraft fire (flak) and he and his crew were forced to bail out. Greening landed in the crater of Mount Vesuvius and was badly injured. He was captured, interrogated and shifted from prison to prison. At one point he escaped and, with the help of Italian civilians, hid out in a cave in the mountains. He was recaptured and eventually incarcerated for the rest of the war in a prisoner of war camp named Stalag Luft I near Barth, Germany.

While in prison, Greening painted an amazing pictorial record of the war – that of his own experiences as well as those of dozens of other prisoners who related their accounts to him.

Ross Greening's story is more colorful and compelling than this short biography, therefore readers are referred to his memoirs, entitled *Not As Briefed: From the Doolittle Raid to a German Stalag,* published in 2001 by Washington State University Press. The book is illustrated with over a hundred of Greening's paintings and drawings. This highly decorated veteran died in 1957 from health problems caused by depredations suffered as a prisoner of war.[2]

Staff Sergeant Carl Hall
European Theatre of Operations
Battle of the Bulge
Dean, WSU College of Engineering

On December 7, 1941, "the day that will live in infamy," Carl Hall was 17 years old, a senior in high school and living on a dairy farm in northwestern Ohio. He heard the news of the Pearl Harbor attack from a radio in the barn where he was feeding cattle. In the fall of 1942, he enrolled at Ohio State University, hoping to finish his first two years of college before being drafted. However, within a few months the draft-eligible age was reduced from 20 to 18 and, in March 1943, he was drafted.

Hall received his basic training at an Infantry Replacement Training Center, and was assigned to Company C, 59th Infantry Battalion at Camp Wolters, near Mineral Wells, Texas. Basic training was 15 weeks and in early summer Hall qualified for the Army Specialized Training Program (ASTP), a college-based program designed to train soldiers for technical and engineering work. The ASTP was cancelled after only six months of training as the men involved were needed for the war in Europe. In March 1944, Carl was assigned to the 99th Infantry Division at Camp Maxey near Paris, Texas, with the rank of private.

In September, his division was declared "combat ready" and dispatched, first to Dorchester, England, and a month later to France. The staging area for the division, before taking up battle positions, was at Aubel, Belgium. Hall's regiment, the 395th Infantry, was the northernmost regiment extending along the front lines, from Hofen on the north to just south of Wahlersheid. By this time, Carl had been assigned to the Regimental S-2 (Intelligence) section, with duties including patrolling ahead of the front line, or staffing outposts 100 yards or more in front of the rifle companies. In November, he was selected as a member of a patrol sent out to make contact with the enemy and bring back prisoners. PFC Hall and his patrol colleagues came under fire many times, but their various missions were mostly successful, with limited battle casualties. Hall recounts:

For the reconnaissance patrols, usually three or four of us would move out under the cover of near darkness, or with protection from a smoke screen, and possible canon fire to explode personnel mines, but the rush of movement didn't always permit such luxury. Our technique was to move expeditiously to the area, keeping a low profile and minimizing noise. We did not have sophisticated equipment to detect mines – that was for the soldiers that followed if we located a minefield. While crawling and lying on our stomachs, we inserted our bayonets into the ground at an angle, deftly and quickly, to detect the mines.[1]

On December 13, 1944, Hall's unit began attacking along the Siegfried Line in an operation that actually turned out to be the Battle of the Ardennes, more commonly known as the Battle of the Bulge. The battle raged hot, but the weather was so cold that Hall and his compatriots fought not only the enemy but the freezing wet winter as well. Many suffered from frostbitten or frozen feet. In his book *Citizen Soldiers*, Stephen Ambrose reported that during the "Bulge" the equivalent of an entire division of American soldiers was put out of action due to frozen extremities, often referred to as "trench foot."[2]

The German attack at the Bulge, the last major offensive of the German Army, was at first successful, but the Allies soon stopped their drive and routed the enemy. Hall's unit crossed the Rhine River near Remagen. The unit was moved to Bamberg April 17 and 18, 1945 to become part of the 3rd Army under General George Patton Jr. From Bamberg, they crossed in rapid succession the Ludwig Canal, Altmuhl River, and the Danube,

near the famous or "infamous" German Mooseberg Prisoner of War Camp. Hall's unit liberated nearly 20,000 American prisoners, including First Lieutenant Leo Bustad (see the Leo Bustad story).

By the end of the war, Carl Hall had been promoted to staff sergeant and awarded the Combat Infantryman's Badge, Bronze Star, Good Conduct Medal, the American Campaign Medal, European African Middle Eastern Campaign Medal with three Battle Stars, World War II Victory Medal, Army of Occupation Medal, Army Meritorious Unit Citation, Belgium Fourragere with two citations, and a Certificate of Merit Citation for patrol activity in 1944-45.[3]

Hall returned to college after the war, earning a B.S. degree in mechanical engineering (M.E.) from Ohio State University in 1948, a master's degree in M.E. from the University of Delaware in 1950, and a Ph.D. in M.E. from Michigan State in 1952. After a distinguished engineering career, Hall became professor of mechanical engineering in 1970 and, later, dean of the College of Engineering at Washington State University. He retired from WSU in 1982 as dean emeritus.[4]

Colonel Jack D. Holsclaw*
Cougar Baseball Player
Tuskegee Airman and "Red Tail" Fighter Pilot
Member of the Famous All-Black P-51 Mustang Air Group
Distinguished Flying Cross Recipient

Jack D. Holsclaw, son of Mr. and Mrs. Charles W. Holsclaw, was born March 21, 1918 in Spokane, Washington. He graduated from Spokane's North Central High School in June 1935 and enrolled at Whitworth College that fall. After a year at Whitworth, he transferred to Washington State College in Pullman. An outstanding baseball and basketball player in high school, he was determined to play baseball for WSC Coach Arthur "Buck" Bailey. However, because of his transfer status, he was not eligible to play until the 1937-38 school year. That year he played third base, then centerfield, for the Cougars. The Cougars ended the season as co-champions of the Northern Division of the Pacific Coast Conference.

At WSC, Jack majored in political science with an emphasis in prelaw.[1] He wanted to attend medical school but found acceptance into a chiropractic program easier, so he transferred for his senior year to Western State College in Portland, Oregon.

Jack completed the naturopathy (chiropractic) program in 1942 and passed the state board examination to become a licensed chiropractor in Oregon. By this time, World War II was raging, and Jack, like most Americans, wanted to do his part for the war

Lieutenant Jack D. Holsclaw with his P-51 *Bernice Baby*.
(Photo courtesy Bernice Holsclaw.)

effort. While attending college in Portland, he trained as a private pilot and obtained his license; therefore, his preference for military duty was the Army Air Force. He enlisted and volunteered for flight school, but the waiting list was long and on October 5, 1942, before he could report for flight training, he was drafted for active duty in the Army. It took several months for the military to straighten out Jack's orders. On July 27, 1943 he was discharged from the Army and awarded a commission as a second lieutenant in the Army Air Force. He, along with other Black trainees, was sent to the Tuskegee Institute (now Tuskegee University) in Tuskegee, Alabama, for flight school. His training included flying P-40s, then P-39s. In December 1943, he and his fellow Tuskegee pilots shipped overseas to an airfield near Naples, Italy. Initially his outfit was assigned to conduct coastal patrols and escort ship convoys in the Mediterranean. The P-39s were not supercharged and could fly only at limited altitudes, so the squadrons were soon equipped with P-47s and ultimately P-51s, the fastest and most powerful fighters in the European Theatre of Operations. Due to their distinctive tail markings, they were called "Red Tails" by the Allies and *Schwartze Vogelmenshen* (Black Birdmen) by the Germans.

In July 1944, and now a first lieutenant and combat veteran with many missions under his belt, Jack made history by earning the Distinguished Flying Cross. By this time, his unit, the 332nd Fighter Group, was composed of four complete squadrons with 16 P-51 Mustangs in each squadron. The day's mission was to provide cover protection for American B-17s on bombing runs over German and Italian targets. The bombers were constantly under attack by enemy fighters, and the P-51 pilots had to fight them off as best they could while remaining as cover for the bombers. Nevertheless, with four squadrons in the air, it was possible to assign three to protect the bombers and designate one "attack" squadron that could pursue the enemy aircraft. On that day, Lieutenant Holsclaw's squadron went on the attack, closing with the enemy fighters and pursuing them to make them pay for attacking the bombers. Following the ensuing air battle over Munich, Germany, a news dispatch for the Associated Press reported that Lieutenant Holsclaw had shot down two German Messerschmitt 109s (Me-109s). Also reported was that overall, the squadron under his leadership had bagged a total of 11 German planes in a spectacular action.[2] Because of his leadership and heroic action, Major General Twining awarded Lieutenant Holsclaw the Distinguish Flying Cross. The citation read:

For extraordinary achievement in aerial fight of a P-51 type aircraft, on 18 July 1944, Lieutenant Holsclaw led his flight as escort to heavy bombers attacking enemy installations in Germany. Despite severe and adverse weather conditions, he brought his flight through to engage an enemy force of approximately 300 enemy fighters. In the ensuing engagement, despite the superiority in numbers of enemy aircraft, with complete disregard for his personal safety, Lieutenant Holsclaw with an outstanding display of aggressiveness and combat proficiency, destroyed two (2) enemy fighters and forced the remainder to break off their organized attacks. By his outstanding courage, professional skill, and devotion to duty, as evidenced throughout his combat career, Lieutenant Holsclaw has reflected great credit upon himself and the Armed Forces of the United States of America.[3]

In a February 1998 interview, Colonel Holsclaw vividly remembered that day, recalling that his air group of 64 P-51 Mustangs faced nearly 300 German fighters. The weather was threatening and, as they took off from the airfield near Naples, their flight leader had engine trouble, forcing his return to the field. For a moment, the group circled the field waiting for instructions, but to rendezvous with the bombers on time, Holsclaw took over and led the group into battle. Three of the squadrons formed an umbrella over the bombers and one squadron, under Holsclaw's leadership, engaged the enemy.[4]

A writer for *Liberty Magazine* detailed the good fortune of the Tuskegee pilots in a story called "Dark Angels of Doom." He reported that, fresh from training in America, the unique band of all Black pilots, to which Holsclaw belonged, began its overseas career with a flourish. They won weekly commendations from General Montgomery for their close support of the British 8th Army in North Africa, by dive bombing and strafing, and knocking out enemy machine gun nests, tanks, and transportation lines. In an initial assault on Italy, the Red Tails shot down 17 enemy fighters and bombers in one day over the Anzio beachhead.[5] Despite their success pursuing enemy aircraft, the main task of Holsclaw's fighter group was to protect U.S. bombers against enemy fighter attacks, an assignment they performed with miraculous success. "Not a single bomber was lost to German planes while being escorted by the Red Tails."[6] To Holsclaw, this was their crowning achievement, and his 24 medals and citations, including the Distinguished Flying Cross, were simply "icing on the cake."

Holsclaw participated as a fighter pilot in seven major campaigns, including southern France, the Po Valley, North Apennines, Rome-Arno, the Balkans, northern France, and Germany. He completed 68 missions, at one time flying 18 in 20 days. To avoid battle fatigue, his commanding officer grounded him after his 68th mission, assigning him to desk duty as operations officer for the Red Tails.

Germany surrendered May 8, 1945, and Jack's unit returned to U.S. soil, where he was assigned to flight gunnery school in Texas. Soon afterward he transferred from reserve to regular status, committing to a career in the Air Force. He later directed Air Force Reserve Officer Training Corps (ROTC) units on three university campuses, and saw flight duty in Japan from 1954 to 1957. He also flew support missions between Japan and Vietnam during the early stages of the Vietnam War. On January 1, 1965, Jack retired from the Air Force with permanent rank of lieutenant colonel.

Besides the Distinguished Flying Cross, Colonel Holsclaw also received the Air Medal with five Oak Leaf Clusters, Distinguished Unit Citation Emblem, American Campaign Medal, European-African-Middle Eastern Campaign Medal with seven Bronze Service Stars, World War II Victory Medal, National Defense Service Medal, and the Air Force Longevity Service Award Ribbon with four Bronze Oak Leaf Clusters. At his retirement, Jack received the Air Force Commendation Medal for which the citation read:

Lieutenant Colonel Jack D. Holsclaw. *(Photo courtesy Bernice Holsclaw.)*

Lieutenant Colonel Jack D. Holsclaw distinguished himself by meritorious service while serving as Chief, Training Division, Sixth Air Force Reserve Region, from 27 May 1962 to 31 December 1964. During this period, Colonel Holsclaw displayed outstanding job knowledge, management ability, and skill in organizing and conducting training programs. Under his guidance, two volumes of a textbook, using keen program learning methods, were prepared and a valuable Orientation Course for newly

assigned personnel was implemented, that significantly improved the Air Reserve Training Program. The distinctive accomplishments of Colonel Holsclaw culminate a distinguished career in the service of his country, and reflect credit upon himself, the Continental Air Command, and the United States Air Force.

As a civilian, Jack Holsclaw was the manager of the Marin County Housing Authority in northern California, and later worked at the People's National Bank in Bellevue, Washington, for 10 years. He and his wife Bernice, his Whitworth College sweetheart, retired permanently in 1983.

Jack Holsclaw showed himself to be a true pathfinder by breaking the color barrier as an Eagle Scout at age 15, being on the Cougar baseball team, attending chiropractic college, and as a highly successful and decorated Air Force pilot and member of the now famous Tuskegee "Red Tails." During his combat days, Jack's favorite P-51 fighter was christened *Bernice Baby* in honor of his beloved wife. Jack died on April 7, 1998.

* *The Jack Holsclaw story previously appeared in the April 2004 issue of* **The Pacific Northwesterner***.*

Army Colonel Lester B. Johnson
42nd Rainbow Division Combat Veteran

Lester B. Johnson was born in Olympia on December 2, 1915 to May W. and Lester B. Johnson Sr. He graduated from Olympia High School in 1933 and enrolled at Washington State College where he joined the Beta Theta Pi fraternity and Sigma Delta Chi journalism society. He graduated from WSC in June 1938 with a degree in economics and a second lieutenant's commission in the Army. In 1940, he was among the few selected from 1,000 reserve candidates for a commission in the regular Army. After training, he was assigned to the 42nd "Rainbow" Division and served in combat with the unit throughout the war in the European Theatre of Operations. Lester was decorated with the Bronze Star with Oak Leaf Clusters, the Combat Infantryman's Badge, the Meritorious Service Medal, along with several other unit citations.

Lester completed 30 years of active service that took him to the Aleutian Islands, Germany, Korea, Japan, the Presidio of San Francisco, Fort Dix, the Defense Language Institute at the Presidio of Monterey, Fort Lewis in Washington State, and a stint as advisor to the Imperial Iranian Gendarmerie in Iran. Colonel Johnson retired in 1970 and died in 1998.

Army Corporal Randall A. Johnson
Creator of the Famous WSU Cougar Logo

Randall A. "Randy" Johnson was born in LaCrosse, Washington, on March 2, 1915. His family moved to Pullman in 1930 and he graduated from Pullman High School in 1933. A budding artist in high school, Randy enrolled in fine arts at Washington State College. He graduated on June 6, 1938.[1]

Corporal Randall A. Johnson. *(Photo courtesy the Johnson family.)*

When he was a junior, Randy designed the now famous Cougar logo, featuring the letters WSC (later modified for WSU) molded into a facsimile of a Cougar head. The following is Randy's account when asked to describe his famous achievement:

I worked for Physical Plant for about three years as a specialist. Instead of 25 cents an hour, I was paid 30 cents . . . I also worked for a number of other university departments and a lot of merchants in town . . . I had been working under the supervision of Fred Rounds, the college architect. He was bossing the work that I did at the time. George Grimes was the head of the department . . . they were rebuilding the football stadium and they needed names and numbers painted and sign lettering done. One job involved one of the agricultural departments that had acquired a new pickup truck, and they asked me to paint the appropriate label on the door . . . a lot of big long-winded names and a lot of lettering. Mr. Rounds said, "That is a handful of words to put on a door," and I replied, "It's about like copying the New Testament on the head of a pin." He then said, "Randall, what this place needs is some sort of a trademark, something that would stand for the college so we wouldn't have to do all of this lettering." I said, "I couldn't agree more." We talked about it for a while and thought it would be nice to work the "Cougar" [mascot] into it someway. I liked the idea because, in those days, we had a live Cougar mascot, and I had been making sketches of him, just for my own fun as I like animals. Mr. Rounds and I talked about it awhile, and then he said, "Why don't you, on your own time, see what you can come up with?" . . . I doodled around and realized that the design had to do several things; it had to identify the college, we wanted it to look like a cougar, and we also wanted it to be a positive statement with some animation in it . . . I came up with an arrangement I liked, so I worked on it some more and thought, "By golly, this will work." I then made a color layout of it and took it into Mr. Rounds, who took one look at it and said, "I like it. Let's take it up to the president." Dr. Holland was in Japan on sabbatical at the time, and the acting president

was Dean Herbert Kimbrough, so we took my design to Dean Kimbrough and he immediately said, "That's good, I like it, go ahead and we'll make it official." [2]

Randy Johnson with WSU designs. *(Photo courtesy WSU.)*

In 1959, more than 20 years later Randall modified his original design to match the new university designation, and turned the copyright over to Washington State University.

Randall joined the National Guard in Pullman during his first year in college; he was assigned to Company E, 161st Infantry. The Guard appealed to him for its $1.00 per week and the chance to avoid early morning drills required of Reserve Officer Training Corps (ROTC) cadets. During summer 1935, the National Guard was activated for riot control in Tacoma, Aberdeen, and Hoquiam. The riots were presumably started by the Young Communist League and led to battles in the streets, drive-by shootings, and houses and lumber mills set afire. Randall and his guard unit were thus introduced to hand-to-hand combat.

Once finished with the National Guard, Randall worked for Washington Water Power Company in its advertising department. Being a licensed pilot, he volunteered for the Army Air Corps but was turned away because he was married. On a second attempt to volunteer, he was again turned away for not meeting the weight requirement. In 1943, Randall was drafted into the Army Infantry. Because he already had Infantry experience, he was assigned to train medical corpsmen on how to stay alive on the battlefield. The training included showing how to dig foxholes, move under fire, and everything infantrymen need to know.[2] However, it was not too long before Private Johnson's commanders discovered his artistic ability and talent, and he was dispatched to the Command and General Staff School (C&GSS) at Fort Leavenworth in Kansas and more aptly assigned to the Instructional Aids Department. For the remainder of the war, his job was to design and prepare training aids and related visuals to assist in training field officers who were being prepared to join the fronts in Europe and the Pacific. Randy refers to his job as head of the creative design section and the C&GSS as the "school that trained colonels to become generals." He recounted, "There was urgency and immediacy about their work that made them feel like they were right in the middle of the war." [3] For example, much of his work involved receiving enemy equipment and related material straight from the battlefronts. His team would then prepare lectures and visuals to train the student officers on what they could expect when they returned to battle. Corporal Johnson remained on the job at Fort Leavenworth through the end of the war and until July 1946 when he was discharged from service.

Randall returned to his job in Spokane and had a long and varied career with the Washington Water Power Company. He became international president of the Public Utilities Advertising Association. In 1956, he was named "Spokane Ad Man of the Year." In 1970, the American Gas Association awarded him the Golden Anvil Award, and in 1976, he received the American Advertising Federation Silver Medal. He served two terms as president of the Eastern Washington State Historical Society (Cheney Cowles Museum). Randy was honored by WSU with an Alumni Achievement Award in 1979 and, in 1997, he and his wife were designated as WSU Benefactors. In 1999, an international group specializing in western history, known as Westerners International, designated Randall their "Living Legend" (there have been just 39 designations in over 100 years).

Photo of a poster of Randall Johnson and samples of his artwork.
(Courtesy the Johnson family.)

Randall and his wife Jeanne, married since 1940, have five children. Three of the children, Arthur, Roxanne and Thomas, graduated from WSU. Edwin James Johnson, Randall's younger brother, WSC class of 1939, was a first lieutenant in the Infantry, and served in numerous battles in the Pacific, including Guadalcanal.

Robert L. Loeffelbein
Navy Quartermaster Second Class

Robert Le Roy Loeffelbein was born June 24, 1924 in Wenatchee, Washington, to Mr. and Mrs. R. E. Loeffelbein. He graduated from Wenatchee High School in June 1940 and enrolled at the Lewiston State Normal School (now Lewis-Clark State College) in Lewiston, Idaho, and then joined the Navy. After the war, he enrolled at Washington State College and lived at South House, one of the old World War II Navy prefabs that housed up to 400 men. Robert majored in English and journalism, and was active on the Rally Committee, serving as yell king for two years. He wrote for the campus newspaper and various other publications, and served as a part-time scriptwriter for the campus radio station. He was a member of Alpha Phi Omega, the National Service Honorary. He received a bachelor of arts in English in May 1948.[1]

Navy QMST 2nd Class Robert Loeffelbein. *(Photo courtesy United States Navy.)*

During World War II, Quartermaster Loeffelbein served aboard the USS *Grimes*, a new assault troop transport. The following are excerpts from the log he kept as his ship steamed toward Tokyo to take part in the occupation of Japan:[2]

July 21, 1945
I had just walked into the wheelhouse for my evening watch when four people all started shouting orders: "Cease Zigzag Lights!" "Full Speed!" "Full Left Rudder!" "Danger Signal!" We barely managed to avoid the incoming off-course AP 6, then went hard right and managed to miss the AP 173 we were being forced into on the other side. Exciting few moments. Some OD on the "6" is going to get a fancy fanny chewing.

August 10
Pulled into Ulithi this afternoon and got the scoop on the peace talk rumors we've been hearing. The atom bombings of Hiroshima and Nagasaki have forced the Japanese to talk surrender. But there's a stumbling block – what to do with Hirohito, Japan's living God.

August 15
Official word came over the radio: THE WAR IS OVER! Every ship in the convoy let loose with horns and whistles until we couldn't even hear orders being given on the bridge.

August 16
The war isn't over after all! Papers haven't been signed, or some such formality. Anyhow, we're still heading for

rendezvous with the Third Fleet . . . Discovered about two hundred extra Gyrenes [Marines] aboard, from the Fourth and Sixth Divisions, when we ran out of chow and started checking billets. Turns out they are AWOL stowaways who wanted to be in at the end, the invasion of Japan proper. The skipper said, "Who's going to charge them with anything?"

August 17

We've now counted closer to 250 Gyrene stowaways. And the other transports all report the same.

August 19

Task Force 31 formed up: about a dozen carriers, three or four battleships, dozens of cans and DMS [destroyer minesweepers], half a dozen or so cruisers and oilers, hospital ships, LSVs [landing craft], repair ships, little of everything, just one big floating naval base. More gold braid aboard now than you'd see at a doorman's convention.

August 25

Word came yesterday the Japanese peace envoy was cabined with Admiral Halsey aboard the U.S.S. Missouri. Headed in slow, seven knots, today for Sagami Wan, the outside harbor of Tokyo Bay, all guns manned, and ever alert for possible Pearl Harbor-type surprises.

August 27

Everyone's fears have been laid to rest. It's to be a peaceful invasion . . . I wanted to be ringside for the land-ing tomorrow, so I finagled a job as signalman on one of the landing barges. I had to get three watch replacements, plus approvals from the watch commander, CPO [chief petty officer], DO [division officer], and boat officer. I didn't have that much trouble getting into the Navy!

August 30

Went on into Tokyo Bay and began off-loading troops and supplies. I was in boat 17 in the sixth wave. On the second trip, we were the first boat into Red Beach [the original invasion name] taking the headquarters officers in. Everyone was tense, guns at ready, but we were met only by a very polite Japanese officer with a working party still in the wool khaki uniforms that gave them a slightly comical look, sort of like our World War I uniforms. They unloaded for us.

After becoming a Navy journalist first class, Loeffelbein returned home after his service. He was recalled for duty during the Korean War, serving in Hawaii in the Navy Special Services and the Quartermaster. As a civilian, he earned several advanced academic degrees and taught at several universities, including Princeton University, SEAS (School of Engineering & Applied Science).

Army Captain Russell A. Long
European Theatre of Operations
Purple Heart and Bronze Star
French Croix de Guerre

Russell Alger Long was born January 29, 1912 in Spokane. His father was the sheriff of Spokane County and superintendent of the Washington State Penitentiary in Walla Walla. Russell graduated from Walla Walla High School in June 1929 and entered Washington State College that fall. He lived in the newest men's residence hall on campus, Stimson Hall, his first year before pledging Sigma Phi Sigma fraternity. He received a B.A. degree in economics, graduating in June 1933 with honors and a second lieutenant's commission in the Army Reserves.[1]

Lieutenant Long went on active Army duty in early March 1942, starting with training assignments in Utah, California and Georgia. In July 1943, he reported to Fort Benning, Georgia, for training as an Infantry troop leader. On July 10, 1944, Lieutenant Long, four other officers, and 200 enlisted men formed an Infantry company and boarded the USS *General Meigs*, an Army transport headed for the European Theatre. D-Day and the invasion of France had occurred about one month earlier, June 6. 1944.[2] The ship docked at Naples, Italy. Lieutenant Long and his men were bivouacked near Naples for several months and, on August 20, were again aboard ship heading for the invasion on the coast of southern France.

On August 25, they were on landing craft headed for the beach. Once on shore, they traveled north toward the front, first by truck, then on foot. By this time, Lieutenant Long's outfit had been assigned to I Company, 141st Infantry Regiment, 36th Division.

Attempting to cross the Moselle River, they came under enemy fire and were forced to pull back. Later they moved ahead, eventually digging in about five miles east of a small French town, Bruyeres, an area that had recently been taken by the 442nd Regimental Combat Team (the "Go For Broke" outfit made up of Japanese Americans). The next day Long's unit came under heavy fire from artillery and mortars. They suffered several casualties and managed to do some damage themselves, including capturing several German soldiers. On October 31, after nearly two months of pressure under combat conditions, the Germans counterattacked. Lieutenant Long saw at least a dozen of his men bunched up so close together that a single shell could get them all. Without consideration for his own safety, he hurried toward his men, shouting and signaling them to spread out and take cover. An instant later, a large enemy shell struck a rock no more than four feet from him and exploded. He recalled the episode:

I felt pieces strike me but with no particular pain involved. They seemed to be low down on my legs and I thought that if there were no more of them (shells), it would not be so bad. Then my legs gave way and I tumbled over backwards into a small depression. As I hit the ground, I thought that it was all over; this was the end. Then I began to feel shock and had to fight for a breath of air. [3]

Long was rescued by a medic and transferred by litter to a field hospital. Both legs were nearly blown off and he had shrapnel wounds in his back and right shoulder. Six of his men were also hit, one in worse condition than Long, and one killed. The following day, his surgeon brought in the pieces of metal removed from Long's body to show him; the shrapnel could barely be held in one hand.

The surgeon explained that about seven-eighths of each of his legs had been severed above the knee, but fortunately, the connections remaining held the principal arteries and nerves, so the surgeon thought the legs might be saved. Long was placed in a plaster cast from his neck to his toes, and taken by ambulance to a hospital in Aix En Provence, France. Lieutenant Long was later sent back to the U.S. and on to various hospitals, spending nearly three and one-half years hospitalized and having 13 major operations before he was able to walk again. He had gone on active Army duty in March 1942, and was released from the hospital and discharged in March 1948. He was discharged with the rank of captain, and awarded the Combat Infantry Badge, the Purple Heart with Oak Leaf Cluster, Bronze Star, WWII

Victory Medal, American Campaign Medal, and the European Middle Eastern African Campaign Medal with three Battle Stars. The French Government awarded Long the Croix de Guerre, the Medaille de la France Liberee and, most recently, on the 50th anniversary of the landings in Normandy and Provence, the Liberation of France 1944 Medal. [4]

Captain Long returned to civilian life in Spokane, resuming his prewar employment in banking. He retired in 1972, having completed 39 years of faithful service to the Seattle First National Bank. Russell Long died in 2001.

Brigadier General Loren G. McCollom
P-47 Fighter Pilot
Prisoner of War

Loren George McCollom was born in Ritzville, Washington, on April 15, 1914, the son of Mr. and Mrs. George W. McCollom. He graduated from Ritzville High School in 1932 and entered Washington State College that fall with a "general" major. He completed the mandatory two years of Reserve Officer Training Corps (ROTC) training but chose not to enter the advanced program. Loren graduated from WSC in June 1937. In 1939, he enlisted as a flying cadet, earning his wings and second lieutenant's commission in the Reserves the following year. [1]

After graduation from flight school, Lieutenant McCollom's first assignment was as aircraft commander in the 8th Pursuit Group at Langley Field in Virginia. Two years later, at the beginning of World War II, he assumed command of the 61st Fighter Squadron, 56th Fighter Group; he and his squadron were relocated to England.

In August 1943, he assumed command of the 353rd Fighter Group in England and was promoted to lieutenant colonel. He flew 40 fighter combat missions over enemy occupied territory, developed new fighter flight patterns and attack tactics, destroyed or seriously damaged four German Me-109s, and was shot down and captured. For his leadership and gallantry, Lieutenant McCollom was awarded the Silver Star with the following citation:

For gallantry in action, while leading a Group of P-47 aircraft on a dive-bombing mission over enemy occupied Europe, 25 November 1943. Colonel McCollom was assigned the task of testing the potentialities of the P-47 aircraft for dive-bombing. After weeks of untiring effort spent in planning and developing new untried tactics, he led his Group against a heavily defended military installation. Though subjected to intense, accurate antiaircraft fire, Lieutenant Colonel McCollom maneuvered his unit over the objective and bombed it with a high degree of success. After releasing his bombs,

he was forced to bail out when his aircraft was practically demolished by a burst of flak. The knowledge gained on this first bombing mission by P-47 aircraft furnished information that will be of great value in future operations. The gallantry, determination, and leadership in battle displayed by Colonel McCollom were an inspiration to his fellow flyers. [2]

McCollom was awarded the Distinguished Flying Cross with the following citation:

Loren G. McCollom, Lieutenant Colonel, Army Air Forces, United States Army. For extraordinary achievement, Colonel McCollom has accomplished forty fighter combat missions over enemy occupied Continental Europe, and has destroyed one enemy airplane in aerial combat. The skillful and zealous manner in which Colonel McCollom has sought out the enemy and destroyed him, his devotion to duty and courage under all conditions serve as an inspiration to his fellow flyers. His actions on all these occasions reflect the highest credit upon himself and the Armed Forces of the United States.

After being wounded and captured, McCollom was imprisoned in Stalag Luft I, a German POW camp, where he remained until the end of the war. There he joined a Cougar classmate, Colonel

Ross Greening from Tacoma. In his memoirs, Greening recounts how he came upon McCollom in Stalag Luft I:

I looked up and suddenly saw a familiar face in this crowd of strangers. I was flabbergasted! It was Mac McCollom, my fraternity brother from Washington State College! "Mac! You old SOB," I screamed. "What in the hell are you doing here?" . . . I noticed burn marks on his face and hands, which was common for men who'd been shot down or had crash landed . . . Lieutenant Col. Loren "Mac" McCollom, a fighter pilot, had been hit by a burst from an 88 mm AA gun just as he started to dive on an objective. His fighter burst into flames and he suffered severe burns before he could bail out. The outline of his helmet could be seen where it had protected the rest of his head from the flames.[3]

While incarcerated, McCollom provided extraordinary services to his fellow prisoners. For this he was awarded the Bronze Star:

Lieutenant Colonel Loren G. McCollom, serving while a prisoner of war, as [an] A-2 of the Wing Organization in Stalag Luft I, Germany, displayed exceptionally meritorious conduct in the performance of outstanding services from 14 December 1944 to May 14 May 1945. Through his organization, he performed duties of great value to the War Department. In addition, he perfected a system of news service for all Prisoners of War confined to Stalag Luft I, which materially contributed to the maintenance of a high state of morale throughout the camp. His services for the War Department and for his fellow prisoners were performed despite risk of detection and consequent grave punishment by his captors. The courage, initiative, and professional skill displayed by Colonel McCollom reflect highest credit upon himself and the armed forces of the United States.

Recalling his forced captivity and the lack and poor quality of food in Stalag Luft I, McCollom was quoted by a news reporter as telling his wife, "By the way, I don't want you ever to serve me cabbage in our home. I ate enough cabbage in Germany for several life times . . . The same thing goes for horse meat . . . I don't want horse meat, either."[4]

After repatriation, McCollom remained in the Air Force, serving in Korea and Japan as well as assignments in the continental United States. In 1958, he was awarded the Legion of Merit, which contained these words: "Colonel McCollom became a recognized leader in bringing automation to the nation's air defenses and in developing an atomic air defense capability." At the time of his retirement in 1968, Major General McCollom was awarded a second Legion of Merit. His medals and decorations now included the Silver Star with two Oak Leaf Clusters, two Legion of Merit, Distinguished Flying Cross,

Bronze Star, Purple Heart, Air Medal with three Oak Leaf Clusters, the Korean Service Medal, and many other service ribbons and citations.

General McCollom is married to the former Katherine Oliver of Hoquiam, Washington. They have three grown children, Susan, Patti and Scott.

Colonel Naomi M. McCracken
Navy and Air Force Veteran
President, American Association of Collegiate Registrars and Admissions Officers

Naomi McCracken was born December 16, 1921 and raised in Clayton, New Mexico, the youngest daughter of Mr. and Mrs. John M. McCracken. Naomi was a bit of a tomboy and preferred to be outdoors doing the thing boys typically did. She graduated from high school in June 1940 and enrolled at New Mexico Highland University that fall with a combined major in education, science, and mathematics. Concerned about the war and wanting to do her part, she enlisted in the Navy just before graduation and was immediately called to active duty, training as a weather observer. Naomi completed her Navy duty in November 1945 and was discharged with the rank of aerographers mate first class. She returned to New Mexico Highlands University and completed her degree in May 1946.

After graduation, Naomi accepted a position as assistant registrar at Highlands University. To take her interest in registrar's work further, she enrolled in graduate school at the University of Kentucky, studying under the renowned registrar Ezra L. Gillis. She was awarded a master's degree from Kentucky in 1948 and then was appointed registrar at Converse College in Spartanburg, South Carolina.

While hosting an Air Force recruiter on the Converse campus, she was convinced to consider becoming an Air Force officer. She was offered a direct commission as a lieutenant in the Air Force, an offer she accepted.

After completing Air Force training, Naomi was assigned as personnel officer at Warner Robins Air Force Base at Macon, Georgia. She completed one year of basic meteorology training, and then reported for duty to Wiesbaden Air Force Base in West Germany, serving as a weather forecaster. Her duties included weather forecasting and providing Air Force pilots with weather information for their flight schedules. In 1957, the Air Force began accepting students to attend the new service academy in Colorado Springs, Colorado. With construction on the Air Force Academy not yet complete, the new cadets were temporarily located at Lowry Air Force Base in Denver. Captain McCracken was assigned to the new academy, first as deputy director and then director of Cadet Records (Registrar). She was the first female line officer assigned to any U.S. military academy. She completed her tour of duty at the Air Force Academy in September

1963 and was assigned as registrar at the Air Force Institute of Technology at Wright-Patterson Air Force Base in Dayton, Ohio, a position she held until called back to her earlier post at the Academy in January 1966. Her initial work at the Academy included the development and installation of a state-of-the-art electronic records system. Products of the new system included well-balanced student course schedules for each day of the week, faculty teaching schedules, sectioning of courses, final exam schedules that provided each student with a maximum of two exams per day, end-of-term grade reports, and cumulative student transcripts.[1]

For her outstanding and innovative work, Captain McCracken was awarded the Air Force Commendation Medal with the following citation:

Captain Naomi M. McCracken distinguished herself by highly meritorious service as Director of Cadet Records in the Office of the Registrar, United States Air Force Academy, from 1 May 1957 to 1 July, 1963. During this period, Captain McCracken developed a machine record system of such streamlined effectiveness that it became a model copied by other colleges and universities, and merited repeated recognition by the Colorado and the American Association of Collegiate Registrars and Admissions Officers (AACRAO). As Academy advisor to Baptist cadets, as institutional representative for Baptist students of all Colorado colleges, and as one of

Air Force Lieutenant Colonel Naomi M. McCracken. *(Photo courtesy United State Air Force.)*

the most energetic officers of the Academy in support of cadet and community activities, Captain McCracken earned the great affection, admiration, and respect of the Air Force Cadet Wing and the Academy faculty and staff. Captain McCracken's distinctive accomplishments reflect credit upon herself and the United States Air Force.[2]

Naomi retired from the Air Force July 31, 1973 with the permanent rank of lieutenant colonel. During her various tours of duty with the Navy and Air Force, she was also decorated with the Meritorious Service Medal, Air Force Outstanding Unit Award with one Oak Leaf Cluster, American Campaign Medal, World War II Victory Medal, Army of Occupation Medal, National Defense Service Medal with one Bronze Service Star, and Air Force Longevity Service Award with one Oak Leaf Cluster.

Following her military service, Naomi remained active in Registrar's work, serving as Registrar and Coordinator of Academic Advising at the Colorado Women's College from August 1973 to January 1977. While at the Women's College, she stepped up her professional activities, ultimately serving a three-year term as vice president for Data Management and Research for the American Association of Collegiate Registrars and Admissions Officers (AACRAO). She then served another three years as AACRAO president elect, president, and past president. Her presidential duties covered the academic year 1976-77.[3]

When the Women's College closed, Naomi joined Washington State University working on this author's team as associate registrar. She provided exceptional service to WSU having complete responsibility for the Records Section of the Registrar's Office. In addition to her professional responsibilities at WSU, Naomi served six years as trustee for the YMCA, three years as a faculty advisor to the Associated Women Students, three years on the Athletic Advisory Council, and three years as the faculty advisor for the WSU Mom's Weekend Committee.[4] Colonel McCracken retired from WSU in June 1984, returning to Colorado Springs where she continues to volunteer her services at the Air Force Academy and for various Academy-related activities.

Captain Clayton H. Mickelsen
Hero of Bataan
Cavalryman in the Philippines
WSC Veterinarian

Clayton Hileman Mickelsen was born August 16, 1911 in Yakima, Washington, and later moved with his family to Portland, Oregon. He graduated from Lincoln High School in Portland and attended Glendale Junior College in Glendale, California. He transferred to Washington State College for fall semester 1935. He received a bachelor of science degree followed by a doctorate in Veterinary Medicine in June 1939.[1] Immediately following graduation, Clayton entered the Veterinary Corps Reserve of the Army as a first lieutenant. He went on active duty in November 1940, and left for the Philippines in April 1941. He was assigned to the 26th Cavalry Regiment, the Philippine Scouts.

During the battle and fall of Bataan, Lieutenant Mickelsen's heroism and gallantry delayed the advance of Japanese tanks and troops, and he was responsible for saving the lives of dozens of his comrades. His actions were reported in a national magazine:

After the battle of Damortis, our cavalry was assigned to cover the withdrawal of the infantry to the south. Our tanks had withdrawn through us, leaving us as the rear guard . . . There was barbed wire on both sides of the road so we couldn't deploy. If a man was knocked off his horse he was trampled. The rest of the regiment went galloping down the road with bullets going by on both sides. Major T. H. Trapnell wanted to defend the bridge . . . at that moment Lieutenant Clayton Mickelson of the Veterinary Corps came up with the Vets' truck. Why it wasn't blasted off the road I will never know. I helped them push it down and pour gas on it and the bridge and light it. The fire just barely stopped the tanks from crossing the bridge and getting at our infantry.[2]

More information on this heroic action is found in "The Last U.S. Horse Cavalry Charge" (June 1995 *Military History Magazine*):

When they were about halfway to Rosario, the cavalrymen found a wooden bridge spanning the deep, muddy Apangat River, a river that tanks could not ford. They jammed the regiment's veterinary truck sideways on the bridge, shot out the engine's carburetor and, still under heavy Japanese machine-gun and 47mm tank fire, set the truck ablaze. A few Japanese walked onto the burning bridge to check its condition, then turned and ran back to their tanks . . . The lead tank cautiously nosed onto the bridge and into the flames. The weight of the tank was too much for the burning timbers. The bridge buckled, and the tank slowly slid over on its side and splashed into the river.[3]

For his heroic action, Mickelsen was awarded the Distinguished Service Cross with the following citation:

Clayton H. Mickelsen. 0-379323, First Lieutenant Veterinary Corps, 26th Cavalry (PS). For extraordinary heroism in action at Rosario, La Union, Philippine Islands, on December 22, 1941. During a concentrated fire from enemy tanks and infantry at close range against the rear guard of the 26th Cavalry (PS) Lieutenant Mickelsen, with one other officer, with total disregard of his personal safety, remained between the hostile troops and his own force, set fire to a truck placed on a bridge, and remained at the bridge exposed to enemy fire until satisfied that the bridge was in flames. Subsequently, Lieutenant Mickelsen, with the other officer, in a scout car, moved slowly with the rear-most elements of the 26th Cavalry, picking up the wounded, and collecting and giving orders to stragglers. By his heroic actions, Lieutenant Mickelsen prevented un-hindered pursuit by the hostile tanks, saved the lives of a number of wounded, collected many stragglers and set an inspiring example of courage for the entire regiment. By command of General MacArthur. [4]

After surrender of the American forces, Lieutenant Mickelsen was forced, under the threat of immediate death, to join the long and hazardous trek that became known as the "Bataan Death March." He was sent to Bilibid Prison, and then to the Fukuoka Prisoner of War Camp in Japan. There he died on February 4, 1945 of avitaminosis, which is caused by deficiency of one or more essential vitamins.

Mickelsen had been promoted to captain in January 1942. It is believed that Captain Mickelsen was the first and only veterinarian to have been awarded the Distinguished Service Cross.[5] He was also awarded the Purple Heart, Asiatic Pacific Campaign Ribbon, World War II Campaign Ribbon, and American Defense Ribbon.

The student lounge on the main floor of the WSU Bustad Veterinary Sciences Building was dedicated on April 7, 1988 in memory of Captain Mickelsen. A dedication plaque and an oil painting of the hero, along with Mickelsen's medals and citations, adorn the wall of the student lounge in his honor. The dedication plaque reads:

In grateful memory of Captain Clayton H. Mickelsen, who died in the service of his country in the Pacific Area February 4, 1945. He stands in the unbroken line of patriots who have dared to die that freedom might live, and grow, and increase its blessings. Freedom lives, and through it, he lives in a way that humbles the undertaking of most men.

Signed Harry S. Truman, President of the United States.

Lieutenant Robert L. Miller
B-17 Pilot with 21 Missions over Europe

Lieutenant Robert L. "Bob" Miller. Miller flew 21 missions over Germany. *(Photo courtesy Robert Miller.)*

Robert L. Miller, a 1940 graduate of Aberdeen (Washington) High School, entered Washington State College for fall semester 1941 after working for a year to save funds for college. He had learned to fly and soloed before departing for Pullman.[1] A volunteer in the Army Air Force Reserve, Bob was called to active duty as a private in February 1943. His commissioning as a second lieutenant in the AAF in 1944 followed training at several bases including one near Hobbs, New Mexico, where he learned to pilot B-17 bombers. In January 1945, he and his new bomber crew boarded a troop ship for an eight-day voyage to Glasgow, Scotland. He was assigned to the 493rd Bomb Group of the 8th Air Force. Lt. Miller flew 21 missions over Germany, limping home at least twice with a badly damaged aircraft. Once, he and his crew managed to land on three engines with a full load of aviation fuel and bombs. In an oral history interview with this author, Miller described a close escape involving teamwork with a fighter escort: [2]

We were on our way to Aussig, Czechoslovakia. As we approached the target, I heard a loud bang. I looked out to see that our No. 2 engine had blown up. We were then flying on three and we could no longer keep up with the formation . . . I radioed our status to our leader and told him I was going to have to fall out of the formation and head for home. He replied,

Lieutenant Miller (back middle) and his crew in front of their B-17 bomber named *Son of a Blitz*. *(Photo courtesy Robert Miller.)*

"Roger, I understand." I fell out of formation and then followed a procedure that we had been given, radioing "Little friend, little friend, this is big friend."

A U.S. fighter responded, "Roger, big friend, this is little friend, how can I help you?" I told him our problem and asked if he could escort us home. He said he would and asked us to fire a red-red flare so he could find us. Our engineer fired the flare out the top of the plane – next thing I knew a P-51 was flying off my right wing. The pilot waved at me and escorted me to safety out of the range of German fighters, then he waved good-bye, waggled his wings, and peeled off to go hunting down on the deck. He saved our bacon!

At the end of the war in Europe, instead of combat, Miller and his crew flew numerous humanitarian missions, dropping food-stuffs to the starving people of Holland. On another occasion, Miller flew displaced POWs back to their home countries. He flew to Linz, Austria, to pick up the newly-freed prisoners. This was necessary because as the Russian Army took over the German Prison Camps, they simply mowed down the fences and thousands upon thousands of prisoners poured out and began to walk toward their home countries. It was feared that these refugees would forage in the fields and destroy much of the crops that were needed to feed the European people the following winter. The combined air forces, the AAF and RAF, dropped leaflets all over the area advising the home-bound prisoners to go to Linz, Austria, to secure flights home. Miller and other B-17 pilots picked up load after load and flew them home.

First Lieutenant Miller was discharged in October 1945 and returned to Washington State where he completed his under-graduate education and earned a BA degree in music "With Distinction" in 1948. After earning a master's degree from the University of Washington, and teaching high school in Clarkston, Puyallup, and Olympia, he joined the WSC music faculty in 1957. In addition to teaching, he served as department chair for several years, retiring from WSU in 1987.

Douglas A. "Doug" Munro*
U.S. Coast Guard Signalman First Class
Congressional Medal of Honor

The United States entered World War II immediately following the bombing of Pearl Harbor on December 7, 1941. Douglas Munro had already volunteered for duty with the U.S. Coast Guard in September 1939. In the early stages of the war, the U.S. was unprepared and things had gone badly. However, by midsummer 1942, the United States had begun its counterattack and the island of Guadalcanal became the setting of some of the fiercest fighting in the South Pacific.

Artist's depiction of Douglas Munro covering the rescue of 500 Marines off the beach of Guadalcanal. *(Painting by T. Andrea, courtesy United States Coast Guard.)*

Doug was well trained and on hand to help with an amphibious landing of Marines on Guadalcanal. On September 27, 1942, three companies of the 7th Marines set out in landing craft attempting to land, drive out the Japanese, and establish a patrol base on the west side of the Matanikau River on Guadalcanal. The unopposed Marines pushed inland more than 500 yards before being confronted by an overwhelming Japanese force. The Marines, under intense fire, were driven back to the beach and, unless rescued, would have been wiped out. Signalman First Class Douglas Munro, in charge of the boats for the original landing, volunteered to lead a small armada of landing craft to evacuate the troops. As the Marines on the beach boarded, the Japanese began firing from the ridges overlooking the beach. Munro, realizing that the Marines were in extreme danger, maneuvered his boat between the enemy and the heavily laden landing craft leaving the beach. All 500 Marines, including 25 wounded, were able to escape. Nine of the 10 landing craft made it off the beach safely, but one was hung up on a sand bar.

Munro directed another craft to pull it off and soon the landing craft was free, heading out to sea. In the meantime, Munro continued to cover the withdrawal by firing on the enemy. Then he himself was hit by machine gun fire and fatally wounded.[1] For his leadership and heroism, President Franklin D. Roosevelt awarded Munro the Congressional Medal of Honor, the highest commendation that can be conferred by the United States. However, Doug Munro's story should really be told from the beginning.

Douglas Albert Munro was born October 11, 1919 in Vancouver, British Columbia, to U.S. citizens on temporary assignment in Canada. He was raised in South Cle Elum, Washington, where his father, James Munro, served as supervisor of an electrical substation operated by the Milwaukee Railroad. The substation was an important link for the Milwaukee. Trains from the east switched from electricity to steam at Avery, Idaho, and then back to electricity at Othello, Washington, before continuing west over the mountains to the Puget Sound area. The South Cle Elum sub-station was crucial in the process as it essentially downloaded high-voltage power to convert it into lower voltage power to drive the Milwaukee engines.

Douglas, or rather Doug as his friends called him, graduated Cle Elum High School in June 1937. His father was a Coast Guard reservist and active in Cle Elum American Legion Post 166. The Legion sponsored the Sons of the American Legion Drum and Bugle Corps. The Drum and Bugle Corps had nearly 20 young boys who played various drums, a bass drummer, and about 30 buglers. The kids were five to fifteen years old, with James Munro as their sponsor. Doug had an excellent background in music, playing in the band and orchestra in high school years and in his college band.[2] Because of Doug's interest and experience in music, he became music director as well as marching leader for the corps. The corps practiced its music and close-order drill twice a week, except for times of too much snow. Practices were held on the parade ground adjacent to the Milwaukee substation in South Cle Elum.

In the late spring and early summer, the Drum and Bugle Corps marched and played in civic events throughout the state including the Spokane Lilac Festival, Puyallup Daffodil Festival, Wenatchee Apple Blossom Festival, and Ellensburg Rodeo parade. My brother and I (the author) played snare drums, and because I was one of the smallest boys in the corps, I always marched in the front row. My drum was about as big as I was;

Drum and Bugle Corps in 1938, sponsored by American Legion Post 166 in Cle Elum, Washington. Doug Munro, wearing a white hat, stands in the back row (on the left). His father, James Munro, also wearing a white hat, is to the right in back row. Inset is of the Quann brothers, Tom (left) and James (the author of this publication), in Cle Elum. *(Photo courtesy James Quann.)*

after marching and playing for five or six city blocks, I would grow tired and begin to lag behind. Doug Munro would come up behind me, lift my drum with his left hand, and place his right hand in the small of my back, nudging me back in line with the formation.

Although he never fully matriculated at Washington State College, records indicate that he attended the WSC Summer Music Camp, a highly selective two-week summer program to which outstanding musicians from Washington high schools were invited. Doug attended Central Washington College of Education (CWCE) from fall 1938 through spring quarter 1939. CWCE was only about 30 miles from home, so one can assume that Doug chose Central to be able to continue his leadership responsibilities with the Drum and Bugle Corps. Doug's work with the corps throughout high school and college years provided an early indication of his leadership potential.

In late summer 1939, with the ominous threat of war on the horizon, Munro did some research on the responsibilities of the various branches of the military and decided that the Coast Guard was his cup of tea. He told his sister that he chose the Coast Guard because the Guard was dedicated to saving lives. Only 20 years old and a man of small stature, he spent a week stuffing himself with enormous amounts of food to gain the extra pounds needed to meet the Coast Guard's minimum weight standard. Once this was accomplished, he passed his physical, was inducted, and reported to his first duty station at Port Angeles, Washington.[3] At enlistment, Doug weighed 136 pounds and was 5 feet 8-1/2 inches tall.[4]

After his training, Doug volunteered for duty aboard the Coast Guard cutter *Spencer*, where he served until 1941. While aboard, he earned his signalman third class rating. With war already looming in June 1941, President Roosevelt directed the Coast Guard to man four large transports, and for Coast Guardsmen to serve along with Navy personnel aboard other Navy vessels. When the call went out for signalmen, Munro was given permission to transfer to the *Hunter Liggett*. The *Hunter Liggett* carried nearly 700 officers and enlisted men in addition to 35 Landing Craft Personnel (LCPs) carriers or Higgins Boats, and two Landing Craft Tanks (LCTs).

In early August 1942, the United States embarked on its first major amphibious assault of the war in the Pacific. After initial battle successes at Coral Sea and Midway, the U.S. decided to counter the Japanese advances in the Solomon Islands. These islands form two parallel lines that run southeast approximately 600 miles east of New Guinea. Tulagi and Guadalcanal, both at the end of the chain, were chosen for assault.

Guadalcanal was strategically important because the Japanese were building an airfield there and, if finished, it would inter-fere with the Pacific campaign. Of the naval troop-carrying ships that were attached to the campaign's task force, 18 carried Coast Guard personnel aboard. The Coast Guardsmen were assigned a very important task in the amphibious landings: the operation of the landing craft. Many of the Guardsmen had come from life-saving posts or stations, and their experience made them the most seasoned small boat handlers available to the Navy. Hence, Doug Munro's assignment to temporary duty in charge of landing craft.

During the summer of 1942, the *Hunter Liggett* and other transports played prominent roles in the initial landings at Guadalcanal, Tulagi, and other nearby islands in the Solomon chain. Munro, then signalman first class, was assigned to temporary duty on the staff of the Commander of Transport Division Seventeen. During the preparations for the invasion of Guadalcanal, Munro was transferred from ship to ship as his talents were called for.

The task force rendezvoused at sea near the end of July and, on August 7, the *Hunter Liggett* led the other transports to their anchorage off Guadalcanal. The ship then served as the command post until the Marines secured the beaches. At the time of the invasion, Doug was assigned to the staff of Rear Admiral Richmond K. Turner on board the USS *McCawley*. He made the landing on Tulagi Island, where fierce fighting lasted for several days.

On September 20, Munro volunteered to lead a search and rescue mission after a Navy dive-bomber was forced down off the coast of Savo Island. Munro and several others set out in a small powerboat in search of the downed pilot and his gunner. As their boat maneuvered to within 300 yards of the beach, Munro and his small crew heard the angry buzzing of machine gun fire directed at them. He zigzagged his small craft so that he and his crew escaped with only minor injuries. It later unfolded that the aviators had been picked up by a patrol bomber flying boat. Meanwhile Munro and his companions, unaware of that fact, braved intense fire in their effort to save the airmen.[5]

Weeks into the campaign, the Marines on Guadalcanal were reinforced and decided to push beyond their defensive perimeter. They planned to advance west across the Matanikau River to prevent smaller Japanese units from combining and forcefully striking U.S. positions. For several days, they tried to cross the river from the east and each time they met tremendous resistance. On Sunday, September 27, Marine Lieutenant Colonel Lewis B. "Chesty" Puller embarked three companies of his First Battalion, 7th Marines in landing craft. They planned to land west of the river, drive out the enemy, and establish a patrol base on the west side of the Matanikau. Doug Munro, just two weeks short of his 23rd birthday, took charge of eight LCPs and two LCTs to transport Puller's men from Lunga Point to a small cove west of Point Cruz.

The Marines landed with the support of the destroyer USS *Monssen*, which laid down a covering barrage with her five-inch guns. The 500 unopposed Marines pushed inland and reorganized on a ridge several hundred yards from the beach. The Marines were then struck by an overwhelming Japanese force and had to pull back. In the meantime, Munro and his boats had returned to their Lunga Point base. Word soon arrived at the base that the Marines were in trouble and being driven back toward the beach. The Marines had no functional radio, so they had to improvise. Flying overhead, Second Lieutenant Dale Leslie spotted the word "HELP" spelled out with the Marines' undershirts on a ridge not far from the beach. He radioed the message to another Marine unit, and by 4:00 p.m. Colonel Puller, realizing that his men were isolated and under fire, embarked on the *Monssen* to personally direct covering fire to protect his men.

At the Lunga Point base, the same boats that had put the Marines on the beach were assembled to extract them. Doug Munro, in charge of the landing craft for the original landing, volunteered to lead the boats back to the beach. The Higgins boats were blunt-nosed wooden craft, 36 feet long, and not one was heavily armed or well protected. They had plywood hulls, were slow and vulnerable to small-arms fire, and were armed only with two .30-caliber machine guns. As Munro led the boats ashore, the Japanese fired on their small craft from the ridge earlier abandoned by the Marines, and from positions east of the beach. The intense fire from the strong, interlocking positions disrupted the landing, and a number of the nearly defenseless crew members in the boats were wounded. In spite of these obstacles, Munro led the boats ashore in shifts of two or three at a time. With Munro taking the lead, he and a crewmember provided covering fire from an exposed position near the beach.

As the Marines embarked again, the Japanese pressed toward the beach, making the withdrawal more dangerous with each passing second. Munro skillfully maneuvered his boat to act as a shield between the advancing enemy and the withdrawing Marines. All of the Marines, including 25 wounded, managed to escape.

Munro steered his LCP offshore. As he passed Point Cruz, he noticed an LCT full of Marines grounded on a sand bar. Munro guided his craft toward it and directed another LCT to help pull the craft off. Twenty minutes later, both were heading out to sea with Munro's boat remaining behind to cover their withdrawal. One of Munro's crewmen saw a line of waterspouts heading toward the boat. It was Japanese machine gun fire. The crew member shouted a warning to Munro, but the roar of the boat's engine prevented Munro from hearing, and a single bullet hit him at the base of the skull. When out of range and after briefly regaining consciousness, he asked just one question, "Did we get them off?" Assured that the troops were out of harm's way, Munro smiled, and died.[6] In recognition of Munro's bravery and heroism, he was awarded the Congressional Medal of Honor and the Purple Heart. The citation for Doug Munro's Congressional Medal of Honor read:

The President of the United States takes Pleasure In Presenting The MEDAL OF HONOR Posthumously to Douglas Albert Munro, Signalman First Class United States Coast Guard for Service As Set Forth In The following CITATION. For extraordinary heroism and conspicuous gallantry in action above and beyond the call of duty as Officer in Charge of a group of twenty-four Higgins boats engaged in the evacuation of a battalion of Marines trapped by enemy Japanese forces at Point Cruz, Guadalcanal, on September 27, 1942. After making preliminary plans for the evacuation of nearly five hundred beleaguered Marines, MUNRO, under constant strafing by enemy machine guns on the island and at great risk of his life, daringly led five of his small craft toward the shore. As he closed the beach, he signaled the others to land and then in order to draw the enemy's fire and protect the heavily loaded boats, he valiantly placed his craft, with its two small guns, as a shield between the beachhead and the Japanese. When the perilous task of evacuation was nearly completed, MUNRO was instantly killed by enemy fire, but his crew, two of whom were wounded, carried on until the last boat had cleared the beach. By his outstanding leadership, expert planning and dauntless devotion to duty, he and his courageous comrades undoubtedly saved the lives of many who otherwise would have perished. He gallantly gave up his life in defense of his country.

Signed by Franklin D. Roosevelt

On October 27, 1942, a month after Doug's death, his parents received an official letter from the Navy Department advising them of the Medal of Honor award. On May 27, 1943, Doug's mother and father received their son's Medal of Honor from President Roosevelt in a ceremony at the White House. Doug's commanding officer, Lieutenant Commander D. H. Dexter, sent a personal letter to Mr. and Mrs. Munro containing the following passages:

. . . On Sunday the 27th of September an expedition was sent into an area where trouble was to be expected. Douglas was in charge of the ten boats which took the

men down. In the latter part of the afternoon the situation had not developed as had been anticipated and in order to save the expedition it became necessary to send the boats back to evacuate the expedition. Volunteers were called for and true to the highest traditions of the Coast Guard and also to the traditions with which you had imbued your son, he was among the first to volunteer and was put in charge of the detail. The evacuation was as successful as could be hoped for under fire. But as always happens, the last men to leave the beach are the hardest pressed because they have been acting as the covering agents for the withdrawal of the other men, and your son knowing this is so, placed himself and his boat so that he could act as the covering agent for the last men, and by his action and successful maneuvers brought back a far greater number of men than had been even hoped for. He received his wound just as the last men were getting in the boats and clearing the beach. Upon regaining consciousness his only question was "Did they get off?" And so died with a smile on his face and the full knowledge that he had successfully accomplished a dangerous mission . . . In the year and a half that I have known Douglas I have grown to admire him and through him, you. He was the true type of American manhood that is going to win this war and I hereby promise that I will make all efforts to call on you whenever it is my privilege to be near Cle Elum and to pay homage to you as the parents of Douglas . . .[7]

Doug Munro's heroism and self-sacrifice are now a part of American history – a history Coast Guard volunteers learn the first day of boot camp. Doug's story is recorded in an exhibit at the U.S. Coast Guard Academy's museum in New London, Connecticut. His heroism also inspired a young poet, Janice Coombs, to write the following poem:

The Death of Doug Munro

The bullets whistled overhead,
and men fell at his feet,
But caring not for death or pain,
he steered his tiny fleet
Into the thick of battle,
where the trapped five-hundred lay
Crouched in steaming foxholes
through the sweltering night and day
The sky above was filled with smoke –
the water bullet sprayed,
And bombs fell wild among the boats,
their giddy red displayed.
The men before and side him fell,
their rafts were blown sky-high,
But he stood straight, unharmed and safe
as the bullets whistled by
Perhaps a spirit guided him,
or an angel brave and true,
Perhaps he thought mission more

than life, as all Coast Guardsmen do.
For he kept in mind the saying
where the Coast Guards never slack,
"You must go forth to battle,
but you need not come back."
When the journey was completed,
and the precious cargo lade,
A boat full still remained on shore–
a second trip must be made.
Though the danger was increasing,
for the fire stronger grew
Munro cared not and went again
with the rest of his gallant crew.
A second time they braved the storm–
a second time embarked,
But while Munro was coming back,
the bullet found its mark.
It seemed as if a spirit strong,
his courage did uplift
To offer up his manly life–it was a holy gift.
He whimpered not of sickening pain,
or asked for loved one dear,
His dying thoughts were not of self,
but of duty strong and clear,
"Did they get off? Did they get off?"
the young Coast Guardsman cried.
And with these words upon his lips,
the hero smiled and died.[8]

Douglas Munro was buried on Guadalcanal. After the war, his remains were brought home and interred with full military honors at the Laurel Hill Memorial Gardens Cemetery in Cle Elum, Washington. His gravesite includes a special monument honoring his life and heroism, and a flagpole from which the U.S. and Coast Guard flags fly daily. The grave is surrounded by concrete pillars supporting a large anchor chain taken from a Coast Guard ship. Doug's mother, Edith, and his father, James, are also buried within the enclosure. Doug's monument includes a bronze engraving with an abbreviated version of his Guadalcanal story, and announces that the Coast Guard cutter *Munro* was named in his honor. However, the Munro story does not end here.

*This Doug Munro story previously appeared in **Columbia: The Magazine of Northwest History**, published by the Washington State Historical Society, Fall 2000.*

Lieutenant Edith F. Munro
Mother of Signalman First Class Doug Munro

The U.S. Congress established the Women's Reserve of the Coast Guard (SPARS) on November 23, 1942, just two months after the heroic death of Doug Munro. SPAR, the name given to the women volunteers, is an acronym of the Coast Guard's slogan with an English translation: *Semper Paratus–Always Ready.* Doug's mother, Edith, distraught over her son's

Lieutenant Edith Munro as a cadet in training at the Coast Guard Academy at New London, Connecticut, 1943. *(Photo courtesy the United States Coast Guard.)*

death, yet extremely proud of his heroism, was one of the first of approximately 10,000 women to volunteer to serve their country as a SPAR. On May 27, 1943, she completed training at the Coast Guard Academy in New London, Connecticut, and was commissioned a lieutenant junior grade (Lt.JG). At 48, and older than most women volunteers, Edith Munro was assigned to the 13th Coast Guard District and took command of the SPAR barracks in Seattle. She also served as the Women's Reserve Personnel Officer and had assignments that took her to Long Beach, California; Houston, Texas; Washington, D.C., and Philadelphia, Pennsylvania.

Promoted to lieutenant on July 1, 1944, she served until her retirement November 1, 1945.[1] Although retired, Mrs. Munro continued to represent the Coast Guard at important military events and ceremonial functions, including the commissioning of the Coast Guard cutter *Munro* in 1972. In 1944, she helped christen the navy destroyer escort *Munro*. Her husband, James Munro, was a captain in the Washington State Coast Guard Reserve, and their grandson, Douglas J. Sheehan, named for his uncle Doug, served as an officer in the Coast Guard.

Edward R. Murrow
War Correspondent in Europe
Pioneer Radio and Television
News Broadcaster

Edward R. Murrow was not a military veteran per se, although he did complete the advanced Reserve Officer Training Corps (ROTC) course at Washington State College. His story, contributed by Pat Caraher, senior editor of *Washington State Magazine*, is included in this book because of Murrow's significant contributions as a war correspondent during World War II and the tremendous influence he had on the development of radio and television broadcasting industries in the United States.

Edward R. Murrow
(Photo courtesy WSU.)

Who can forget Edward R. Murrow's famous words "This ... is London" preceding his live radio accounts of the bombing of Britain during World War II? The American public became familiar with his distinctive voice delivering accounts of the important events during the war. Sometimes his reports came from London's rooftops, while on other occasions, from its streets.

Morrow joined the Columbia Broadcasting System as director of talks and education in 1935 and was director of CBS's European Bureau from 1937 to 1946. When Murrow spoke, people seemed to listen. The same was true during his student years at Washington State College, during wartime London, at the famous McCarthy hearings in the mid-1950s, and on the many television shows and documentaries that he hosted during his career.

First on radio and later on television, the famed CBS reporter gained the public's trust. His integrity in reporting the news defined a standard for the profession. In addressing a 1958 meeting of the Radio and Television News Directors' Association in Chicago, Murrow spoke of the power of television:

This instrument can teach, it can illuminate, yes, and it can even inspire. But, it can do so only to the extent that humans are determined to use it to those ends. Otherwise, it is merely wires and lights in a box.

Television was meant to be more than a means of entertainment, the late broadcast journalist contended. He saw it as a tool against ignorance, intolerance, and indifference. He encouraged those in the media, and viewers alike, to never lose sight of this potential.

Murrow came to Washington State College from Blanchard, Washington, a logging community in the western part of the state.

While pursuing a degree in speech, he became a big man on the Pullman campus. In fact, campus politics proved to be his forte. He was elected president of the junior class and, as a senior, student body president. He also was president of his fraternity, Kappa Sigma. He was a cadet colonel in the Army Reserve Officer Training Corps (ROTC) program and inducted into Crimson Circle, the senior service honorary. After graduating in 1930, he served two years as president of the National Student Federation of America, an organization that represented students from more than 400 colleges and universities nationwide. At WSC, he was enrolled in the first collegiate radio broadcasting program taught anywhere in the nation. At the time, the college catalog listed the course as *Community Drama* since broadcasting was not yet considered academically respectable.

He credited two of his speech professors, Ida Lou Anderson and Maynard Lee Daggy, for their interest in him and for influencing his career in a positive direction. It was Ms. Anderson, a tiny disabled woman, who suggested that he insert a long pause after saying, "This…" in his famous introduction to his London reports.

While in London, Murrow earned the reputation as America's unofficial ambassador to Great Britain. He and Sir Winston Churchill established a close friendship. After the war, Murrow returned to New York, where he became director of Public Affairs. After a year in administration, he chose to return to the

United States. His newscasts for CBS radio became regular evening fare for Americans from 1947 to 1959. In the early 1950s, Murrow reportedly declined an offer to return to his alma mater as president of Washington State College.

Murrow and Fred J. Friendly produced the CBS radio program "Hear It Now." The three albums of records wove together the important and dramatic stories of three decades. In 1951, Murrow and Friendly co-produced "See It Now," which pioneered television news documentaries. Murrow narrated the program. The series was a network feature for seven years.

On March 9, 1954, Murrow risked his career with a "See It Now" attack on Senator Joseph McCarthy highlighting McCarthy's anticommunist scare tactics of the time. Murrow concluded the report with these words:

We cannot defend freedom abroad by deserting it at home. The actions of the junior senator from Wisconsin have caused alarm and dismay amongst our allies abroad and given considerable comfort to our enemies, and whose fault is that? Not really his, he didn't create the situation of fear, he merely exploited it and rather successfully.

In his 1960 CBS documentary "Harvest of Shame," Murrow exposed the deplorable conditions and treatment of migrant farm workers in America. At one point, he looked into the camera and said:

The migrants have no lobby. Only an enlightened, aroused, and perhaps angered public opinion can do anything about the migrants. The people you have seen have the strength to harvest your fruit and vegetables. They do not have the strength to influence your legislation. Maybe we do.

Radio and television's top news analyst and reporter concluded a quarter-century with CBS on January 28, 1961 when President Kennedy appointed him director of the U.S. Information Agency. Murrow was credited with revitalizing that agency and giving it a worldwide acceptance that it had not received previously.

In 1962, Murrow returned to Washington State University to deliver the commencement address and receive, from WSU Regents, the Distinguished Alumnus Award, a new award established to honor the university's most esteemed graduates. Murrow resigned from the U.S. Information Agency in mid-January 1964 because of his failing health. He died on April 27, 1965 of a brain tumor, following a protracted illness with lung cancer. He was 57.

The annual Edward R. Murrow Symposium was established at Washington State University in his honor in April 1973. The following day, the new Edward R. Murrow Communications Center was dedicated on campus. In 1994, the U.S. Post Office issued a postage stamp with Murrow's image and the ceremony of this commemorative was held in the Edward R. Murrow Communications Center.

Those who knew Murrow best, his peers, considered him a man of reason and common sense with an old-fashioned sense of patriotism and a firm belief in the democratic process: a conviction that the majority of Americans, if fully informed both of events and the meaning of those events, will draw wise conclusions. Murrow also believed passionately in the right of dissent, or, as he once said, "the right to wrong."

Murrow married Janet Brewster in 1934. She was a former World War II correspondent and radio news writer for the British Broadcasting Corporation. Janet retired after a career in television and radio broadcasting. She died at her home in Needham, Massachusetts, in December 1999 at age 88.

Jeanne Lewellen Norbeck
WASP Test Pilot
Volunteer Women's Air Force Service Pilot
Killed In the Line of Duty

During World War II, women service pilots flew missions on the home front that had been previously flown by men who were now serving as fighter and bomber pilots abroad. In September 1942, the Women's Air Force Service Pilots (WASP) Corps was formed. More than 1,800 qualified volunteers paid their own transportation to Sweetwater, Texas, for training. The WASP meant travel, danger, self-fulfillment, usefulness and,

above all, the opportunity to take to the air in the world's most sophisticated airplanes.[1]

From 1942 until the Corps was disbanded in December 1944, the WASPs flew over 60 million miles and logged nearly 300,000 flying hours in every airplane in the American air arsenal, from P-51 Mustang fighters to the B-29 Super fortress. A few of the more experienced pilots served as test pilots, and other WASPs towed targets to train air-to-air gunners, others flew simulated strafing and smoke-laying

WASP Test Pilot Jeanne Lewellen Norbeck. *(Photo courtesy Washington State University.)*

missions, and many flew on radar jamming and searchlight tracking missions. In addition, WASPs spent thousands upon thousands of hours ferrying 12,650 aircraft to bases abroad, and many of the WASPs served as flying instructors training male Air Force pilots.

All in all, the WASPs flew as regularly and as long as male pilots in the same jobs, showing no difference in physical, mental or psychological capabilities.[2] The WASPs performed every vital flying mission in America's massive war effort, and flew longer hours with a lower accident rate than their male counterparts not serving in combat.[3] Jeanne Lewellen Norbeck volunteered for WASP duty and, because of her ability and experience, she was one of the first to be assigned responsibilities as a female test pilot and light-test engineer.

Jeanne Marcile Lewellen was born November 14, 1912 in Columbus, Indiana. She entered Washington State College in the fall of 1930. Jeanne came to Pullman and WSC at the invitation of her two aunts, Ivy and Amy Lewellen, who were administrators at college. Jeanne's aunt Ivy was the longtime executive secretary and aide-de-camp for President E. O. Holland, and Amy was in charge of the Dictaphone Office and later the Office of Duplicating and Mailing.

On campus, Jeanne joined Kappa Kappa Gamma sorority, declared a major in English, and became an outstanding student and leader. She was active in the Women's Athletic Association, the Young Women's Christian Association, the Spurs (a national sophomore women's honorary association), and the WSC Women's Council. During her senior year, she served on the Associated Students Board of Control, was a Reserve Officer Training Corps (ROTC) sponsor, and Mortar Board treasurer. She was also active in the American College Quill Club, a group dedicated to literature and writing. She graduated in June 1933 with a B.A. degree in English.[4]

After graduation, Jeanne became secretary to the chief surgeon in the hospital at Coulee Dam, headquarters for the Grand Coulee Dam project on the Columbia River. Her soon-to-be husband, Edward Norbeck, also worked on the dam project. Later, Edward took a position in Hawaii, Jeanne followed, and they were married there. They settled on one of the outer islands where Edward had a position as manager of a large plantation. Given the lack of transportation between the islands, Jeanne and her husband learned to fly, and Jeanne became an outstanding pilot. They were at home on the plantation when the Japanese attacked Pearl Harbor, December 7, 1941. With war raging, they returned to the mainland where Edward joined the Army and Jeanne the WASP Corps.

Jeanne logged many hours in the air, enjoying every minute of flying. She felt triumphant over her contribution to the war effort and the fact that she was at the top of her unit, having been promoted to Commander of her WASP Group.[5] After hundreds of hours of flying under routine as well as extremely hazardous conditions, Jeanne earned a well-deserved reputation as a competent and outstanding flyer, testing aircraft that had been damaged in war, or worn out, then rebuilt to fly. Her test pilot work freed male pilots from such dangerous work, allowing them to report for combat in one of the war zones.

On October 16, 1944, just two months before the WASP Corps was disbanded, two WASP flight test engineers at Shaw Army Airfield in South Carolina flipped a coin to see who would flight test a recently repaired aircraft. Jeanne Lewellen Norbeck was one of those engineers. In her book about the WASPs, Yvonne Pateman describes what happened based on her personal recollection and Norbeck's radio communications:

. . . The flashing coin spins and falls. Jeanne Norbeck, engineering test pilot, checks the toss. "O.K. Marybelle, it looks like I get to check this BT." Marybelle Lyall nods. She will wait for the next BT available. Jeanne looks at the Form I-A. Plane was grounded because its left wing was heavy, but a mechanic says it is okay now. Jeanne takes off. Once off, Jeanne puts the BT-13 through light maneuvers to test whether its left wing is indeed 'heavy' as reported by a cadet on Form I-A. It seems O.K. That's the problem right there because it seems to be good enough. Jeanne senses something not quite right, but so far, nothing has shown up to give a basis for her uneasy feeling about the old BT. Better head back to the field. Her gut feeling was that something is definitely wrong. In preparation for entering the landing pattern, WASP Norbeck slows the BT to accommodate to the minimum airspeed acceptable. Yes, the left wing does feel heavy! Without further warning, the BT flips over. At the landing pattern altitude, there is not the slightest chance that WASP Norbeck can save herself from the ensuing initiation of a spin.[6]

The WASP pilots were considered civilian employees, not military, and thus were accorded none of the normal benefits afforded our fighting men (insurance and medical benefits). Jeanne's friends were shocked to find out that neither the Army, Air Force, or the U.S. Government assumed the expenses for Jeanne's funeral, or a military escort, or even an American flag for her coffin. In fact, Jeanne's WASP friends and other military officers shared expenses for transportation and funeral expenses, and one of her WASP comrades volunteered to escort Jeanne's body home and help comfort her family. An unidentified WASP voiced what all of Jeanne's friends believed, which was that "we serve our country, and when one of us dies, the parents are met with a pine box and a message, thanks a lot, here's your daughter." [7]

Three other WASP test pilots were killed in the line of duty, as were 34 other women pilots, all without the usual military benefits or honors. On November 23, 1977, after several years of congressional infighting, President Jimmy Carter quietly signed a bill, originally introduced by Senator Barry Goldwater, granting veteran status for the Women's Air Force Service Pilots of World War II. For Jeanne Lewellen Norbeck and many of her fellow WASPs, it was a gesture long overdue. Jeanne was buried in Garland Brook Cemetery in Columbus, Indiana. On Veterans Day, November 11, 1997, in a ceremony in the center of the campus of Washington State University, Jeanne Lewellen Norbeck's name was added to the lengthy roster of names inscribed on the WSU Veterans Memorial. She made the supreme sacrifice for her country, and she will be remembered!

Lieutenant Glenn E. Oman
WSU Associate Athletic Director
Australia, New Guinea and Philippine Islands

Glenn E. Oman was born on April 29, 1919 in Pullman, Washington, to Mr. and Mrs. Harry F. Oman. He graduated from Pullman High School in 1937 and enrolled at Washington State College, majoring in business administration. He was enrolled through the spring semester 1940 when he joined Company E of the 161st Infantry, 41st Division of the Washington National Guard.[1] He was called to active duty well before the December 7, 1941 attack on Pearl Harbor and sent to Ordnance School at the Aberdeen Proving Ground in Maryland. In March 1942, his division was shipped to Australia. He was assigned to the Division Headquarters Company then to Ordnance Company where he received promotion to the rank of sergeant.[2]

Based on his outstanding qualifications and performance, Sgt. Oman was selected (he said he had no choice) for Officers Candidate School (OCS) in Brisbane, Australia. Upon successful completion of OCS, he was commissioned as a second lieutenant.

Lieutenant Oman's unit, the 3469th Infantry, was shipped from Australia to New Guinea for "mop up" operations against the Japanese. From New Guinea, he was sent to Leyte in the Philippines as part of the drive to recapture the islands from the Japanese. At this point, Lieutenant Oman was assigned to S-2

Intelligence and given the assignment of inspecting battlefields to help determine how well the enemy was equipped and supplied. He suffered a battlefield wound while on Luzon, and was shipped home shortly thereafter.

The sergeant turned officer was discharged on January 10, 1946 and once again became a civilian. He was awarded the Legion of Merit, American Defense Service Medal, American Campaign Medal, World War II Victory Medal, Philippine Liberation Medal, and the Asiatic Pacific Campaign Medal. (Glenn was not awarded a Purple Heart because he was in a hurry to rotate home and did not report his wound.)

Glenn returned to Washington State College for the spring 1946 semester, earning his B.A. degree in business administration in 1947. He joined Vice President Lauren Shelton in the Accounting Office shortly after graduation, and in 1948 became ticket manager for the Athletic Department. He progressed through the ranks from ticket manager to business manager, then assistant athletic director, and later associate athletic director. He retired on July 1, 1981, following 32 years of outstanding service to the university, the coaches, and its young men and women athletes.[3] Glenn died in 2002.

Captain Eugene G. "Pat" Patterson
Soldier in the Pacific
WSU Alumni Director and Coach
Washington State Senator

Born on October 8, 1921, Eugene G. "Pat" Patterson graduated from Pullman High School in June 1937 and entered Washington State College that fall. The war may have interrupted his education, but Pat returned to WSC after it ended to earn a B.A. degree in political science.[1]

Pat Patterson, WSU Alumni Director and Washington State Senator. *(Photo courtesy WSU.)*

Pat joined the Washington National Guard in 1937 and was called to active Army duty shortly after his marriage to his classmate Maxine Margaret Weeks in August 1940. He was later commissioned a second lieutenant in the Infantry. He and his outfit were en route to the Philippines when, on December 7, 1941, the Japanese bombed Pearl Harbor. They were redirected to Hawaii, and then on to join the battles on Guadalcanal and New Georgia. Captain Patterson was wounded during the New Georgia campaign and evacuated to New Zealand for medical treatment and rest.

Company E squad at Ft. Lewis, 1939. Back row, from left: Pat Patterson, Edwin Johnson, Wayne Arrasmith, Bob Speaks, Virgil Gass. Front row: Kenny French, Bob McCalder, Cliff Cochran. French and McCalder were later killed in action. *(Photo courtesy Patterson family.)*

After his recovery, he rejoined the 25th Infantry. His division was shipped to New Caledonia for amphibious training in preparation for the invasion of the Philippines. By that time, Captain Patterson had been overseas longer than most, earning him enough points to be rotated stateside. Pat was awarded the Bronze Star for heroic service, Purple Heart, Combat Infantryman's Badge, Asiatic-Pacific Campaign Medal, and the American Defense Service Medal.[2]

Following the war, Pat returned to Pullman and WSC, finished his degree in 1946, and became commander of the newly founded Veterans of Foreign Wars (VFW) Post in Pullman. His outstanding VFW work earned him the position of state junior vice commander of the VFW with an office located in Seattle. In 1952, he returned to his alma mater as WSU alumni director, a position he held for the next 25 years.

As director, Pat coached the WSU golf team and served the university as legislative liaison. He was elected to the Washington State Legislature in 1972 and served with distinction for 20 years, spending eight years in the House of Representatives and 12 years in the Senate. Pat retired from the university in 1977, but continued his legislative duties until 1992.[3] Pat and Maxine have seven children and seven grandchildren. Pat died in February 2004.

First Lieutenant Scotty Rohwer
A Palouse Pilot

Scotty Rohwer was born August 9, 1918 in Spangle, Washington, to Jake and Pauline Rohwer. In 1936, he graduated from Spangle High School, enrolling at Washington State College that fall. He was a member of Sigma Alpha Epsilon fraternity and a four-year member of the Lariat Club, serving as president his senior year. He received a bachelor of science in agriculture in 1941.[1]

After the attack on Pearl Harbor, Scotty became an Army Air Force cadet, training in California and Arizona. A commissioned officer and B-25 pilot, he left Homestead Field in Florida for an air base on Corsica, an island south of France in the Mediterranean. His unit was the 486th Squadron of the 340th Bomb Group, 57th Wing of the 12th Air Force, and its mission was to attack the retreating Germans in northern Italy and support the allied landings in southern France.

First Lieutenant Scotty Rohwer was awarded the Distinguished Flying Cross "for extraordinary achievement while participating in aerial flight."[2] He was also awarded the Air Medal with seven stars and the ETO Ribbon. His 67 combat missions, expertly detailed through his own daily log and letters home, are reprinted in an insightful book by Spangle, Washington, author Nona Hengen.[3]

Lieutenant Colonel Ira Christian "Chris" Rumburg
WSC Student Body President
Football Team Captain
Missing In Action in the English Channel

Chris Rumburg was everything a young man could be – and more. He was born and raised in the Spokane Valley, graduating in 1934 from West Valley High School. He was an outstanding student and a big, strong lad who excelled in all sports, particularly football. He enrolled at Washington State College in fall 1934 and turned out for football. The first year on campus he lived in a boarding house, but later joined Alpha Tau Omega fraternity. Chris sat on the bench for part of his first year, but his 6-foot 4-inch, 200-plus pounds frame, and great heart and strength soon earned him the starting center position on varsity and a leadership role on the team. When football season ended, he joined the Cougar wrestling team, winning three letters as a heavyweight. In his senior year, his teammates elected him captain of the football team.

Chris was a natural leader on and off the field and one of the most popular men on campus. He excelled in the classroom as well, and rose to the rank of cadet lieutenant colonel and battalion commander in the Army ROTC program. He also played numerous roles in campus theater productions and became a force to be reckoned with in student political circles.[1] In the spring of his junior year, Chris was elected WSC student body president serving in that role from fall 1937 to his graduation in

Student Body President Chris Rumburg. *(Photo courtesy Washington State University.)*

the spring of 1938. The 1938 yearbook listed him as one of the "Big Men On Campus" and his credits, in addition to football, wrestling, and acting included memberships in the Crimson Circle, Scabbard and Blade, Publications Board, Gray W, Accent on Youth, and a leader in winter sports.[2]

The same day Chris Rumburg received his bachelor of arts degree he was also commissioned a second lieutenant in the Army (Infantry). Since his campus life and leadership experience in student government prepared him well for the real world, Rumburg's call to active duty in March 1941 provided the opportunity to put his talented leadership skills to work. His first duty station was the Hunter Liggett Military Reservation in California, followed by command training in England. Following his schooling in England, he returned to the states as an Infantry instructor training young men in preparation for the invasion of Europe. He was then shipped back to England, and on Christmas Day 1944, Battalion Commander Lieutenant Colonel Chris Rumburg and his men were aboard a troop ship headed from England to the beaches in France. His ship was torpedoed by a Nazi U-boat, and it was here that his courage and leadership earned him the Bronze Star. Although badly damaged, the ship was slow to sink, allowing Colonel Rumburg to save countless lives.

Although he might have directed the rescue effort from a safe position on the bridge, he chose to personally lead his men to safety. The official report stated that, on Christmas Day 1944, an Army transport ship was torpedoed in the English Channel, resulting in the loss of hundreds of men. Colonel Rumburg played a hero's role in the tragic sinking, saving many lives, and "the memory of his deeds will remain long in the minds of scores of men he succeeded in saving from death."[3]

Chief of Staff John Keating was on the transport with Chris when it went down. Excerpts from his letter to Chris's wife Naomi provided details of the events:

. . . Colonel Rumburg worked for more than two and one-half hours extricating trapped men from the wreckage and leading others to safety they could not find for themselves. Every ounce of his enormous strength, which has become a legend among us, was expended in those trying hours. Those who were there tell of seeing him several times carrying two men at a time to safety. You can be sure that his life was not a useless sacrifice. Because of his bravery, the lives of at least 100 soldiers were spared. He must have had that smile on his face that he always had when he foiled the wits of someone, when he knew he got the best of the bargain – knowing that 100 or so would live for another Christmas . . . He had initially suffered a hand wound and during his repeated acts of bravery, he received a blow on the head. His loss of blood and exhaustion eventually weakened him to the point where he could no longer help himself.

Needless to say, his battalion as well as his regiment, with a grim look of determination, are now making the "Boche" pay for the life of their beloved "Earth Shaker." To his men and the lives of other men in the division, he is now a monumental inspiration and he will continue to live in the hearts and minds of each one of us. I doubt if there ever will be a gathering of men in the division where reverence will not be paid to him . . .[4]

Captain Robert D. Campbell provided the specific information that resulted in Lieutenant Col. Rumburg being awarded the Bronze Star, posthumously, as recounted here:

. . . I am working at present with the 66th Infantry Division, Chris Rumburg's old outfit. Chris was aboard a troop ship that was hit by a German submarine's torpedo. A section of the stairs leading to the top deck was blown away. Chris went about organizing his men to leave the ship and finally let himself down into the hold to help lift the injured to the top deck. Not long after he let himself down into the hold, a timber fell across his hand cutting off two fingers. Chris refused first aid and went right on lifting injured men to the top deck. After he had all the men out that were still alive, he climbed to the top deck himself. One of his men was about to enter the water without his Mae West [life jacket], so Chris took his off and gave it to him. Chris then jumped into the water and swam around getting his men to the rafts and seeing that they stayed calm. He found one fellow having trouble getting to a raft, so he helped him to the raft and shoved him on. Then, after using up all the great strength that God gave him, his hand slipped from the side of the raft and he sank from sight . . .[5] [Because Rumburg's body was never recovered, he remains officially listed as Missing in Action.]

Lieutenant Colonel Ira Christian "Chris" Rumburg was survived by his wife, parents, three sisters and three brothers, two of whom also served their country: Corporal Harold "Hal" Rumburg at McChord Army Air Force Base near Tacoma, Washington, and Sergeant Dean L. Rumburg on duty with a tank battalion in France. Like Chris, his siblings also graduated from West Valley High School in Spokane.

In a letter to WSC President Holland, Chris's mother wrote, "If we had to lose him, we are happy he could use his great strength in saving lives instead of taking them." [6]

Colonel Jerry M. Sage
OSS Operative Behind Enemy Lines
"The Cooler King" of North Africa, Italy, and Germany

World War II and his experiences as a prisoner of war were the central themes throughout the military and civilian lives of Jerry Sage, and he shared those experiences in his book, *SAGE*, published in 1985.[1] He earned the reputation as the "Cooler King" for the 24 months he spent, much of it in solitary confinement as a German prisoner of war in North Africa, Germany, and Poland. The exploits of Sage and some of his fellow POWs were the basis for the epic movie *The Great Escape*, which starred Steve McQueen. An Army colonel, Office of Strategic Services (OSS) officer, paratrooper, guerilla fighter, saboteur, and persistent escapee, Sage spent two years in German POW camps, including a 15-month stay at Stalag Luft III between Berlin and Breslau near the old German-Polish border. A *Seattle Times* newspaper article published in 1987 quoted Sage as saying, "I escaped fifteen times and was recaptured fourteen." [2] Colonel Sage retired from the Army in March 1972 and died in March 1993.

Jerome M. Sage (he later changed his name to Jerry) was born on May 27, 1917 in Spokane, Washington. He attended Spokane's North Central High School and was a four-sport athlete. In good company, he played right end with Bob Carey (Colonel Robert Carey of this book) playing left end on the team coached by Archie Buckley (Navy Lieutenant Archie Buckley of this book) that won the 1933 Spokane City football championship. He graduated from North Central High School in 1934 and enrolled at Washington State College that fall.

While at WSC, Sage was very active in campus life and politics. He was a member of Kappa Sigma fraternity, the WSC Associated Students Board of Control, a company commander in Reserve Officer Training Corps (ROTC), and president of his senior class. He was a member of Crimson Circle and played tackle for four years on the WSC varsity football team. He received his Phi Beta Kappa key at the same time he received his bachelor of arts degree in political science, and graduated with high honors in June 1938.[3]

An extremely active student politically, Jerry Sage was one of the leaders of the 1936 student strike over the arduous rules laid down by the dean of women, Annie Fertig. Sage was convinced that students should be in control of their own lives and actively protested the onerous policies and social rules of the dean. He and others formed a group that later became known as the "Strike Committee." Robert Yothers, a prelaw student, was appointed chair of the group. "Yothers, accompanied by an early instigator of the protest by the name of Jerry Sage, and a half-dozen others representing various living groups carried their protest to President E. O. Holland . . ." Yothers was Phi Beta Kappa, and Sage soon would be. One person who knew both men said the difference between them was that ". . . Yothers was brilliant and sober, while Sage was brilliant and brash . . ." The previous fall,

Yothers had been chosen as one of two students to represent WSC in competition for a Rhodes Scholarship. He would go on to become an attorney, legislator, and an official of the Republican Party.

Sage, a big, blond football player, was known to some as the "wild man" because he would try anything that looked interesting. The combination of the two personalities must have taken its toll on President Holland. Yothers, the articulate political science student, would logically and methodically argue with Holland towards concessions, to which Holland would concede, but then seek a counter concession. Yothers would put the question to the other representatives, and Sage would say "no." Once Holland pointed a stern finger and said, "You pain me, Sage!"[4]

Negotiations between the two student leaders and the strike committee, including the president, continued until ultimately a "strike day" was called for May 7, 1936. The faculty supported the students and ultimately the president conceded to the changes demanded by the students. Dean Fertig and Dean of Men Carl Morrow both resigned.[5] Sage's tenacity and inspired leadership during his college years seems to have foreshadowed his leadership and prowess in the military.

In June 1938, Sage received his degree in political science along with a commission as second lieutenant in the Army Reserves. After college, he went to work for Proctor and Gamble Distributing Company in San Francisco. He worked for three and one-half years, but with World War II approaching, he volunteered for active duty just before Thanksgiving of 1941, reporting to the Presidio of San Francisco for training. Then came the attack on Pearl Harbor.

In January 1942, he was transferred to Fort Lewis, Washington, where he received a top-secret telegram ordering him to report, by the earliest available aircraft, to an office in Washington, D.C. Unbeknown to him, he had been recruited by Colonel William "Wild Bill" Donovan of the Office of Strategic Services (OSS). After an extensive interview, Sage was asked if he wished to volunteer for OSS duty and he emphatically agreed. He was sent for training at a mountain retreat in Maryland. He soon discovered that the goal of the OSS was "to collect and analyze strategic information, to plan and operate special services including sabotage, psychological warfare, and similar clandestine operations that did not fall within the jurisdiction of the regular armed forces." He received extensive training in the martial arts, other forms of self-defense, and silent killing; the skills he would need for behind-the-lines operations.

In July 1942, Sage and several colleagues were sent to England for six weeks of special training with the British Special Operations (SOE) School of Industrial Sabotage, the counterpart of the U.S. Office of Strategic Services. In December 1942, he shipped overseas to take part in the North Africa campaign. He joined a convoy bound for North Africa, coming ashore at Oran.

He and his buddies, infiltrators all, were dispatched to Algiers where they reported for their first assignment. The assignment was for Sage and his crew to infiltrate enemy lines and harass General Rommel's Afrika Korps. At the time, the Nazi general's tanks had the advantage over Allied Forces, and were wreaking havoc on American armor.

The desert sands limited enemy tanks and trucks, as well as our own, to traveling only on improved roads and dry riverbeds. To counteract the threat of enemy contact, Sage and a fellow officer developed an effective weapon, the "manure bomb." Since the natives traveled primarily by camel, donkey, and horse, piles of dung were the most common sight along the roadways. The manure bomb was made by molding composition C explosives into the same shape, texture and color of camel or donkey dung. These homemade bombs were placed along the roadways used by Rommel's troops. Because the disguised manure bombs appeared to be part of the regular landscape, they proved very effective in stopping enemy vehicles and troops. Treads were blown off tanks, trucks were damaged or destroyed, and German infantrymen were killed or wounded.

Sage's men also blew up bridges, ammunition dumps, and railroads. Later, when bivouacked just forward of the town of Feriana, Tunisia, Sage, code named "Dagger," observed enemy soldiers laying antitank and antipersonnel mines in the exact location of a planned U.S. attack scheduled for the following day. Dagger was asked to reconnoiter behind enemy lines in an attempt to find out what the Germans were doing. He and another operative worked their way through the minefield and radioed back coordinates and the disposition of the German troops. They came under fire and were wounded and captured. Sage was put aboard a truck headed for Gafsa, Tunisia. During the next several days, although wounded in a leg and shoulder, Sage attempted to escape twice.[6]

He and other captured and wounded U.S. soldiers were loaded aboard a boxcar. While the train was moving, Sage and two comrades pried a window open and escaped in the dark. They dropped beside the tracks and wandered about freely for the remainder of the night, but were recaptured the next day when presumably friendly Arabs reported their presence to German officials. Sage was careful not to let the Germans know he was an OSS agent, passing himself off as a downed flyer. He and other American flyers were placed on a German transport plane headed for a German prison camp in Italy. They landed in Naples where, due to his now numerous attempts to escape, Sage was placed in solitary confinement. The treatment was rough and the food was poor to nonexistent. His leg wound became infected and he suffered diarrhea and exhaustion.

Sage was hospitalized in Naples, then shipped by rail to Frankfurt, Germany, arriving in early March 1943. While the train traversed the Italian mountains, he escaped through a lavatory window of one of the railcars, only to be recaptured almost immediately. He arrived in Frankfurt on March 12 and spent the next 18 days in solitary confinement. Interrogation followed, as did brutal treatment, both physical and psychological.

In early April, Sage and a large group of British and Americans were sent to Stalag Luft III, a prison camp for flyers. The camp was near Sagan, a town of about 20,000 people located in the pine forest of Silesia, 90 miles southeast of Berlin. The stalag was Sage's home for the next 15 months. In this camp, he was introduced once again to "the cooler" (solitary confinement), and his numerous solitary confinements earned him the title "The Cooler King." His confinements resulted from his many escape attempts and his resistance to the bullying tactics of his guards and captors. In his first few days in North Camp (of Stalag Luft IIII), Sage attempted to escape several times but each attempt was thwarted.

While in solitary confinement, Sage whiled away the hours planning his next escape. When not confined, he was a key member of an escape team with responsibility for creating diversions to keep the guards from discovering the three tunnels (Tom, Dick and Harry) that they were digging. He was also responsible for a team of "penguins" whose job it was to dispose of the tons and tons of sand and dirt being excavated from the tunnels. Stalag Luft III and the activities that occurred there are detailed in a book by Paul Brickhill titled *The Great Escape,* which prompted the movie by the same name.

When not in solitary, Sage and several of his fellow college-educated buddies established "Sagan University" within the barbed wire to teach their comrades German, French, Norwegian, and other subjects of interest to them. Sage taught salesmanship, self-defense, and unarmed combat, earning himself yet another nickname, "The Silent Killer." He and his students also made all types of weapons including knives, hatchets and spears, and managed to keep them concealed from the guards. They also collected bits of wire and rope to be used if it became possible or necessary to eliminate the guards and take control of the camp.

Just before the day set for the great escape, Major Sage and his fellow American airmen were purged from South Camp where the escape tunnel was located and sent to North Camp, thus separating them from the British prisoners. This transfer made it impossible to participate in the great tunnel escape planned for March 23, 1944, perhaps saving Sage's life. The break was scheduled for 8:30 p.m., but problems, including an allied air raid, delayed the escape. When the tunnel was finally opened, the diggers were stunned to find that the escape hatch was out in the open, 10 feet from the woods that were to hide the escapees. Nevertheless, the men continued to escape one by one, and when dawn came and they were discovered, more than 80 men were outside. An alert was sounded and most of the escapees were recaptured within 24 hours. Within two weeks, at least 50 of these fine courageous men were executed by firing squad.

Sage licked his wounds in North Camp and began planning his next escape. Because of his reputation for resistance and propensity for escape, Major Sage was transferred from prison to prison, eventually ending up at Oflag 7B near Mooseberg, Bavaria. There, he was again searched, suffered many hours of interrogation, and was placed in solitary confinement. On January 20, 1945, Sage and his colleagues were told they would be evacuated deeper into Germany, ahead of the advancing Russian troops. In preparation, Sage packed his earthly belongings of the time and put on all of his clothes including two pairs of socks, long johns, two pairs of pants, a heavy shirt and sweater, a battle jacket, an overcoat, and a knitted head piece that covered his head and face with holes for eyes, nose, and mouth.

On January 21, they were marched out of camp at Schubin into a blinding snowstorm. After marching all day in the bitter cold, the prisoners took refuge in a farmer's barns and outbuildings that bordered along the route of the march. Sage was convinced his chances for escape were better alone than with the mass exodus of prisoners. During that night, he hid himself away in a cellar under a pile of vegetables. At daylight, the prisoners were marched out, but Sage stayed hidden. Later in the day, he and several others who had hidden out were fed and cared for by friendly Polish citizens.

The following morning they heard the guns of the advancing Russian Army; Major Sage left his hiding place and marched forward, intercepting a Russian officer. He convinced the Russian that he and his fellow escapees were in fact American soldiers and allies. The Russians helped them escape to the east across Poland and the Ukraine to Odessa, Russia. Major Sage then went by ship back to OSS headquarters in Egypt and then on to the United States in late March 1945. During his two-year ordeal, Sage went from a healthy 220 pounds down to 130 pounds. Like his fellow POW, Lieutenant Leo Bustad (see the Leo K. Bustad story in this book), he remembered the friendship and support of his fellow prisoners, but also the tremendous cold and hunger.

After a short leave at home in Spokane, Sage was promoted to lieutenant colonel and assigned to the OSS Training Center on Catalina Island, off the coast of California. There he taught OSS recruits headed for the Pacific silent killing, demolitions, sabotage, and methods of evasion, survival, and escape from behind enemy lines. Although the fighting had ended in mid-August, World War II ended officially on September 2, 1945 when Japanese Foreign Minister Mamoru Shigemitsu signed the instrument of surrender on board the battleship *Missouri* in Tokyo Bay.

Colonel Sage remained on active duty through the Korean War and most of the Vietnam War. He earned a master's degree in public law and government at Columbia University, and finished all of his coursework for a Ph.D. in International Affairs at Columbia. However, the Korean War broke out before he could finish his doctoral dissertation. In 1963, he was given command of the 10th Special Forces Group (Airborne), the Green Berets, with headquarters in the Bavarian Alps. He taught at the U.S. Military Academy at West Point for three years and was a member of the U.S. Army Command and General Staff faculty. He retired with the rank of full colonel in 1972. He then returned to his family in Enterprise, Alabama, and started his second career, teaching. He taught high school for several years and, in the late 1970s, was named "South Carolina Teacher of the Year."

Colonel Sage's military decorations include the Order of the British Empire, Legion of Merit, Bronze Star, Purple Heart, Medal for Humane Action, and Prisoner of War Medal. The colonel's son, Captain Terry Sage, a West Point graduate, was killed in action in the counterattack to the Communist Tet Offensive in January 1968.

Second Lieutenant Howard A. Scholz
Palau Island Campaign
Killed In Action

Howard Allison Scholz died on September 14, 1944 of wounds received during the battle for Palau Island. The son of Mr. and Mrs. Albert J. Scholz of Colfax, Washington, the lieutenant graduated from Washington State College in 1943 with a B.S. degree in agriculture and with honors. He was the only one of his graduating class to receive a commission in the United States Marine Corps. Called to active duty in September 1943, he was involved in various South Pacific campaigns for approximately one month before his death. In a letter received by his wife, the former Nancy Rogers, Lieutenant Scholz said he would be receiving campaign ribbons by the time he could write to her again.[1] The letter arrived two weeks after his death. Scholz attended WSC from fall 1939 through spring 1943.

Private First Class Toll Seike
Combat Infantryman
442nd "Go For Broke"
Regimental Combat Team

Toll Seike, son of Mr. and Mrs. Shizu Seike, was born October 9, 1923 in Seattle, Washington. He graduated from Highline

High School in 1942 and enrolled at Washington State College that fall. Toll's older brother Benjamin was already at WSC, majoring in horticulture. In those days, the department operated many greenhouses, and each had modest living quarters for the students who helped care for the greenhouses and their growing plants. Since both boys had to work to afford college, Toll lived with his brother in one of the greenhouses; hence, his name does not appear in the *Chinook* or other WSC publications of the era.[1]

On February 19, 1942, only two and a half months after Pearl Harbor and the declaration of war on Japan, President Roosevelt, acting under his emergency war powers, issued Executive Order 9066. The order provided broad powers for the "protection of the national security." As a result, all Japanese Americans from the western half of Washington and Oregon, all of California, and the southern half of Arizona, were subject to forced removal from their homes, farms, and places of business, to relocation centers (detention camps) in remote areas of the United States.[2] Toll Seike's family was sent to the Tulelake Relocation Center in northern California. Because he was in college, Toll could stay in school until the end of the semester, choose to be "relocated" with his family, or join the Army. He left WSC at the end of the fall semester 1943-44, volunteering for Army duty.

After training at Camp Shelby, Mississippi, he joined the all-Japanese American 442nd Regimental Combat Team and was sent into battle in Europe. The combined 100th Infantry Battalion and the 442nd landed in France on September 30, 1944. On October 23, after nearly two weeks of intensive fighting in the Vosges Mountains, Toll's unit was pulled back from the front lines for a respite. The rest was short lived because the First Battalion of the 141st Regiment, a Texas outfit, had been surrounded and cut off by the Germans, and the 442nd was ordered to rescue the "lost battalion."

The 442nd moved out on October 25, facing an entrenched enemy, sniper and machine gun fire, heavy mortar and artillery barrages, land mines, barbed wire, enemy tanks, and miserable weather. The fighting was intense and the troops could only move ahead foot by foot. By October 28, the lost battalion's situation had become desperate, and the 442nd was ordered to reach them "at all cost." Rescue came on October 30, but PFC Toll Seike was killed in action the day before.

For this and other actions, the 442nd Regimental Combat Team became the most decorated unit in United States military history, receiving 18,143 individual decorations, including 9,486 Purple Hearts, 4,000 Bronze Stars, 560 Silver Stars, and one Congressional Medal of Honor.[3] Toll Seike, the young Japanese American who chose to fight for his country rather than remain with his family in a California Relocation Camp, was awarded the Combat Infantryman's Badge, Bronze Star, Purple Heart, Victory Medal, and several service medals.[4]

The Smawley Brothers
Patriots All

Seaman Bob Smawley

R obert B. "Bob" Smawley, best known as an early advocate of the WSU Alumni Center, has had a long and distin-guished career at Washington State University. He was born and raised in Pullman, graduated from Pullman High School in 1946, and immediately joined the Navy. He served from May 1946 through March 1948. Although World War II had ended, Bob served his country well, first as a naval seaman and later as an aviation storekeeper on Ford Island in Pearl Harbor, Hawaii.

After the service, he enrolled at Washington State College in fall 1948 to major in business administration. While at WSC, he joined Sigma Nu fraternity and was involved in numerous campus activities. He received his B.A. degree in June 1952 and, after a short career in Spokane working in sales, he returned to Pullman to join the WSC staff.[1]

Along the way, Bob became a prime player in the renovation of a large old cattle barn into a beautifully restored and elegant WSU Alumni Centre. The new facility became the center for all alumni activities and other various university events. Bob joined Keith Lincoln of WSU, former San Diego Charger football player, in the planning and fund-raising projects that led to the

Seaman Robert "Bob" Smawley. *(Photo courtesy Washington State University.)*

renovation of the old barn. At this writing, Bob, in retirement, serves as the WSU goodwill ambassador and involves himself in public relations activities and alumni business. Bob also serves as chief gardener for the Alumni Centre, maintaining beautifully adorned gardens with flowers in season and caring personally for the expansive grounds. In 1999, the University family acknowledged Bob's many years of dedication and service by naming the Alumni Courtyard and Gardens in his honor.

In April 2000, Bob was presented with an Alumni Achievement Award acknowledging his many years of service to WSU and the Lewis Alumni Centre:

Bob Smawley . . . for unequalled loyalty, enthusiasm and dedication to WSU and the Alumni Association, and for . . . timeless investment in future generations of Cougars. During a career that has spanned nearly half a century, the 1952 WSU graduate has served the university in many capacities . . . as athletic ticket manager and coordinator of the Cougar Club. Later he became manager of University Purchasing, Director of General Services, Director of the Beasley Coliseum and Director of University Relations. He retired as assistant to the vice president for University Affairs in 1993, but has continued to work for the WSU Alumni Association . . . joined the association board in 1967 and served as secretary for 20 years. He cochaired the Alumni Associ-

ation Centennial Committee and was association president during its centennial in 1989-90. Recognized as a Pullman and WSU historian, Smawley developed and narrates a host of slide presentations for various community and university constituencies. Throughout his career at WSU, he has served as a mentor for many WSU students and is a past adviser to his fraternity, Sigma Nu. Since the Lewis Alumni Centre was remodeled, he has devoted countless hours to planting and maintaining the flowers that grace the centre's landscape.[2]

Wilber Smawley and Donald Smawley

Older brothers, Wilber K. (Bill) and Donald E., left Pullman High School during World War II to enlist in the Armed Forces. Donald was in the Coast Guard and Bill was in the Army. Don served from 1944 to 1947. His primary service was aboard armed Coast Guard vessels that escorted American ships between East Coast locations and England. Bill joined the National Guard at the age of 17 as a member of Company E, 161st Infantry, which was activated in 1941. He was a courageous and daring infantryman, serving in combat in the battles for Guadalcanal and New Caledonia. Not content with those skirmishes, Bill volunteered to serve with "Merrill's Marauders" in the Burma Theatre.

The "Marauders" were commanded by Brig. General Frank D. Merrill and were foot soldiers in a regiment-sized unit, the Army 5307th Composite Unit, consisting of volunteers who joined to fight the Japanese in Burma. The unit reached India in October 1943 and was in constant combat in Burma from February to August 1944. The unit not only fought the enemy, but also constantly struggled against disease, leeches, insects, harsh terrain, and weather.[3] Although victorious in five major and 30 minor battles, by the time the 5307th was disbanded, it had suffered more than 80 percent casualties.[4] Bill Smawley survived the battles without a serious wound, but died of typhus fever on June 10, 1944 in India. He was buried in Hawaii in the Punchbowl Memorial Cemetery.

Lieutenant Allan H. Smith
Navy Interpreter
Anthropology Department Chair
WSU Vice President Academic

Allan H. Smith was born on September 8, 1913 in Norwood, Pennsylvania. His family moved to New Haven, Connecticut, in 1915 where his father taught at Yale University. Allan received a bachelor's degree from Yale in 1935 and a Ph.D. in anthropology from Yale in 1941. He joined the faculty at Washington State College in 1947 as an associate professor of anthropology. In 1965, Professor Smith became the first chair of the newly designated Department of Anthropology, a post he held until being chosen as WSU vice president academic in 1969. He retired in 1978 and died in 1999.

Smith served in the Navy in the central and western Pacific from 1943 through 1946. Fluent in speaking and writing Japanese, he was a Japanese language officer with the rank of lieutenant. His Navy duties included interrogation of Japanese prisoners and translation and deciphering of captured enemy documents. He was wounded during the battle for Okinawa and awarded the Purple Heart.[1]

During Dr. Smith's tenure at Washington State University, he taught both undergraduate and graduate classes, was heavily involved in anthropological research, and published many books and technical research papers. In 1949, Dr. Smith was granted a leave of absence from WSC to conduct ethnological research in the southern part of Ryukyu Island in the Pacific. He later served as the Ryukyu civil administration advisor to Ryukyu University and as the anthropology advisor to Ryukyu Army Command. Still later, he served as high commissioner of the Trust Territory of the Pacific Islands. His research interests included the cultures of the Kalispel Tribe in Washington State, ethnological research in the Ryukyu Islands, archaeology of Mount Rainer National Park, and many other topics related to Northwest Indian cultures, resulting in more than 25 publications. His study of the Kalispel Indians was so extensive that when other scholars visited that group to inquire about their cultural past, their response was, "Ask Dr. Smith." [2]

Professor Smith and his wife Trudy traveled extensively conducting research in Asia, Europe, Egypt, Sudan, and other locations throughout the world. Dr. Smith was preceded in death by his wife. Although they had no children, Professor Smith was the favorite teacher of many, and treated his students, especially graduate students, as family.

Lieutenant (JG) Shirley K. Stewart
Navy WAVES

Shirley Kathleen Stewart was born July 1, 1915, the daughter of Mr. and Mrs. Frank Stewart in Johnson, Washington. She graduated from Johnson High School in June 1933 and entered Washington State College, majoring in home economics. She joined Mu Beta Beta and the 4-H Club Honorary, becoming their historian. She was also a member of the Lohese Club, founded in 1913, and served as its president.[1] Since this period was in the depth of the Great Depression, Shirley needed to work her way through school, first as a live-in housekeeper and baby-sitter, then in the Library Reserve Room, and later as a laboratory assistant for a home economics instructor. She also

served as president of Stevens Hall while a resident in the same women's residence hall where her mother had lived years earlier. Shirley graduated with a B.S. degree in home economics with honors at the end of summer session 1937.[2]

In June 1943, Miss Stewart joined the Navy Women Accepted for Volunteer Emergency Service (WAVES) and reported to Smith College in Northampton, Massachusetts, for training. After training, she was commissioned with an ensign's rank and transferred to a new unit of the Pacific Fleet, serving as a ship's secretary with offices in downtown Seattle. Her duties involved assembling Navy crews for the new ships being built on the West Coast.

Navy Lieutenant (JG) Shirley Stewart (Waugh). *(Photo courtesy the Waugh family.)*

Her second post was at a WAVES barracks in Boston serving as executive officer and commissary officer. In both assignments, her primary job, the job of all women in the services at that time, was to take over the work and responsibilities of men, releasing them for active duty on the front lines or, as in her case, on the high seas.

Ensign Stewart was discharged at the end of the war. She married Burton Waugh of Burlington, Washington, and started a family and a second career that included teaching. She also received a master's degree in library science. Her career included serving two years at Yakima Valley College, seven years at Central Washington University, and six years at Centralia College.[3] Shirley Waugh died March 22, 2002.

Infantry Captain Glenn Terrell
D-Day Fighter
WSU President, 1967-1985

Glenn Terrell graduated from Davidson College in June 1942, receiving his bachelor's degree in political science and a commission as a second lieutenant in the Infantry. With World War II raging, Glenn went on active duty almost immediately after graduation. He received Basic Infantry Officer's training at Fort Benning, Georgia, after which he helped take the 30th Infantry Division through basic training at Camp Blanding, Florida. He was then transferred to the VII Corps Headquarters Company in England in preparation for the D-Day invasion.[1]

On D-Day, June 6, 1944, he and his comrades were loaded on an LCT (Landing Craft, Tank) headed for Utah Beach on the western coast of France. Utah and Omaha Beaches were the landing sites for the American troops, while Gold, Juno, and Sword Beaches were assigned to the British and Canadian soldiers. According to historian Stephen Ambrose, these landings were:

> *. . . not only the biggest amphibious operation in history but the most thoroughly planned and practiced. In preparation for going ashore on D-Day, 170,000 soldiers, British and Canadian and American, participated in exercises from January through May of 1944. Every one of them knew what was expected of him and what he could expect in the way of German resistance. They knew that Hitler had erected defenses called the Atlantic Wall to stop them. The Atlantic Wall consisted of reinforced concrete forts, trenches, minefields, and anti-landing craft devices of all kinds, and it was backed up by panzer (tank) divisions and manned by battle-hardened Nazis. The Allied soldiers were carried across the English Channel by ship or plane and were commanded by the best officers their countries could produce. They would be supported by 5,000 planes, including four-engine bombers and all types of fighters, dropping 500-pound bombs or firing rockets or strafing with .50-caliber machine guns, and by over 2,000 fighting ships firing cannons on the German positions.* [2]

Although he was not one of the first to land on the Utah beachhead, Terrell, one of thousands storming the beach, assumed the duty of finding and securing the VII Corps Headquarters on the march through France, Belgium, and into

Germany. Brigadier General Teddy Roosevelt Jr., son of Teddy Roosevelt, the 26th president of the United States, led the onslaught. "Ignoring enemy fire and mortar explosions, Roosevelt paced the beach waving his cane, bellowing orders at the incoming troops . . . to make sure that the invasion proceeded inland without slowing down." [3] VII Corps remained in the fight, leading the break-out from the Normandy beachhead, and into the area around Aachen, the first major German city to fall to the Allies. Later, VII Corps attacked to the Rhine River, captured Cologne, and helped exploit the Remagen bridgehead.

Ultimately, Terrell participated in five ETO campaigns. He was discharged in 1946 with the rank of captain. Captain Terrell was awarded the Bronze Star (for meritorious achievement), French Croix de Guerre, European African Middle Eastern Campaign Medal, and the World War II Victory Medal. Terrell returned to civilian life, earned his master's and Ph.D. degrees, and made higher education his profession for life. Dr. Glenn Terrell became Washington State University's seventh president when appointed by the Board of Regents in the summer of 1967. He served for 18 years, retiring on July 1, 1985 at age 65. Pat Caraher, editor of *Hilltopics*, summed up Terrell's tenure in these dramatic words:

The late 1960s, the decade of the '70s, and the first half of the '80s were neither the 'golden age of American higher education' nor the best time to be a college president. At the start of that period, schools across the country, including Washington State University, became centers of student unrest. The focus was on the U.S. involvement in the Vietnam War, correcting social injustices, eliminating racism and protecting the environment. The early '70s brought the first of a series of economic recessions that continue to plague higher education . . . through it all, one thing remained constant at WSU – President Glenn Terrell. His belief in WSU, his insight into what a university should be, the courage to 'stick to his guns' in the face of adversity, and his ability to 'keep a cool head while keeping the peace,' allowed WSU to survive some admittedly tough times, and to flourish.[4]

WSU Vice President Allan H. Smith added to the Terrell legacy:

It is impossible to think of a president more dedicated to the good of a university and its constituencies and, more broadly, of higher education at the state and national levels, and more indefatigable in his pursuit of this good. The meetings that he attended within the state and across the nation in the course of his tenure, the varied groups to which he talked concerning significant academic issues, and the important committees relating to higher education and its future on which he served, often as chairman, are staggering in their numbers. President Terrell will be remembered by this university for a very long time.[5]

Finally, at the time of his retirement, the WSU Associated Students named President Terrell an "honorary student." For a university president, always known as a friend of the students, no other tribute could have been more appropriate.

Army Lieutenant Glenn Terrell, circa D-Day. President of WSU, 1967-84. *(Photo courtesy Bob Smawley.)*

Captain Jerry R. Williams*
P-38 Fighter Pilot in the Pacific
WSC and NFL Football Great

Jerry Ralph Williams was born November 1, 1923 in Spokane, Washington, the son of Mr. and Mrs. Ralph D. Williams. He started high school at Lewis and Clark. He graduated from North Central High School following a fabulous high school career in sports. His friend Bob Carey (see the Robert Carey story in this book) introduced him to North Central football coach Archie Buckley (see the Archie Buckley story) and his transfer to North Central ensued. Jerry became Spokane's Number One Athlete (*Spokesman-Review* poll), was captain of his football team at North Central, and led all scoring. He was a four-sport varsity athlete in baseball, track, football, and basketball. He graduated from North Central in June 1942 and enrolled that fall at the University of Idaho. He was drafted after one semester. Encouraged by Bob Carey, Jerry joined the Army Air Corps and, like his friend Bob, became a P-38 fighter pilot.[1]

After 18 months of training, Lieutenant Jerry Williams was sent to the Pacific where he flew 23 missions before the war ended. He was on a flight over Japan when the atomic bomb was released over Hiroshima. He flew escort for the leaders to the Peace Conference aboard the USS *Missouri* where Japanese officials signed the surrender agreement that ended World War II. Jerry was awarded the Air Medal and several other combat citations. He called his favorite P-38 *Buck* after his high school

Captain Jerry Williams, WWII P-38 fighter pilot, WSC and NFL football great. *(Photo courtesy the Williams family.)*

coach, Archie Buckley. He was discharged from the service in August 1946 and enrolled at Washington State College the next month.[2]

In 1947, Jerry played football on the WSC team coached by Phil Sarboe, and joined Sigma Nu fraternity. During the school year 1948-49, he served as vice president of the junior class, was president of the Grey W Club, and was the greatest ground gainer on the football team. He also played right field on the Cougar baseball team that won the Northern Division championship. During 1949-50, he was ranked third in the nation in kickoff returns, played left halfback on the East-West Football Team, and was voted the second most valuable player on the team. On the Cougar team that fall, he carried the ball 98 times, gained over 500 yards, and scored 36 points.[3] In one memorable game against Oregon State in November 1948, Williams scored three times for the Cougars, including once on a 29-yard pass from Frank Mataya.[4] He won the "Bohler" inspirational award his senior year, and was chosen to play in the college All-Star Hula Bowl in Hawaii, and the East-West game in Los Angeles. Williams was named the most valuable player in both games.

Jerry graduated from Washington State College in 1950 and signed with the Los Angeles Rams to play professional football. He was a member of the World Championship Ram Team in 1951, and later was named to the All-Time Ram Team. Williams was traded to the Philadelphia Eagles where he set a new record for receptions and served as defensive player-coach. "Jerry was extra bright and always two or three steps ahead of everybody else…George Allen made a big deal out of running the nickel defense (five defensive backs), but it originated with Jerry Williams." [5]

Williams began coaching at the University of Montana in 1956, and then joined the Philadelphia Eagles as defensive coach. His team won the World Championship in 1961. He left the Eagles to serve first as coach, and then head coach, of the Calgary Stampeders, leading them to a Grey Cup victory in 1968. He left the Canadian team to return to the Eagles as head coach from 1970 to 1972. He then returned to the Canadian football league to coach the Hamilton Tiger-Cats to a championship. Williams retired at the end of the 1975 season with a career CFL record of 44-28-1 and moved to his cattle ranch in Arizona. He also pursued his second love, flying. [6]

Jerry Williams was honored with membership in the WSU Athletic Hall of Fame, the Inland Northwest Athletic Hall of Fame, the Washington State Athletic Hall of Fame, and the All-Northwest All-Time Pro Team. [7] Jerry died in 1999 survived by his wife Marian, three sons and two daughters.

*The Jerry Williams story previously appeared in the April 2004 issue of **The Pacific Northwesterner.***

Major John H. Wills
WWII Army Engineer and Depot Commander
Persian Gulf Service Command, Abadan, Iran

John H. Wills was born January 26, 1915 in San Diego, and moved with his parents to Spokane, Washington, when he was less than a year old. He attended public schools in Spokane and graduated from Lewis and Clark High School in 1934. He enrolled at Washington State College where he majored in electrical engineering for four years. [1] He pledged Alpha Kappa Lambda fraternity, played in the college orchestra, and was a member of the ROTC rifle team. Because the country was in the depths of the Great Depression and jobs were scarce, John's WSC faculty advisor suggested that he transfer to Purdue University to enhance his chances of employment. He took the advice, graduated from Purdue with its class of 1939 and was commissioned as an Army second lieutenant based on his four years of ROTC training while at WSC.

Lt. Wills went on active Army duty in early 1941 well before the attack on Pearl Harbor. Following training and several assignments stateside, Wills was assigned to help create and operate the Army's Persian Gulf Service Command Depot near Abadan, Iran, at the far north end of the Persian Gulf. Army personnel assigned to the depot enlarged the existing ports, built or repaired the main road heading toward Russia, and operated the Trans-Iranian Railway to deliver supplies, equipment, arma-

Army Major John H. Wills. *(Photo courtesy the John Wills family.)*

ments, ammunition, and other materials to Russia's backdoor. By all accounts, the materials supplied through the depot were responsible for the great turnaround that allowed the Russian Army to counterattack and ultimately reroute the Germans, pushing them back to and beyond their own borders.

Captain Wills, later Major Wills, in an interview with this author, recounted some of the depot activities:

There were two railroad spurs out of Ahwaz, one was the main line to Khorramshahr, and the other went right to a small port on the Persian Gulf. They had four docks and we in Khorramshahr had sixteen or more, so we could unload twenty-plus Liberty Ships at a time, twenty-four hours a day, seven days a week for the entire two and one-half to three years . . . We had a plant to assemble GMC and Studebaker two and one-half ton trucks. They were shipped over in crates, and our troops put them together and then turned them over to Russian drivers who drove them to the front. We also had a great number of truck drivers as well as railroad people and operating and construction personnel. We rebuilt the railroad and during the first six or eight months, the U.S. shipped fifty diesel locomotives over . . . we were running the diesel locomotives and full-sized trains in both directions on a single track with sidings to allow trains to pass each other . . . the trains moved out at three-minute intervals.

Also, we had an assembly plant for fighter aircraft in Abadan. Single-seat fighters were shipped to us in crates, and our men put them together. They were test flown by Russian pilots, loaded with ammunition, and flown from Abadan to the Russian Front . . . All in all, we had truck transport, rail transport, and air transport, all working at the same time to supply the Russian war effort . . . We shipped everything. Guns of all types, planes, tanks, ammunition, explosives, trucks, jeeps, food, clothing, boots, medical supplies, locomotives, tractors, road building equipment, everything the Russians needed . . . It was all top secret . . . My wife didn't even know where I was for three years.[2]

By the end of the war, the Persian Gulf Command had delivered nearly 17,000,000 tons of Lend-Lease materials valued at over $9,000,000,000.00 to support the Russian fight against Nazi Germany. According to the Foreign Economic Administration, the Persian Gulf Command shipped the following Lend-Lease materials to support the Russian offensive:

Year	Value	Gross Long Tons
1941	$545,000	194,000
1942	$1,351,788,000	2,468,999
1943	$2,965,928,000	4,794,000
1944	$3,429,345,000	6,218,000
1945	$1,371,598,000	2,977,000

These totals included nearly 14,000 aircraft, more than 400,000 trucks and Jeeps, and many thousands of other military vehicles, such as artillery movers, tank transports, scout cars and tanks, and more than 4,000,000 tons of foodstuffs.[3]

Major Wills completed his Army service in early 1946. He then worked as a civilian engineer for several multinational companies throughout the United States. Returning to Spokane, he and his wife Betty founded several successful engineering-related businesses before retiring. After retirement, John became a stockbroker. In 1999, WSU named Mr. and Mrs. John H. Wills "Benefactors of Washington State University," a designation reserved for major donors to the university.

Going to the Front With Class

Late in World War II, two Washington State College classes were inducted en-mass and sent to the various fronts. They were Army Specialized Training Program (ASTP) trainees and the entire 1943 junior class of the Reserve Officer Training Corps (ROTC).

Army Specialized Training Program

The Army Specialized Training Program was created by Secretary of War Henry Stimson. His plan called for 150,000 bright young men to be trained in regular subjects including mathematics, engineering, and foreign languages – specialties that would be required by the Army later in the war. The students would be assigned to colleges and universities under contract with the War Department. The students, designated as privates, received $50 a month and the Army paid tuition and room and board.[1]

There were about 250 ASTP soldiers enrolled at WSC in the fall of 1943, but their educations were cut short due to anticipated forces needed on the front lines. In February 1944, the national ASTP program was reduced from 150,000 to just 30,000.[2] The announcement from the Secretary of War read:

Because of the inability of the selective service system to deliver personnel according to schedule, the Army is now short 200,000 men who should have been in uniform before the end of 1943.[3]

Consequently, instead of completing their college work and going on to Officer Candidate School (OCS) as planned and promised, most of the students enrolled as ASTP found themselves in rifle companies on the front lines. The WSC students were scattered throughout the European Theatre of Operations (ETO) and the Pacific. At least nine of the WSC contingent were killed in action. They included Jack Snyder, Rudolph Schmitz, Ferman Elley, Albert Novey, Ora Bollinger, Thomas Nabby, Harry Pearce, Charles Stoops, and Stephen Zoradi.[4]

Advanced Reserve Officer Training Corps

The WSC senior class of Advanced Reserve Officer Training Corps (ROTC) was exempt from active duty until the students received their degrees and became commissioned officers. Therefore, the WSC junior ROTC class of 1943 was assigned to active duty in their place. Requirements for them to be commissioned as second lieutenants included 17 weeks of basic training and completion of their college degrees. However, in May 1943 the entire third-year class was ordered to report to Camp Roberts, California, for active duty. At Camp Roberts, they received training in Infantry or Tank units.

The training was rough and hot. They were to complete the 17-week basic training course and then attend Officer Candidate School (OCS) at Fort Benning, Georgia. Unfortunately, OCS was over enrolled, so these 33 ROTC cadets were sent back to WSC with instructions to enroll in physics and mathematics courses, and military training. They were housed in fraternities and sororities, and marched to classes.

In June 1944, this WSC group was back on active duty receiving further training at either Camp Roberts (Infantry) or Fort Sill, Oklahoma, (Tank training), then assigned to OCS at Fort Benning. All but one completed OCS, were commissioned, and either assigned to the ETO or the Pacific.[5] The following initial Army directive dated May 20, 1943 was given to the 33 ROTC students from WSC:

Following-named enlisted reservists first year advanced ROTC . . . are ordered AD effective June 7, 1943, on that date WP for address indicated, to Presidio of Monterey, California, reporting to the CO Recp Center for processing and assignment to Camp Roberts, California reporting there at no later than June 12, 1943, to receive Military Training in lieu of that normally given during 2nd year advanced course ROTC (Inf) instructions. Enlisted Reservists herein reporting to Recp Center will present to Classification Officer transcript of college academic and ROTC records.

The 33 privates from WSC were:
Edwin B. Abbott, Cashmere, Washington
Frederick J. Anderson, Kalispell, Montana
William A. Bakamis, Renton, Washington
Alvin Bauer, Vancouver, Washington
John R. Bayton, Port Angeles, Washington
Richard A. Beckman, Tacoma, Washington
John S. Carver Jr., Pullman, Washington

Joseph A. Cochran, Walla Walla, Washington
Alfred B. Coppers, Fall City, Washington
Lloyd D. Damewood, Spokane, Washington
George A. Davison, Twin Falls, Idaho
Leland H. Nelson, Walla Walla, Washington
Daniel M. Ogden Jr., Spokane, Washington
Thomas F. O'Neill, San Francisco, California
Vincent N. Pfaff, Centralia, Washington
Howard G. Schuster, Wilbur, Washington
Langdon H. Tannehill, Glendale, California
George M. Todd Jr., Snoqualmie, Washington
Scott J. Witt, Longview, Washington
William C. Dent, Pullman, Washington
Milan F. DeRuwe, Pomeroy, Washington
Charles D. Dietrich, Vancouver, Washington
John D. Gillis, Washtucna, Washington
William H. Gustafson, Tacoma, Washington
John E. Halver, Woodinville, Washington
Donald R. Hayward, Tacoma, Washington
Earnest Hento, Sumas, Washington
Clarence R. Hix, Pullman, Washington
William W. McCanse, Pomeroy, Washington
Arthur R. MacKelvie, Zillah, Washington
Virgil L. Michaelson, Colfax, Washington
George P. Mooney, Kent, Washington
Edward J. Myers, South Bend, Washington

WORLD WAR II and KOREA

Lieutenant Ace Allen
WSU Distinguished Military Graduate
Served in World War II
Killed In Action in Korea

Ace Allen was born on October 7, 1923 in Glacier Bay, Nova Scotia. He attended grade school in Pullman, Washington, and graduated from Jefferson High School in Tampa, Florida. His permanent home was with his mother, Mrs. Emma J. Allen, in Spokane. Shortly after graduating from high school, Ace volunteered for service in the Army Air Corps, serving 30 months of World War II in the European Theatre of Operations. He went on active duty January 19, 1943, serving until after the end of the war and was discharged November 13, 1945 with the rank of sergeant.

He enrolled at Washington State College in February 1946 and immediately joined the Army Reserve unit in Pullman. At WSC, Ace lived in Waller Hall, majoring in business administration.

He was involved in many campus activities including Scabbard and Blade and the National Independent Students' Association. He was named Waller Hall's Windsor of the Year (an honor bestowed on the hall's outstanding senior) and Outstanding Military Graduate in 1950. He received his degree in June 1950 and a commission as an Army second lieutenant.[1] Ace's brother Louis Allen was also a WSC graduate and an outstanding boxer on the varsity boxing team coached by Ike Deeter.

Lieutenant Allen completed a short training session at Fort Lewis, Washington, and was immediately sent to Korea as an Infantry platoon leader. He was killed in action in Korea on August 9, 1950, just two months after graduation from WSU, already having served his country once before.

Lieutenant Allen had joined the front line combat troops on August 7, 1950, leading his platoon assigned to clear out enemy positions in a valley near Taegu, South Korea. His unit suffered heavy casualties, but accomplished its mission bravely and heroically.[2] Frank Pace Jr., Secretary of the Army, wrote to Ace's mother announcing that her son had been awarded the Purple Heart, posthumously. He stated:

The medal, which you will receive in a short time, is of slight intrinsic value, but rich with the tradition for which Americans have so gallantly given their lives ever since the days of George Washington, whose profile and coat of arms adorn the medal . . . Little that we can do or say will console you for the loss of your loved one. He has gone, however, in honor and in the company of patriots.[3]

An editorial in the *Spokane Daily Chronicle* provided a fitting and final honor for the World War II sergeant who, as an officer and platoon leader gave his life for his country. Referring to the recent Reserve Officer Training Corps (ROTC) Military Review held on the WSC campus that spring, the editorial writer wrote:

. . . Hundreds who beheld the moving spectacle in the college stadium little more than three months ago must have been sobered by a sense of the transience of life when they read Wednesday of the death of Ace Allen. They could see him marching at the head of the crack drill squad of the ROTC, barking orders with precision learned in 30 months of service in the air force . . . And they could hear the call of taps, played by three buglers, one on the field, one stationed outside and the third far in the distance. . . There must have been blurred eyes as the throng that sat in the sunshine of that spring morning reflected on the suddenness with which that scene has been transformed into one of tragedy and heartbreak . . . Let us hear taps again for Ace Allen, and for the last time. Death has left him in the quiet dignity that hovers over the last resting place of all who love their country more than the vibrant adventure of living.[4]

Lieutenant Allen was awarded the American Theatre Service Medal, European African Middle Eastern Service Medal, Good Conduct Medal, Victory Medal, and the Purple Heart.

First Lieutenant James B. Baker
Infantry Company Commander
Navy and Army Veteran

James Brygger Baker was born October 12, 1924 in Tacoma, Washington, and graduated from Stadium High School there in 1942. He entered Washington State College in February 1943 as a speech major. He joined Sigma Nu fraternity and was involved in the Arena Theatre Productions.[1] He joined the Navy in May 1943 and received training at Great Lakes Naval Training Center, followed by aviation radio school in Memphis, Tennessee. When the war in Europe was over, he attended gunnery school in Florida before being discharged.

James "Jim" Baker returned to WSC in fall 1946 to continue work on his degree using his GI Bill benefits. He was enrolled in advanced Reserve Officer Training Corps (ROTC), and earned a bachelor of arts in speech and a commission in the Army Reserves in June 1949. Two years later, he was recalled into service as a second lieutenant in the Infantry. He trained at Camp Roberts in California and Fort Benning in Georgia. By January 1952, after studying biological, radiological, and germ warfare

Infantry Platoon Leader Lieutenant James Baker at the front in Korea. *(Photo courtesy the Baker family.)*

in Japan, he was sent to Korea to serve with "I" Company, 3rd Battalion, 15th Infantry Regiment.

Lieutenant Baker first served as an Infantry platoon leader on the front lines. On March 2, pinned down by enemy fire in a sector near Maktae-dong, his heroism later earned him the Bronze Star as noted here:

Lieutenant Baker, the patrol leader, completely disregarded his personal safety as he made his way through the lethal hail of hostile bullets toward the enemy trench, firing his weapon and throwing grenades as he advanced. Forced to take cover within ten feet of the enemy emplacement, Lieutenant Baker continued to throw grenades until the enemy weapons were effectively silenced. His outstanding aggressiveness and determination enabled the patrol to withdraw and move its casualties to safety.[2]

During his solo advance on the enemy, Lieutenant Baker was hit by shrapnel, but ignored the wound and kept on. He was awarded the Purple Heart and the Combat Infantry Badge with one star. In May 1952, Baker became company commander, a post he held until rotated home late that summer.

Following his discharge in August 1952, he worked in real estate in Portland, Oregon. Baker owned and operated his own commercial brokerage company, earning CCIM designation from the Commercial Investment Institute, where he also taught part time.

Jim Baker and wife, Fran Landerholm Baker (WSC '50), have four sons, all WSU graduates and all members of their dad's fraternity. The Bakers are now retired.[3]

Lieutenant Dale C. Gough
Land-based Bomber Pilot – Flew 100 Missions

Dale Clifford Gough was born August 9, 1922 in Salt Lake City, Utah. He graduated from Lewis and Clark High School in Spokane and joined the Marines at the end of World War II. After the war, he enrolled at Washington State College. With a combination of credits from GED test scores and six semesters of college course work, he graduated in June 1949 with honors and a bachelor of arts degree in business administration.[1] He was reactivated as a Marine pilot in April 1952 and served with distinction in the Korean War. In February 1953, he was awarded the Silver Star Medal for his daring and heroic actions, as noted by the following citation:

For conspicuous gallantry and intrepidity as pilot of a plane in Marine Attack Squadron One Hundred Twenty-One in action against enemy aggressor forces in Korea on 3 February 1953. Assigned the mission of attacking hostile artillery positions which were inflicting heavy casualties upon friendly troops, First Lieutenant Gough scored a direct bomb hit on one of the enemy gun emplacements, although the positions were surrounded by precipitous terrain. During his second attack on the target, his plane became severely damaged by hostile defensive fire and he was forced to discontinue his run. Despite the concentrated enemy antiaircraft fire, he maneuvered his crippled aircraft into position for a third attack and succeeded in destroying another gun emplacement and in successfully suppressing artillery fire in the area. By his heroic actions, First Lieutenant Gough was directly responsible for the destruction of two hostile weapons which were endangering the security of friendly ground forces. His outstanding skill, indomitable courage and gallant devotion to duty reflect great credit upon himself and were in keeping with the highest traditions of the United States Naval Service.

Signed for the president by R. B. Anderson, Secretary of the Navy.[2]

The following month, Gough was awarded the Distinguished Flying Cross:

For heroism and extraordinary achievement in aerial flight as pilot of a plane in Marine Attack Squadron One Hundred Twenty-One during operations against enemy aggressor forces in Korea on 28 March 1953. Serving as Tactical Air Controller Airborne for repeated aerial assaults against heavily defended and well-entrenched enemy strong points that were blocking a major advance by the First Marine Division, First Lieutenant Gough conducted repeated low-level rocket assaults in order to mark the objectives clearly for the several flights under his control, although handicapped by extremely adverse weather and intense hostile antiaircraft fire. Maneuvering his plane to minimum altitude through increasingly accurate enemy fire, he scored direct rocket hits that enabled the attacking aircraft to strike with devastating effect. By his exceptional accuracy and superb airmanship, he was largely responsible for the success of seven flights of planes that inflicted heavy enemy casualties and substantially aided the advance of friendly frontline ground forces. His courage, exemplary leadership, and devotion to duty throughout reflect great credit on First Lieutenant Gough and were in keeping with the highest traditions of the United States Naval Service.

Signed for the president by C. S. Thomas, Secretary of the Navy.

Captain Gough flew 100 missions over Korea. In addition to the medals cited above, he was awarded the Air Medal with five Gold Stars.[3]

Brigadier General John F. Kinney
Wake Island Pilot
Japanese Prisoner of War in China
Pilot and Squadron Leader in Korea

John Franklin Kinney was born on November 1, 1914 in Endicott, Washington, the son of Mr. and Mrs. E. A. Kinney. He graduated from Endicott High School in 1932 and entered Washington State College that fall. Kinney took nearly all the mechanical and electrical engineering courses available. He was an active student leader serving as Junior Class president, vice president of Crimson Circle honorary, and officer in the Scabbard and Blade Military Honor Society. He graduated from WSC in June 1936 with an Army Reserve commission.[1] He volunteered for pilot training but was initially rejected for color blindness, which proved to be an incorrect diagnosis. He had always wanted to fly; to stay near the flying scene, he took a job as an aircraft mechanic with Pan American Airways. Unbeknown to him at the time, his training and experience as a mechanic with Pan Am would serve him well in the future on Wake Island.

He was appointed an aviation cadet in the Marine Corps Reserves in July 1938 and assigned to active duty at the Naval Air Station in Pensacola, Florida. In August 1939, Kinney accepted a commission in the Marine Corps as a second lieutenant. From September 1939 to May 1940, Lieutenant Kinney attended basic training at Philadelphia. He was then assigned to Marine Bombing Squadron Two, Second Marine Air Group, and Fleet Marine Force in San Diego. In December 1940, he joined the Second Marine Air Group at Pearl Harbor, Hawaii. He was on duty there and at Ewa, Oahu, during most of 1941. While in Hawaii, Kinney and his cohorts had an opportunity to fly F4F-3 Wildcats, the latest single-wing fighters produced by the Grumman Corporation. Both the USS *Yorktown* and USS *Enterprise* were in Hawaiian waters at the time, and Kinney practiced Wildcat takeoffs and landings on the flight decks of those carriers.[2]

A few days before the attack on Pearl Harbor, Lieutenant Kinney and his fellow pilots were transferred to Wake Island to patrol and defend it against a possible Japanese invasion. In the early morning hours of December 4, Kinney and his mates took off from a carrier and landed on Wake Island. They had only a dozen Wildcat fighters, spare parts were almost nonexistent, as were qualified mechanics. In spite of this situation, the patrol missions began as scheduled on December 5. On December 7 (December 8 on Wake Island), Pearl Harbor was attacked and, almost immediately, a bomber attack was made on Wake Island. Kinney was on air patrol, but unable to close on the enemy. Upon landing, he was shocked by the devastation that included numbers of killed and wounded, and two-thirds of their aircraft destroyed.

In addition to flying patrol and attack missions on the lookout for enemy planes and ships, Kinney was designated assistant engineering officer. When, during the first attack, the head engineering officer was killed, he took over the job. A second attack came on Monday, December 9 and was followed by

Lieutenant Colonel John Kinney receiving an Air Medal. *(Photo courtesy Washington State University.)*

another on December 10. Lieutenant Kinney fought in the air and on the ground, where he was charged with keeping as many aircraft airworthy as possible. He was credited with a virtual miracle in keeping crippled planes functioning with almost no tools and a complete lack of regular equipment. He performed all types of repairs and replacement work including changing engines, propellers, and other critical aircraft parts.[3] He, along with his Marine and Army mates, managed to hold off an overwhelming enemy force of air and land invaders for nearly two weeks, even though they were badly outnumbered, poorly equipped, and running short of ammunition and supplies. In one instance, he and three civilian volunteers swapped a complete engine from a badly damaged Wildcat over to a lightly damaged aircraft and had the repaired Wildcat back in the air in just nine hours.

On December 20, 1941, the island was overrun and the commanding officer ordered surrender. Lieutenant Kinney and the other survivors were captured and would spend the next three and a half years as prisoners of war. Later, although as a prisoner he was not aware of it, Kinney was awarded the Legion of Merit with the following citation:

For exceptionally meritorious conduct in the performance of outstanding services to the Government of the United States while serving with Marine Fighting Squadron Two Hundred Eleven, during the heroic defense of Wake Island, from 8 to 22 December 1941. Replacing the regular Engineering Officer at the outset of the action and assum-

ing responsibility for the maintenance of all aircraft in operational status, Second Lieutenant Kinney skillfully affected vital repairs upon the overused planes under extremely primitive conditions, working day and night at his essential task and carrying out his duties in the face of frequent enemy aerial attacks. With little experienced assistance, no instructions or guidance and wholly inadequate tools and equipment, he succeeded in changing parts, assemblies, engines and propellers from one craft to another, enabling Squadron Two Hundred Eleven to put up the sole aerial defense against the overwhelming hostile forces until the last battered plane was hopelessly beyond salvage. Forcing himself to the utmost of endurance despite acute physical suffering, Second Lieutenant Kinney surpassed all his previous resourceful efforts by ingeniously assembling and rebuilding a complete engine and propeller out of scrap parts removed from many aircraft wrecks. Collapsing from sheer exhaustion only at the end of the bitter ordeal, Second Lieutenant Kinney, by his extraordinary technical and mechanical ability and his fortitude, great courage and gallant devotion to the fulfillment of an assignment attaining monumental proportions, inspired the small force gallantly defending the island against terrific odds and upheld the highest traditions of the United States Naval Service.

Signed for the President by James Forrestal, Secretary of the Navy.

On January 12, 1942, Lieutenant Kinney and his fellow prisoners embarked on the Japanese troopship *Nitta Maru* headed for Yokohama, Japan. From Yokohama, the *Nitta Maru* transported the prisoners to the Japanese occupied Chinese port of Shanghai. The prisoners were then moved inland to a prison camp near the port of Woosung. It was the dead of winter and the prisoners were plagued by extreme cold and hunger. The daily ration per man consisted of one cup of cooked rice, two cups of soup, and three cups of weak tea.[4] In May 1942, Kinney's family was notified that he was alive in a Japanese prison camp near Shanghai, China.[5]

In early December 1942, the American prisoners were moved to a camp called Kiangwan, about 10 miles closer to Shanghai. The Kiangwan prison was Kinney's home until May 9, 1945. During that time, he kept busy planning various ways and routes of escape. Applying his engineering skills he produced all sorts of equipment and devices designed to make life a bit easier for his fellow prisoners. He built a shortwave crystal radio set from scavenged materials, a magnet from a Japanese speedometer, and a piece of wire from an ignition coil. He melted lead and sulfur to form crystal. The project consumed six months of trial-and-error work. For his efforts, Kinney was able to pick up English news transmitted by Russian and Vichy French stations in Shanghai that reported where the battles were being fought.[6]

On May 9, 1945, the prisoners were placed in railroad boxcars headed to yet another prison in China. Once aboard the train,

Kinney began planning an escape. He devised a way to conceal the escape attempt from the guards so that he and several others, in the dark, wedged their way through a high window of the moving train car, dropped to the ground, and escaped into the countryside. On June 21, Kinney's parents received word that he had escaped and while still in enemy territory, was well and in the hands of friendly Chinese.[7] After the war, President Truman presented Kinney with a Bronze Star with the following citation:

For meritorious service while interned as a Japanese Prisoner of War at Kiangwan, China, from December 1942 until May 1945. Effecting escape from a moving train on 10 May 1945, while en route from a Prisoner of War Camp at Kiangwan to a camp in North China, Second Lieutenant Kinney, although suffering from malnutrition and faced with tremendous odds, finally succeeded in reaching the United States Armed Forces at Kunming forty-seven days later after traveling nearly seven hundred miles by foot, horse and boat through enemy territory previously untraversed by United States Armed Forces, providing them with valuable firsthand information concerning enemy troops and defenses in the Shanghai area, the location and treatment of prisoners of war, the capabilities and limitations of the Chinese New Fourth Army, and the activities of guerrillas behind enemy lines. By his exceptional foresight, courage and tireless devotion to duty, Second Lieutenant Kinney contributed immeasurable to the success of the final phase of the war in China, and upheld the highest traditions of the United States Naval Service.

On July 2, 1945, Lieutenant Kinney and his companions were ordered back to the United States and arrived in Washington, D.C., on July 9. Kinney recalled the following:

Over a period of 47 days, I had traveled about a thousand miles through and behind enemy lines, although certainly not all in a straight line. I'd covered various parts of the distance on foot, on horseback, by donkey, by boat, and in sedan chairs. During this time, all five of us regained our health rapidly and when we reached Kunming, we were in fairly good physical condition. At Kunming, we had a succession of debriefing conferences where we provided as much information as we could on the strength and disposition of the enemy – as well as that of the Chinese Communist Army units. We related what we could about the defense installations in the Shanghai area so that military planners could schedule them for future air raids . . . We provided the names of POWs in our camp and the names of those who had died . . . We were also able to correct a previous misconception of the prison camp at Kiangwan. American military intelligence had apparently labeled that camp site a Japanese ammunition storage depot and had slated it for a future bombing attack.[8]

After the war ended, Kinney was assigned to various Marine Corps facilities, promoted numerous times, and in July 1949, ordered to attend the Air War College at Maxwell Field in Alabama. While there, he flew nearly every aircraft available to a Marine pilot, including P-51s, C-47s, and B-25s. He graduated in May 1950 just in time to take part in the Korean War, flying the new F9F jet attack aircraft.

Kinney and his squadron provided cover for Army Infantry units on the ground and flew escort missions to protect the B-29s bombing over North Korea. In late August 1951, because of Kinney's experience and success operating fighter jets, he was transferred to Washington, D.C. to draw up specifications for a new and vastly improved jet fighter. His hard work led to the successful development and production of the A-4 Skyhawk, which was ready for testing two years later. This new fighter, in use throughout the Vietnam War, proved to be a durable and effective addition to the U.S. air arsenal. Lieutenant Colonel Kinney's leadership and heroism throughout the Korean War earned him many medals and awards. The following are the citations from several of the accolades Kinney received:[9]

Silver Star: *For conspicuous gallantry and intrepidity as Commanding Officer of Marine Fighter Squadron Three Hundred Eleven in action against enemy aggressor forces in Korea from 10 March to 27 July 1951. Responsible for welding his squadron into an efficient fighting team to provide air support for friendly forces, Lieutenant*

Colonel Kinney personally led strikes on enemy positions and, despite intense hostile ground fire, hazardous terrain and adverse weather conditions, aided his squadron in the infliction of destruction on the enemy. Spearheading a sixteen-plane attack on the hostile stronghold of Hyon-ni, he skillfully fought his plane in the face of enemy antiaircraft fire and assisted in destroying five antiaircraft batteries and in damaging four others. His outstanding leadership, courage, and unwavering devotion to duty in the face of personnel and logistical difficulties served to inspire his squadron in successfully completing its mission and reflect great credit upon Lieutenant Colonel Kinney and the United States Naval Service.

Distinguished Flying Cross: *For heroism and extraordinary achievement in aerial flight as pilot of a plane in Marine Fighter Squadron Three Hundred Eleven during operations against enemy aggressor forces in Korea on 9 May 1951. As commanding officer of a jet fighter squadron spearheading a fighter sweep of the enemy airfield at Sinuiju, involving operations at extreme range in the face of numerically superior hostile jet aircraft, Lieutenant Colonel Kinney led his squadron over the target prior to the arrival of friendly low-level attack aircraft and high-altitude interceptors and succeeded in drawing the enemy jet aircraft from their bases across the Yalu River, thereby destroying their capability of later*

employment against the friendly attack aircraft and assuring the success of the entire fighter sweep. By his courageous leadership, skilled airmanship, and devotion to duty, he upheld the highest traditions of the United States Naval Service.

Ninth Air Medal: *For meritorious acts while participating in aerial flight, as a pilot attached to a Marine Fighter Squadron, from 7 June 1951 to 6 July 1951. Lieutenant Colonel Kinney successfully completed his seventy-second through ninety-first combat missions against the enemy over Korea, where enemy fire was either expected or received. By his skillful airmanship, he inflicted great damage on concentrations of enemy vehicles, materiel, and personnel. Lieutenant Colonel Kinney's conduct throughout was in keeping with the highest traditions of the United States Naval Service.*

In June 1959, Kinney became Brigadier General John F. Kinney, and retired from the Marine Corps with more than 20 years of service, a storied defense of Wake Island, three and one-half years as a prisoner of war, and 125 combat missions in Korea. During his Marine career, Kinney was awarded the Silver Star, Legion of Merit with Combat V, Gold Star in lieu of a second Legion of Merit, Distinguished Flying Cross, Bronze Star with Combat V, ten Air Medals, a Presidential Unit Citation, Army Distinguished Unit Citation with Distinguished Unit Emblem, American Defense Service Medal with Fleet clasp, Expeditionary

Medal with a silver "W", Asiatic-Pacific Campaign Medal with one Bronze Star, Victory Medal, Korean Service Medal, and the Prisoner of War Medal. In 1980, Kinney received the WSU Alumni Achievement Award.

Following retirement, civilian Kinney became a test pilot, flying the A-4D aircraft, the very aircraft for which he had written the specifications in 1952. In 1969, he joined Hiller Aircraft in Palo Alto, California, as head of flight operations responsible for final assembly and production flight testing.

Navy Commander Leo R. Pierson
World War II and Korea Dive Bomber Pilot

Leo Ronayne Pierson was born in Cheney, Washington, February 11, 1920, the son of Mr. and Mrs. W. W. Pierson. He graduated Cheney High School in 1939 and enrolled at Washington State College that fall, majoring in business. He also took courses at Eastern Washington College of Education in Cheney. After completing his degree from WSC in 1942, Pierson joined the Navy, completed pilot training, and was assigned to the USS *Yorktown* aircraft carrier in the Pacific. He was assigned to Bombing Squadron Five as a SBD-5 pilot.[1]

Lieutenant Pierson participated in more than 30 bombing and strafing missions from early August 1943 through May 1944.

His missions are tabulated in Navy records as the following:

Strikes against enemy installations and shipping in the South Pacific on or at Marcus, Wake, Makin, Mille, Kwajalein, Taroa, Wotje, Truk, Saipan, Tinian, Palau Group, Hollandia. Anti-submarine patrols, inner air patrols and searches encountered or expected enemy opposition on each of the flights listed. Enemy aircraft and enemy antiaircraft fire of all calibers were encountered or expected on all flights over enemy held territory. Results of strikes (confirmed reports): Direct hit on gun emplacement at Marcus, hanger partially destroyed at Wake, near-miss on 7,000 ton AK at Kwajalein, heavy AA emplacement destroyed at Taroa, AA emplacement destroyed at Kwajalein, direct hit on enemy troop concentration at Kwajalein, direct hit on stern of 5,000 ton AK at Truk, direct hit on oil storage dump at Truk, near miss on CL (Sendai Class) at Truk – slowed speed to such an extent that it was later sunk by our surface forces, direct hit on 10,000 ton AO at Palau – confirmed sunk by other pilot's reports, hit on concentration of enemy tanks at Hollandia.[2]

Pierson was awarded the Distinguished Flying Cross with three Gold Stars, Air Medal with four Gold Stars, seven World War II Battle Stars, Korean Medal with one Battle Star, and U.N. Medal. The citation for his first Air Medal read:

Meritorious achievement in aerial flight as Division Leader of a Flight of Dive Bombers in Bombing Squadron Five, attached to the USS Yorktown, during operations against enemy Japanese forces on Truk Atoll, April 29-30, 1944. Encountering motor trouble as he came in low over the target under extremely adverse weather conditions, Lieutenant (then Lieutenant, Junior Grade) Pierson immediately dropped out of formation, followed his group over the target and executed a low-level glide bombing attack on an ammunition dump, scoring a direct hit. Although repeatedly hit by the enemy's accurate antiaircraft fire as a result of his plane's reduced speed and consequent loss of maneuverability, he succeeded in clearing the target area and returned safe to his carrier. By his tactical skill and personal valor in the face of great danger, Lieutenant Pierson rendered gallant service, and his conduct throughout was in keeping with the highest traditions of the United States Naval Service.[3]

Pierson was recalled to active duty in December 1952 aboard the aircraft carrier USS *Oriskany*, serving in Korean waters until the end of the Korean War.[4] On July 1, 1969, Pierson was transferred to the retired Reserve with the grade of commander.

Colonel Dallas P. Sartz
Fighter Pilot in the Pacific
F-86 Jet Fighter Pilot in Korea
Boxing Champion and Hydro Jet Boat Racer

Dallas P. Sartz was born October 9, 1922 in Everett, Washington. He graduated from Everett High School in 1940 and enrolled at Central Washington College of Education. He also earned college credits at Montana State College and Mexico City College. He enlisted in the Army Air Corps in 1943 and served as a fighter pilot throughout the South Pacific.[1]

Sartz enrolled at Washington State College in the fall of 1948 and received his B.S. degree in physical education in February 1951. While at WSC, he joined the Air National Guard 116th Fighter Squadron in Spokane. He received training as a jet pilot and went with his squadron to fight in the Korean War. He was one of the first 26 pilots to cross the Atlantic in a jet aircraft. After Korea, he was assigned to an airfield in England, and then returned to Spokane to rejoin the Air National Guard as commander of maintenance. Colonel Sartz retired from active service in 1978.[2] Before going off to war, Sartz was the Washington Golden Gloves middleweight boxing champion in 1942. After the Korean War, he became a part-time hydro-jet-boat racer, driving the *Miss Spokane* as well as *Miss Seattle Too*. He retired from racing in 1962. Colonel Dallas Sartz died October 17, 1998.[3]

KOREA and VIETNAM

Lieutenant Colonel Donald L. Bauer
Air Force Combat Veteran
Distinguished Flying Cross Recipient

Born December 20, 1928 in Spokane, Washington, Donald Lee Bauer graduated from Ritzville High School in June 1947 and entered Washington State College in September, majoring in engineering. He enjoyed college life, joined Phi Sigma Kappa fraternity, but his heart was in flying.[1] He dropped out of school after two years to join the Air Force in August 1949 as an aviation cadet at Williams Air Force Base, Arizona, where he finished flight training and was commissioned with the rank of second lieutenant. While he was in training, the North Koreans invaded South Korea and the Korean War was raging. He was promoted to first lieutenant and assigned to the 8th Squadron, 49th Fighter-Bomber Group based near Taegu, South Korea, flying F-80s and F-84s. After flying 86 hazardous combat missions in F-84 Thunderjets, he had a near-fatal experience that left him hospitalized but the recipient of the Distinguished

Flying Cross. The official Air Force announcement recounted his heroism and near death:

On his 87th combat mission, the Ritzville pilot had started a takeoff run when he realized that the brakes on his Thunderjet were frozen. Bauer's wingman was taking off just behind him in echelon. Each plane was carrying two 1000-pound bombs. The young flier battled his controls to maintain his takeoff run, despite the frozen brakes, in order to protect his wingman.

Finally the wingman cleared the leading ship and Bauer released his bombs a few feet off the ground, and seconds later his plane plunged into a rice paddy and exploded. Badly burned the pilot managed to free himself and drop into the water and mud. Bauer received a commendation [the Distinguished Flying Cross] for his grim struggle to save his wingman's life and while he was hospitalized received credit for a full 100 missions, the normal quota for an airman to be eligible for return to the United States.[2]

After the Korean War, Captain Bauer remained on active duty, assigned to an array of bases and duties stateside. He attended the Armed Forces Staff College in Norfolk, Virginia, and completing tours at Truax Air Force Base in Wisconsin, Goose Bay, Labrador, and Stewart Air Force Base in New York. Bauer was sent to Vietnam in 1969 as Air Liaison Officer to IV Corps Headquarters. There he flew numerous combat missions and was responsible for the Forward Air Controllers at 13 forward operation locations in the Mekong Delta.

In 1970, Lieutenant Colonel Bauer was assigned to a base in Texas, and from 1971 to 1973, he worked in Taipai, Taiwan, with senior staff officers of the Ministry of Defense for the Republic of China. Bauer retired from active duty in July 1978 after having completed 29 years of service with over 5,000 hours in jet fighters.[3]

Lieutenant General Keith A. Smith*
Distinguished Flying Cross Recipient

Keith Alfred Smith was born November 11, 1928 in Cheney, Washington. His parents owned and operated a dairy farm just outside of town. Keith graduated from Cheney High School in 1945. In 1948, after several years of employment on the Ed Edwards' wheat and cattle ranch near Hartline, Washington, he entered Washington State College on a scholarship offered by an anonymous donor. Keith made the most of his college experience. Besides majoring in animal husbandry, he was a boxer on Ike Deeter's team, was president of East House, his residence hall, and became an effective student leader involved in many campus groups including the Newman Club, Independent President's Council, Lariat Club, and the Intercollegiate Knights. He volunteered for Marine training after completing two years of mandatory Reserve Officers Training Corps (ROTC) training.[1]

Lieutenant General Keith A. Smith. *(Photo U.S. Marine Corps.)*

Smith graduated from WSC in June 1952 and immediately reported for active duty as a Marine second lieutenant.[2] He completed the basic school at Quantico, Virginia, in January 1953 and reported for flight training at the Naval Air Station, Pensacola, Florida. He was designated a naval aviator on May 12, 1954 and reported for duty with Marine Night 542nd Fighter Squadron in El Toro, California, prior to being transferred to Marine Night Fighter Squadron 513 in Korea. He was promoted to first lieutenant in August 1954 and captain in July 1956.

Keith returned to civilian life in February 1957 but remained active in the Reserves. In 1960, he returned to active duty. In April 1965, he was a member of the first Marine F-4B squadron to see action in Vietnam, where he flew 156 combat missions. For his service, he was awarded five Flight Strike Air Medals and one Single Mission Air Medal. His squadron was awarded the Navy Unit Commendation Medal for its superior performance in South Vietnam. His efforts earned him the Silver Star in lieu of a sixth Air Medal. The citation read:

> *For meritorious achievement in aerial flight while serving with Marine Fighter/Attack Squadron 531 in the Republic of Vietnam. On 31 May 1965, as pilot and flight leader of a section of F-4B Phantom jet aircraft, Major Smith led his flight on a night close air support mission in support of an Army of the Republic of Vietnam outpost at Ba Gia which was under heavy attack and in danger*

> *of being overrun by a numerically superior insurgent communist [Viet Cong] force. Despite the fact that he had no previous experience or training with para-flare illumination, Major Smith displayed great professional skill and aggressive determination as he made repeated attacks in the face of intensive enemy small arms and automatic weapons fire. By rapidly locating new targets and delivering devastatingly accurate bombs and rockets, Major Smith and his flight destroyed enemy gun positions and decimated a final assault on the friendly outpost. The superior airmanship, exceptional judgment and professional skill of Major Smith were directly responsible for saving the outpost of Ba Gia and blunting a major enemy offensive. His heroic actions, accomplished in the face of strong enemy fire and under extremely difficult flying conditions, were in keeping with the highest traditions of the United States Naval Service.[3]*

Smith returned to the United States in July 1965 and attended the Command and Staff College at Quantico. Upon graduation, he was assigned as head of the technical training section in the Office of the Deputy Chief of Staff for Aviation, Marine Corps Headquarters. He was promoted to lieutenant colonel in October 1967. In August 1969, he assumed command of Marine Fighter Attack Squadron 542, participating in 389 combat missions. These actions earned him the Legion of Merit award, for which the citation read:

For exceptionally meritorious conduct in the performance of outstanding service while serving in various capacities with Marine Aircraft Group Eleven, the Republic of Vietnam from 22 June 1969 to 30 January 1970. Throughout this period, Lieutenant Colonel Smith performed his demanding duties in an exemplary and highly professional manner.

Initially assigned as Group S-1, he reorganized his staff section, consolidated office spaces, reassigned tasks on a more equitable basis, and established management and control techniques which ensured the expeditious processing of personnel actions during a phase of excessive rotations and reassignments. In addition, he monitored the Group Civic Action Program and was instrumental in the completion of many projects to aid the local populace. Reassigned as Commanding Officer of Marine Fighter/Attack Squadron 542 on 11 August 1969, Lieutenant Colonel Smith molded his air and ground crews into a well-coordinated force and displayed exceptional initiative and sound judgment in his planning and execution of air strikes against heavily defended hostile targets.

Under his dynamic leadership, his aircrews completed thousands of combat sorties, frequently tested new strike tactics, and delivered enormous volumes of high explosive ordnance with an effectiveness which signifi-

cantly reduced the enemy's combat capability and enhanced the security and maneuverability of friendly ground units. Constantly concerned for the well-being of his men, Lieutenant Colonel Smith initiated many projects to improve working and living facilities, including the expansion of recreational areas and the installation of water heaters in living quarters. When his Squadron was designated for redeployment to the Continental United States in accordance with Phase III of the Redeployment Program, he supervised the preparation of all aircraft and support equipment, coordinated the reassignment and movement of personnel and succeeded in relocating the entire unit within established time limits.

His ability to evaluate operational requirements under extremely adverse conditions and initiate appropriate actions earned the respect and admiration of all who served with him and contributed immeasurable to the accomplishment of his unit's mission.

By his leadership, extraordinary professionalism, and unwavering devotion to duty, Lieutenant Colonel Smith rendered distinguished service to his country and thereby upheld the highest traditions of the Marine Corps and of the United States Naval Service.

In September 1969, Lieutenant Colonel Smith was awarded the Distinguished Flying Cross and the citation read:

For heroism and extraordinary achievement in aerial flight while serving as Commanding Officer of Marine Fighter/Attack Squadron 542, Marine Aircraft Group Eleven, First Marine Aircraft Wing in connection with combat operations against the enemy in the Republic of Vietnam. On the night of 16 September 1969, Lieutenant Colonel Smith launched as Section Leader of a flight of F-4 Phantom Aircraft assigned the mission of eliminating a major hostile machine gun emplacement deep in enemy controlled territory. En route, he skillfully led his flight through a heavy line of thunderstorms and arriving over the designated location, received a thorough briefing from the tactical Air Controller (Airborne) which revealed that the target area lay in a valley surrounded by hills and ridgelines. Undaunted by the hazards of maneuvering his aircraft over the rugged mountainous terrain, in darkness and through clouds, Lieutenant Colonel Smith maneuvered his Phantom to elude intense hostile fire triggered by flare illumination and fearlessly executed repeated bombing runs, delivering all of his ordnance on the target with pinpoint accuracy. His flight's devastating attacks caused two large secondary explosions and silenced the enemy weapons. Lieutenant Colonel Smith's courage, superior airmanship, and unwavering devotion to duty in the face of grave personal danger were instrumental in accomplishing the hazardous mission and were in keeping with the highest traditions of the Marine Corps and of the United States Naval Service.

In February 1970, Colonel Smith brought his squadron home from Vietnam and assumed command of Marine Fighter Attack Squadron 323 stationed at El Toro, California. He was promoted to colonel in August 1972. He attended the Industrial College of the Armed Forces from August 1973 to June 1974, was promoted to brigadier general in May 1976, and assumed duty in July as assistant deputy chief of staff for Marine Aviation. He then served in Okinawa and received a promotion to major general in April 1979. General Smith was assigned duty as commanding general, 2nd Marine Aircraft Wing, Fleet Marine Force (FMF), Atlantic, Marine Corps Air Station (MCAS) Cherry Point, North Carolina, in June 1981. He earned his third star for lieutenant general in August 1984, and until his retirement in 1988, he was deputy chief of staff for aviation at Marine Corps Headquarters in Washington, D.C.

When he retired, the cowboy from Cheney, Washington, was the third highest-ranking officer in the entire Marine Corps. Keith and his wife Shirley (Shirley Lee of Hoquiam, Washington) were the author's good friends at WSC, and Keith and the author worked together as breakfast cooks in the Stadium Commons dining hall. Keith and Shirley have nine children. Their oldest child and son, Vincent, followed his dad into the Marine Corps. As a Marine captain, Vincent was killed in Beirut, Lebanon, when his Marine barracks was blown up by terrorists.

*The Keith Smith story previously appeared in the April 2004 issue of **The Pacific Northwesterner**.*

VIETNAM

Brigadier General Harold B. Adams
SR-71 Pilot (Spy in the Sky)
Deputy Director, Joint Chiefs of Staff

Harold Benny Adams was born January 20, 1943 in Albuquerque, New Mexico, to Mr. and Mrs. Joe C. Adams. Harold graduated from Bridgeport High School in Bridgeport, Washington, in June 1961. He enrolled at Washington State University that fall, majoring in fine arts. He graduated from WSU in February 1966 as a distinguished graduate and was commissioned as a second lieutenant in the Air Force.[1] In July, Harold was assigned as a pilot trainee with the 352nd Student Squadron at Williams Air Force Base in Arizona. His next assignment was as a B-52 copilot with the 28th Bombardment Squadron at Homestead Air Force Base in Florida. In 1970, he became an aircraft commander at Wright-Patterson Air Force Base in Ohio. While at Wright-Patterson, Harold completed several B-52 Arc Light tours in the skies over Vietnam.

In July 1972, Captain Adams was assigned to the 1st Strategic Reconnaissance Squadron at Beale Air Force Base in California as an SR-71 aircraft commander flying hazardous and highly secret reconnaissance missions.[2]

For his superb performance on such reconnaissance missions, Adams was awarded a sixth Oak Leaf Cluster to add to his original Air Medal. The citation read:

Captain Harold B. Adams distinguished himself by meritorious achievement while participating in aerial flight as an SR-71 Aircraft Commander, 1st Strategic Reconnaissance Squadron, 9th Strategic Reconnaissance Wing, Beale Air Force Base, California, from 26 March 1973 to 7 May 1973. During this period, the airmanship and courage exhibited by Captain Adams in the successful accomplishment of these important, highly sensitive, special category reconnaissance flights [read spy in the sky], under extremely hazardous and adverse conditions, demonstrated his outstanding proficiency and steadfast devotion to duty. The professional ability and outstanding aerial accomplishments of Captain Adams reflect great credit upon himself and the United States Air Force.[4]

In September 1974, Captain Adams set a world speed record of three hours and forty-seven minutes flying the SR-71 between London and Los Angeles. While still at Beale Air Force Base, Captain Adams was awarded the Distinguished Flying Cross:

To fully appreciate the significance of the awards bestowed on Captain Adams, the following provides information about this highly secret aircraft. The SR-71, code-named "Blackbird" is the world's most advanced strategic reconnaissance aircraft, and its crew includes a pilot and a reconnaissance officer. Part jet, part spaceship, the SR-71 is capable of sustained speeds in excess of three times the speed of sound (Mach 3 – faster than a bullet) at altitudes of 80,000 feet. It was designed to replace the aging U-2 and could penetrate enemy airspace without being intercepted. Each SR-71 mission was planned with all the precision of a space flight, and the two-man crew wore pressurized astronaut suits while flying. From 80,000 feet, the Blackbird can survey 100,000 square miles of the earth's surface with a variety of photographic, radar, and infrared equipment. For 25 years, it was taken on routine flights over the Soviet Union and Red China without meeting resistance.[3]

Captain Harold B. Adams distinguished himself by extraordinary achievement while participating in aerial flight as an SR-71 Aircraft Commander ... on 25 January 1974. On that date, his courageous accomplishments and superior professional skill resulted in the successful collection [read spy in the sky] of significant intelligence vital to the highest national interests. While operating in a hazardous environment and despite conditions which threatened the effectiveness of this flight, Captain Adams applied his exceptional airmanship and successfully concluded this unique and important mission. The professional competence, aerial skill, and devotion to duty displayed by Captain Adams reflect great credit upon himself and the United States Air Force.

Captain Adams completed Air Command and Staff College in June 1975, and then served as an air operations staff officer in Air Force Plans and Operations at U.S. Air Force Headquarters in Washington, D.C. In January 1980, he was assigned to the 93rd Bombardment Wing, Castle Air Force Base in California, where he re-qualified in B-52 bombers. That April, he assumed command of the 51st Bombardment Squadron at Seymour Johnson Air Force Base in North Carolina. After completing National War College in 1982, he returned to Air Force Headquarters where, for his outstanding performance, he was awarded the Legion of Merit. The citation read:

Colonel Harold B. Adams distinguished himself by exceptionally meritorious conduct in the performance of outstanding services to the United States as Chief, Bomber Division, and Directorate for Strategic Force Analyses, Assistant Chief of Staff Studies and Analyses, Headquarters United States Air Force, the Pentagon, Washington, District of Columbia, from 28 June 1982 to 8 July 1984. Analyses accomplished under Colonel Adams' direction led the Air Staff and the Department of Defense in defining the scope and direction of the President's highest priority national program, strategic modernization. As the spokesman of choice by the Air Force leadership, Colonel Adams persuasively defended major strategic program decisions against serious challenges from other Services and Congressional committee staffs. His contributions to future strategic deterrence and to the defense of the United States set him apart as an effective advocate of strategic air power and far exceeded the normal requirements of his position. The singularly distinctive accomplishments of Colonel Adams reflect great credit upon himself and the United States Air Force.

On August 1, 1988, following several additional assignments, Adams was promoted to brigadier general. One of his more interesting positions was as commander of the 99th Wing at Andrews Air Force Base in Maryland. His mission was to support the presidential fleet of Air Force I and II.

General Adams is a command pilot with more than 3,500 flying hours and 127 combat missions. His military decorations and awards include: the Legion of Merit with one Oak Leaf Cluster, Distinguished Flying Cross, Meritorious Service Medal with two Oak Leaf Clusters, Air Medal with seven Oak Leaf Clusters, Air Force Commendation Medal with one Oak Leaf Cluster, Presidential Unit Citation with two Oak Leaf Clusters, and Air

Force Outstanding Unit Award with three Oak Leaf Clusters.[5] General Adams is married to Belle Lucille (Hill) of Tacoma, Washington. They have a daughter, Betina.

The Fabian Family
Three Air Force Officers

In 1950, Professor Felix M. Fabian Sr. left his position on the police force of Houston, Texas, to move his family to Pullman, Washington, to accept a faculty appointment with the Police Science Department at Washington State College. In Texas, he served in the National Guard and was dedicated to fighting crime and serving his country. His sons, Felix Jr., John, and William, were imbued with the same values. After college, each became an officer in the Air Force. Felix Sr. earned a master's degree from WSC and a Ph.D. from neighboring University of Idaho. He ascended through the faculty ranks to serve as department chair. For two years in the late 1950s, Felix Sr. was sent by the U.S. State Department to South Vietnam to assist in the training of the National Police Force. The stories of his sons follow.

Colonel John M. Fabian
Astronaut

John Fabian was born in Texas and moved to Pullman with his family when he was eleven. He graduated from Pullman High School in June 1957 and started at Washington State College that fall, majoring in mechanical engineering. He graduated in June 1962 with a bachelor's degree in mechanical engineering, with honors, and a commission as a second lieutenant in the Air Force.[1]

John reported for active duty two months after graduation and was assigned to the Air Force Institute of Technology in Dayton, Ohio. He earned his wings at Williams Air Force Base in Arizona, flying KC-135s for five years in the Strategic Air Command as a tanker pilot. Later, he was selected to attend the University of Washington Graduate School where he earned a Ph.D. in mechanical engineering. His flying duties included 96 combat missions over Vietnam.

John's interest in space and his excitement about it began with the 1957 Russian flight of *Sputnik*. He was selected by the National Aeronautics and Space Administration (NASA) in 1977, and reported for NASA training in 1978. His first five years were spent training in backup roles for the then-current astronauts. More importantly, due to his training and expertise in engineering, he was assigned to help design and oversee the development and construction of a robotic arm for future spacecrafts. He first used the robotic arm operationally on his 1983 *Challenger* space mission.[2] The *Challenger* crew included Commander Bob Crippen, John Fabian as mission specialist number 1, Sally Ride as mission specialist number 2, Norm Thagard as mission specialist number 3, and Rick Hauck as pilot. Sally Ride was the first American woman to fly in space.

Colonel Fabian's second space mission, aboard *Discovery* in 1985, also utilized the robotic arm that he had helped design and build. In an interview with this author, Colonel Fabian narrated the following regarding his two missions:

> *I put up five communications satellites in my brief NASA career, and four of those were for foreign countries and one was for an American company. Then we used the robotic arm to put a Spartan satellite into space to look for "black holes" near the center of our galaxy. A few days later we used the robotic arm to bring it back.*[3]

Describing the function of the robotic arm in placing a German satellite into space, Fabian said:

> *We used the arm to put it in space and it flew free in space for a period of time, and then we later went back and used the arm to retrieve it and put it back in the shuttle's cargo bay and bring it back to Earth. That's the unique aspect of the robotic arm; it is the only tool that we have which allows us to reach out and grab another*

Astronaut John Fabian, WSU class of 1962, aboard the 1983 *Challenger* flight. *(Photo courtesy NASA.)*

object flying in space at 18,000 miles per hour, and latch onto it and bring it back to earth . . . without damaging the satellite or the shuttle.[4]

When asked what he was feeling during the first shuttle lift-off, he responded, "Proud, worried, excited, concerned, ready, alert, eager, focused, and prepared."[5]

Colonel Fabian retired from the Air Force in 1987, having received at least 20 medals and commendations, including the French Legion of Honor, the King Abdul Aziz Medal from Saudi Arabia, and the Defense Superior Service Medal. The citation for the Defense Superior Service Medal read:

Colonel John M. Fabian, United States Air Force, distinguished himself by exceptionally superior achievement as an Astronaut with the National Aeronautics and Space Administration, Lyndon B. Johnson Space Center, from 18 June 1983 to 24 June 1985. Colonel Fabian served as the Mission Specialist for the Space Transportation System's seventh mission, and his preflight and in-flight performance made a significant contribution to the success of the flight. As the Mission Specialist in charge of orbit operations, his prime responsibilities were communication satellite deployments and the German Shuttle Pallet Satellite operations. During the flight, Colonel Fabian actively participated in the precise deployment of two communications satellites, one each for Canada and Indonesia; the first deployment and retrieval of a free-flying satellite by the Orbiter; the conduct of another in a series of commercial experiments leading to a low-cost production of scarce pharmaceuticals in space; and the expansion of the dynamic envelope for the use of the Orbiter's robot arm. His professional performance during the mission resulted in the high rate of capture of a free-flying satellite speak highly of him as a Remote Manipulator System Operator. The distinctive accomplishments of Colonel Fabian reflect great credit upon himself, the United States Air Force and the Department of Defense.

In 1983, Colonel Fabian was honored with the Washington State University Regents Distinguished Alumnus Award. John and his wife Donna, a WSU alumna, have a son, Michael, currently serving in the Air Force, and a daughter, Amy.

Colonel Felix M. Fabian Jr.
Dean of the Defense Intelligence College

Felix Fabian Jr. was born in Texas on November 10, 1937 and moved to Pullman with his family, graduating from Pullman High School in June 1956. He enrolled at Washington State College, majoring in economics. He was awarded a bachelor of arts degree in June 1961 and commissioned an Air Force second lieutenant on the same day.[1] Assigned to Randolph Air Force Base in San Antonio, Texas, Felix served as base housing officer and over time was given additional administrative responsibilities ranging from mortuary officer to paymaster. Although he wanted to fly, his eyesight prevented it. He looked instead toward furthering his education, earning a master's degree from Michigan State University. He was assigned to Warner Air Force Base in Georgia. He had two assignments at the Pentagon, and then served in Southeast Asia at Ubon, Thailand, as base finance officer. Upon his return from the Vietnam Theatre, he joined the faculty at the Air Force Academy and taught economics. Felix later earned a Ph.D. at the University of Texas.

Colonel Felix Fabian Jr. finished his military career serving as dean of the Defense Intelligence College in Washington, D.C.[2] After retiring from the military in 1989, he became vice president of finance at Southern Arkansas University. For his numerous military achievements, Felix was awarded the Bronze Star, Meritorious Service Medal with two Oak Leaf Clusters, the Air Force Achievement Medal, Joint Meritorious Unit Award,

Republic of Vietnam Campaign Medal, National Defense Service Medal, Vietnam Service Medal with four Oak Leaf Clusters, and several other ribbons and awards. The citation for the Bronze Star awarded on February 19, 1970 read:

Captain Felix M. Fabian Jr. distinguished himself by meritorious service as Chief of the Accounting and Finance Office, Office of the Comptroller, 8th Combat Support Group, while engaged in ground operations against an opposing armed force at Ubon Airfield, Thailand, from 12 December 1968 to 5 December 1969. During this period, Captain Fabian's outstanding professional skill and initiative enabled the Accounting and Finance Office to provide outstanding service to the personnel in the 8th Tactical Fighter Wing. His extreme dedication to his job and superior efforts contributed significantly to the successful accomplishment of vital combat support functions. The exemplary leadership, personal endeavor and devotion to duty displayed by Captain Fabian in this responsible position reflects great credit upon himself and the United States Air Force.

Colonel Felix M. Fabian Jr. passed away in March 1991. When asked to define the highlight of Felix Jr.'s Air Force career, his brother John said:

In terms of the maximum impact that he had, it was his role as Dean of the Defense Intelligence College. He

From left: Second Lieutenant William "Bill" Fabian, Colonel Bryson Bailey (professor of Air Science), Second Lieutenant John Fabian, Second Lieutenant Felix Fabian Jr., at Washington State University, 1962. *(Photo courtesy WSU.)*

had not only American but also international students who were learning to work within the intelligence community.[3]

Colonel Felix Fabian Jr. is survived by his wife Shirley, son Robert, and daughter Sarah.

Captain William H. Fabian
Distinguished Flying Cross, Silver Star
Killed in Action

Captain William Hilric "Bill" Fabian was born April 20, 1940 in Houston, Texas. He moved to Pullman with his family and graduated from Pullman High School in 1958. He apparently lied about his age in order to join the Washington National Guard while still in high school. He enrolled at Washington State College in the fall 1958, majoring in police science and administration. While in college, he joined the U.S. Army Reserves.

Bill graduated from WSC in June 1962 with a bachelor of science degree, with honors, and a commission as a second lieutenant in the Air Force.[1] Very shortly thereafter, he went on active duty, assigned to Williams Air Force Base in Arizona for pilot training. Captain Fabian served three tours of duty in Vietnam. His first assignment was as a B-47 bomber pilot and later as a KC-135 tanker pilot. He then volunteered to fly fighter aircraft and was trained in F-4 jets and observation aircraft 0-1As.[2] The 0-1A was a "spotter" aircraft used to direct artillery and fighter strikes against enemy forces on the ground.

To be an effective spotter pilot, it was necessary to locate enemy forces or installations, radio in the proper coordinates, and hover in the area to sight-in and direct artillery fire and air strikes. This role required an inordinate amount of gallantry and courage to complete each mission, because the spotter pilot was extremely vulnerable to enemy fire from the ground and in the air. On just such a mission, Bill was shot down and killed.

Having previously been awarded the Air Medal with five Oak Leaf Clusters, Air Force Outstanding Unit Award with two Oak Leaf Clusters, Combat Readiness Medal, National Defense Service Medal, and the Vietnam Service Medal with two Bronze Stars, Captain Fabian was posthumously awarded the Distinguished Flying Cross, Silver Star, and Purple Heart. The citation for the Distinguished Flying Cross read:

Captain William H. Fabian distinguished himself by extraordinary achievement while participating in aerial flight as a Forward Air Controller near Loc Miah, Republic of Vietnam on 14 September 1968. On that date, Captain Fabian directed four immediate air strikes in extremely close proximity to elements of the 1st Brigade, 1st Infantry Division who were pinned down by withering cross fire from hostile automatic weapons. Although, under intense antiaircraft fire, Captain Fabian remained over the target area to direct all ordnance precisely on the hostile positions allowing the friendly troops to extract the wounded and assault the hostile positions. By his professional competence, aerial skill, and devotion to duty, Captain Fabian has reflected great credit upon himself and the United States Air Force.

The citation for the Silver Star medal, dated December 7, 1968, read:

Captain William H. Fabian distinguished himself by gallantry in connection with military operations against an opposing armed force near Phouc Vinh, Republic of Vietnam on 14 November 1968. On that date, Captain Fabian, a Forward Air Controller directed air strikes and artillery in support of friendly ground forces engaged in heavy fighting with hostile forces. Because of his great enthusiasm and intimate knowledge of the ground situation, he voluntarily returned again and again to the scene of conflict to insure that air power was used with maximum effectiveness. His disregard for his own personal safety and his determination to win, were instrumental in turning the tide of battle in favor of the friendly forces. By his gallantry and devotion to duty, Captain Fabian has reflected great credit upon himself and the United States Air Force.[3]

Captain William Hilric Fabian was killed in action on November 14, 1968 and is buried among other heroes in the Arlington National Cemetery in Washington, D.C. He is survived by his wife Deanna and children David, James and Melanie.

Colonel James P. Fleming
Congressional Medal of Honor

James Phillip Fleming, son of Mr. and Mrs. John H. Fleming, was born March 12, 1943 in Sedalia, Montana. He attended school in Washington, graduating from Moses Lake High School in June 1961. He enrolled at Washington State University that fall as a police science major. Fleming resided first in Kruegel Hall then moved into the WSU Fire Station to serve as a volunteer firefighter. He was a member of the Reserve Officer Training Corp (ROTC) Drill Team and the Army ROTC Flight Training Group. In June 1965, Fleming received his bachelor of science degree in police science and a commission as a second lieutenant in the Air Force.[1]

Lieutenant Fleming was assigned to Laredo Air Force Base in Texas for pilot training. In December 1966, he attended helicopter pilot training at Sheppard Air Force Base, graduating in May 1967. In June 1968, he joined the 20th Special Operations Squadron in Vietnam where he served until April 1969.

Air Force Colonel James P. Fleming with his Medal of Honor. *(Photo courtesy the United Stated Air Force.)*

On November 26, 1968, while serving as an aircraft commander in action near Duc Co, he unhesitatingly flew to the aid of a six-man Special Forces patrol in danger of being overrun by a large superior enemy force. Lieutenant Fleming descended twice in his minimally-armed helicopter through a barrage of enemy fire to rescue the beleaguered patrol. Each time, he had to balance his helicopter on the bank of a river with its tail boom hanging over open water. With complete disregard for his safety, he kept his helicopter in an exposed position, with bullets smashing through his windscreen, until the entire patrol had been rescued. For his actions, Fleming was awarded the Medal of Honor, the nation's highest decoration.[2] The citation read:

For conspicuous gallantry and intrepidity in action at the risk of his life above and beyond the call of duty. On 26 November 1968, Captain Fleming (then First Lieutenant) distinguished himself as the Aircraft Commander of a UH-IF transport Helicopter near Duc Co, Republic of Vietnam. On that date, Captain Fleming went to the aid of a six-man Special Forces Long-Range Reconnaissance Patrol that was in danger of being overrun by a large, heavily armed hostile force. Despite the knowledge that one helicopter had been downed by intense hostile fire, Captain Fleming descended, and balanced his helicopter on a riverbank with the tail boom hanging over open water. The patrol could not penetrate to the landing site and he was forced to withdraw.

Dangerously low on fuel, Captain Fleming repeated his original landing maneuver. Disregarding his own safety, he remained in this exposed position. Hostile fire crashed through his windscreen as the patrol boarded his helicopter. Captain Fleming made a successful takeoff through a barrage of hostile fire and recovered safely at a forward base. Captain Fleming's conspicuous gallantry, his profound concern for his fellowmen, and his intrepidity at the risk of his life above and beyond the call of duty are in keeping with the highest traditions of the United States Air Force and reflect great credit upon himself and the Armed Forces of his country.[3]

Upon his return from Southeast Asia in April 1969, Fleming was assigned to the 12th Flying Training Wing at Randolph Air Force Base in Texas. A year later, he became a C-141 Starlifter pilot at McChord Air Force Base in Washington. In 1971, he was assigned as an instructor at the Air Force Academy at Colorado Springs, Colorado. After several other lengthy assignments, he was promoted to colonel and, as a command pilot, clocked more than 5,000 total flying hours and 810 combat missions in Southeast Asia. In addition to the Medal of Honor, his military decorations include the Silver Star, Distinguished Flying Cross, Air Medal with seven Oak Leaf Clusters, Legion of Merit, and the Meritorious Service Medal with one Oak Leaf Cluster. In 1990, Fleming received Washington State University's Alumni Achievement Award.

Colonel Fleming married the former Jennifer L. Hansen of Kelso, Washington. They have three children, Amy, Rebecca and John.

Chief Master Sergeant David A. Guzman
Vietnam, Turkey, Germany, Italy, the Pacific
WSU Veteran Affairs Coordinator, Registrar

David A. Guzman was born March 15, 1940 in Los Angeles, where he attended local area parochial schools. Financially unable to attend a college of his choosing, David volunteered for service in the Air Force. He was too late for the Korean War but in time, following extensive training, was able to do his part in the Vietnam War. Imperfect eyesight kept him from flying, so he chose Air Force administration as his career path, and his specialty became personnel management. David planned to return to school and earn a college degree either under the GI Bill or while on active duty.[1]

After his training and assignments at Long Beach Air Force Base in California, Minot Air Force Base in North Dakota, Misawa and Wakkanai Air Bases in Japan, and Offutt Air Force Base in Nebraska, Staff Sergeant Guzman was posted to Tan Son Nhut Air Base just outside of Saigon, Vietnam. There his initiative and leadership earned him the Air Force Commendation Medal for which the citation read:

Chief Master Sergeant David A. Guzman. *(Photo courtesy the United States Air Force.)*

Staff Sergeant David A. Guzman distinguished himself by meritorious service as Noncommissioned Officer in Charge, Officer, Forecasting, 377th Combat Support Group, Tan Son Nhut Air Base, Republic of Vietnam from 10 December 1965 to 1 December 1966. During this period, Sergeant Guzman's outstanding skill and initiative aided immeasurably in identifying and solving numerous problems encountered in the accomplishment of his duties. The energetic application of his knowledge has played a significant role in contributing to the success of the United States Air Force mission in Southeast Asia. The distinctive accomplishments of Sergeant Guzman reflect credit upon himself and the United States Air Force.

Following his tour in Vietnam, Sergeant Guzman was assigned to March Air Force Base in California, then to Headquarters 5th Allied Tactical Air Forces (NATO) in Vicenza, Italy, as personnel sergeant major. In 1974, Guzman was assigned to head the Test Control Branch at the Military Personnel Center at Randolph Air Force Base in Texas. While there in 1976, he was promoted to chief master sergeant. A Meritorious Service Medal was awarded to him following his duty at Randolph. The citation read:

Chief Master Sergeant David A. Guzman distinguished himself in the performance of outstanding service to the United States while assigned to the Test Control Branch, Airman Promotion Division, Directorate of Personnel

Program Actions, Air Force Military Personnel Center, from 6 May 1974 to 9 July 1976. During this period, the outstanding leadership, professional skill, initiative, and ceaseless efforts displayed by Chief Guzman resulted in significant contributions to the effectiveness and success of the Airman Promotion Program. The singularly distinctive accomplishments of Chief Guzman reflect great upon himself and the United States Air Force.

Guzman then became the senior enlisted advisor to the commander, Space and Missile Systems Organization at the Air Force Station in Los Angeles. He was then assigned to Sembach, Germany, as sergeant major of the largest consolidated base personnel office outside of the continental United States. Following his four-year assignment in Germany, Chief Guzman was reassigned as the senior enlisted advisor to the commander, the United States Logistics Group in Ankara, Turkey. He served in this position for one year before being reassigned to Headquarters, Pacific Air Forces (PACAF) at Hickam Air Force Base, Hawaii, where he served as the senior enlisted advisor to General Robert Bazley, commander-in-chief of the Pacific Air Forces.

Upon retiring from the Air Force in May 1987, Chief Guzman was awarded the Legion of Merit, the fifth highest U.S. military decoration. The citation noted his leadership, exemplary improvements in quality of life programs at all bases within the PACAF command area that consisted of 51 percent of the earth's surface. Chief Guzman's persistent efforts provided greater opportunities for personnel to seek and obtain higher professional military educational goals, and resulted in renovation of the command's leadership schools and Noncommissioned Officers Academy. In addition to those mentioned above, Chief Guzman earned another 36 decorations.

Following a stint at New Mexico State University's Extended Campus in Albuquerque, civilian Guzman and his wife Cathy settled in Moscow, Idaho, where he earned a master's degree in counseling and human services from the University of Idaho. In September 1988, he joined the Washington State University registrar's staff as coordinator of veterans affairs and assistant to the registrar. His new position also placed him on the WSU Veterans Memorial Committee, chaired by Registrar James Quann. When Quann left the university in July 1990, Guzman became chair of the memorial committee. His leadership and fund-raising ability led to the construction and ultimate dedication of the WSU Veterans Memorial on Veteran's Day, November 11, the 11th day of the 11th month, of 1993.

David A. Guzman was promoted to associate registrar in June 1996 and to university registrar in October 1998. He retired from Washington State University in June 2002.

Army Major General Milton Hunter
Architect and Distinguished Alumnus

Milton Hunter was born May 1, 1943 in Houston, Texas. He graduated from Yates Senior High School in Houston in June 1961. He attended Compton (California) College for two years before enrolling at Washington State University in fall 1963. He was an advanced Army cadet in the Reserve Officer Training Corp (ROTC); a member of Scabbard and Blade, the Army ROTC Honorary; SCARAB, the architecture honorary; the American Institute of Architecture; and Crimson Circle. Milton graduated in 1967 with a bachelor of architectural engineering degree and a commission as a second lieutenant in the Army Reserves. He was the 1967 WSU Distinguished Military Graduate of the Army ROTC Program. He later received a master of science in engineering (construction management) from the University of Washington.[1]

Hunter is a graduate of the Engineer Officer Basic and Advance Courses, the Command and General Staff College, the Army War College, the Executive Development Program, Darden School of Business Administration, University of Virginia, and the Construction Executive Program at Texas A & M University. His service assignments include commander and district engineer, Seattle District; assistant director of civil works, Central Region, Directorate of Civil Works; and deputy district engineer, Charleston (South Carolina) Engineer District. He also served

Major General Milton Hunter speaking at the rededication of the newly updated WSU Veterans Memorial, October 7, 2000. *(Photo courtesy Washington State University.)*

in the Directorate of Program Analysis and Evaluation, Office of the Army Chief of Staff; the 339th Engineer Battalion (Construction) at Fort Lewis, Washington; as executive officer and company commander with Headquarters and Headquarters Company, 937th Engineer Group (Combat), 18th Engineer Brigade, Vietnam; as assistant engineer of the 12th Engineer Combat Battalion, 8th Infantry Division at Bad Kreuznach, West Germany; as commander of the 79th Engineer Combat Battalion, 18th Engineer Brigade, at Karlsruhe, West Germany; chief of staff, U.S. Army Corps of Engineers, Washington, D.C. (Pentagon); and commanding general and division engineer of the South Pacific Division.[2]

General Hunter served as military social aide to the White House and, in 1979, was selected as one of the Outstanding Young Men of America. His duties in the White House were during the first year of the Ford administration. The nation was beginning its bicentennial celebration and Hunter was consumed with all the protocol of hosting VIPs – from the Queen of England and her entourage, and other important heads of state from around the world, to well known celebrities from all walks of American life.[3]

Among General Hunter's military decorations are the Legion of Merit, the Bronze Star (for heroic and meritorious achievement), the Legion of Merit, Meritorious Service Medal with Oak Leaf Cluster, Army Commendation Medal with Oak Leaf Cluster, Parachutist Badge, and several other U.S. and Vietnamese service medals. In 1991, Hunter received Washington State University's Alumni Achievement Award and cited for "Outstanding contributions and achievement in a distinguished military career – bringing pride to his alma mater."[4] General Hunter was one of the featured speakers at the dedication of the newly completed WSU Veterans Memorial on October 7, 2000.

General Hunter married Karina Bechtle of Pforzheim, West Germany. They have two sons, Alexander and Patrick.

Lieutenant Colonel Dennis B. Jones
RF-4 Fighter Pilot
171 Reconnaissance Missions over Vietnam
WSU Alumni Association President

Dennis B. Jones was born June 3, 1942 in Spokane to Mr. and Mrs. Kennard Jones. He graduated from Lewis and Clark High School in Spokane in 1960 and enrolled at Washington State University that fall. He received both a bachelor of arts in business administration and a commission as a second lieutenant in the Air Force Reserve in May 1964. While at WSU, he took flying lessons and had his first solo flight as a pilot.[1]

Jones went on active duty in the Air Force, graduating from pilot training in 1966, and then was transferred to Europe as an

Air Force Captain Dennis Jones, RF-4 reconnaissance pilot.
(Photo courtesy the Jones family.)

RF-4 pilot. The RF-4 is a reconnaissance version of the F-4 jet fighter. With the Cold War still on, he spent most of the next year perfecting his piloting capabilities and flying reconnaissance missions over Germany. In 1967, he returned stateside for more training before being assigned to a unit in Vietnam in February 1968. He flew 171 reconnaissance missions over Vietnam in an unarmed RF-4 taking photographs, generally at very low altitudes. His plane was subjected to enemy ground and air fire on most of his missions. Captain Jones was awarded the Distinguished Flying Cross and 10-plus air medals in addition to various campaign ribbons.[2] The citation for the Distinguished Flying Cross read:

Captain Dennis B. Jones distinguished himself by extraordinary achievement while participating in aerial flight as an RF-4C Aircraft Commander over classified targets in North Vietnam on 27 June 1968. On that date, Captain Jones displayed great determination and superior airmanship while flying a high priority reconnaissance mission over a heavily defended area. Although his aircraft was damaged by intense hostile ground fire, Captain Jones skillfully and courageously made a successful recover at his home station. Review of mission film revealed valuable information concerning the disposition of hostile ground forces. The professional competence, aerial skill and devotion to duty displayed by Captain Jones reflect great credit upon himself and the United States Air Force.[3]

Captain Jones described the mission accordingly:

My mission was in support of the action along the DMZ. There were reports from U.S. ground troops that the North Vietnamese were moving their ground troops across the DMZ at night using helicopters. The Pentagon wanted photographs of the helicopters, especially since the North Vietnamese kept denying that they were doing it. I was tasked to try and obtain airborne photos. I stationed myself off the coast of South Vietnam with a KC-135 tanker standing by in case I needed to refuel. I would wait for a call from the ground specialist who was at an outpost just south of the DMZ . . . When he saw them he would call me and I would dive towards the ground, level off at 200 feet, line up over a known position and then fly on a heading towards the specialist's location . . . He would guide me by giving heading changes until I was over the helicopters. I had night filming capability by ejecting photo cartridges when I toggled the camera photo switch. When the cartridge flashed, the whole area and my airplane were lit up. That is when the North Vietnamese would fire at me. Each run I would take five photos in succession . . . I did this several times for the next two hours. I was to be relieved but the next airplane due on station aborted, so I stayed on station for another two hours, doing several more attempts to photograph the helicopters. With each successive attempt, I was getting more and more antiaircraft and ground fire . . .

On my last run my aircraft was hit by 37mm antiaircraft guns, but I was able to recover at my home base. I had been airborne for more than six hours, flying at night and refueling three times.[4]

Discharged in January 1973, Major Dennis Jones became a commercial pilot for Delta Airlines and remained active in the Air Force Reserves. He was also active with the WSU Alumni Association, serving as president in 1997-98, the year of the Cougar Rose Bowl. A reserve lieutenant colonel, Dennis retired from Delta Airlines on July 1, 2002.

Captain Dennis B. Jones in his RF-4. *(Photo courtesy the Jones family.)*

Four-Star General Robert D. Russ
Highly Decorated Vietnam Veteran

Robert Dale Russ was born March 7, 1933 in Portland, Oregon, moving as a child with his parents to Wapato, Washington. He graduated from Wapato High School in 1951 and enrolled at Washington State College that fall. Russ was a member of Phi Sigma Kappa fraternity, serving his senior year as chapter president. He was also active with the Interfraternity Council and the Alpha Kappa Psi professional business fraternity. He was a four-year Air Force ROTC cadet and an officer in the Arnold Air Society. Robert Russ earned a B.A. degree in business administration and second lieutenant's commission in the Air Force in June 1955. He later earned a master's degree in business from George Washington University.[1]

Lieutenant Russ went on active duty in September 1955 at Lackland Air Force Base, Texas. In 1957, he was assigned to the 81st Tactical Fighter Wing at Royal Air Force Station Bentwaters, England, flying F-84F jet fighters. From May 1962 to August 1964, Captain Russ served as chief of the Fighter Section, Directorate of Tactical Evaluation, and 28th Air Division. After graduation from Air Command and Staff College in July 1965, he was assigned to Headquarters Air Defense Command in Colorado. After attending F-4 replacement training at Davis-Monthan Air Force Base in Arizona from July 1967 to January 1968, Major Russ was assigned to the 12th Tactical Fighter Wing at Cam Ranh Bay Air Base in South Vietnam. From there, he flew 242 combat missions, including 50 over North Vietnam.[2]

In Vietnam, Russ distinguished himself as a brilliant pilot and tactician and was decorated many times. A few of his citations follow:[3]

The Silver Star: *Major Robert D. Russ distinguished himself by gallantry in connection with military operations against an opposing armed force as an F-4C Aircraft Commander near the A Shau Valley, Republic of Vietnam on 24 January 1969. On that date, though his aircraft was burning extensively from antiaircraft fire, Major Russ continued his attack and completely destroyed a hostile gun position. With both engines burning and loss of communication with his rear seat pilot, Major Russ maneuvered his stricken aircraft away from the hostile area before ejecting himself and his pilot to safety. By his gallantry and devotion to duty, Major Russ has reflected great credit upon himself and the United States Air Force.*

Distinguished Flying Cross: *Major Robert D. Russ distinguished himself by extraordinary achievement while participating in aerial flight as an F-4C Aircraft Commander near Saigon, Republic of Vietnam, on 13*

May 1968. On that date, Major Russ flew a mission in support of friendly troops attempting to capture a hostile stronghold near the city. In spite of intense ground fire, Major Russ delivered his ordnance with devastating accuracy, inflicting severe damage upon the hostile force. The professional competence, aerial skill, and devotion to duty displayed by Major Russ reflect great credit upon himself and the United States Air Force.

Distinguished Service Medal: *The President of the United States of America, authorized by Act of Congress July 9, 1918 awards the Distinguished Service Medal to General Robert D. Russ for exceptionally meritorious service in a duty of great responsibility. General Russ distinguished himself as Commander, Tactical Air Command, Langley Air Force Base, Virginia from 22 May 1985 to 31 March 1991. In this vital position of responsibility, his outstanding leadership, exemplary foresight, and extraordinary initiative were primarily responsible for developing and fielding the world's most modern and capable tactical forces, thus ensuring the nation's aerial preeminence well into the twenty-first century. Additionally, his professional skill, ceaseless dedication, and ingenuity have resulted in maintaining these forces at the highest state of readiness in the history of the United States Air Force, a fact clearly demonstrated by the outstanding performance of the Tactical*

Air Forces during Desert Shield and Desert Storm. Further, his personal commitment to the systematic improvement of facilities and services throughout Tactical Air Command resulted in vast gains in the quality of life for all Air Force people. The singularly distinctive accomplishments of General Russ culminate a long and distinguished career in the service of his country and reflect the highest credit upon himself and the United States Air Force.

After Vietnam, General Russ continued to serve his country with increased responsibilities in his duties as deputy chief of staff for Research, Development and Acquisition, at U.S. Air Force Headquarters in Washington, D.C., and as commander, Tactical Air Command at Langley Air Force Base. He retired from the Air Force in February 1996. His decorations and awards include the Purple Heart, Distinguished Service Medal, Silver Star, Legion of Merit with Oak Leaf Cluster, Distinguished Flying Cross with two Oak Leaf Clusters, Air Medal with 13 Oak Leaf Clusters, and the Vietnam Service Medal with five Service Stars. In 1992, Russ' alma mater bestowed upon him the WSU Regents Distinguished Alumnus Award.

General Robert Russ married the former Jean E. Johnson of Spokane, Washington. They have three children, Randall, Robin and Robert. General Russ died in 1998.

OPERATION JUST CAUSE (PANAMA) and OPERATION DESERT STORM

Sergeant Kim Michelle Chilberg*
Combat Veteran

Kim Michelle Chilberg was born on October 23, 1966 and raised in the Spokane Valley, Washington. She graduated from Central Valley High School in 1984 and enrolled at Washington State University that fall. After finishing her spring semester, Kim left college to volunteer for the Army. Having a knack for languages, she attended several in-service training schools, earning a rating as a linguist fluent in both Spanish and Korean. After additional training, Miss Chilberg was assigned to Camp Humphries in South Korea, where she served with the Technical Control and Analysis unit and where she earned her sergeant's rating.[1] Sergeant Chilberg was later dispatched on a fact-finding mission to Panama.

In December 1989, for her Spanish language skills, Sergeant Chilberg was sent back to Panama in "Operation Just Cause," the successful mission designed to oust General Manuel Noriega from power. Attached to the 82nd Airborne out of Fort Bragg,

North Carolina, Chilberg, in addition to her intelligence duties, was assigned to an Infantry platoon and issued a 30-calibre machine gun. It was with this unit that she was caught in a live firefight, becoming perhaps the sole female serving in a combat situation during the Panama Invasion.

After completing her Army tour, Sergeant Chilberg returned to WSU, earning President's Honor Roll status each semester. She received her degree in criminal justice in July 1994, graduating summa cum laude.[2]

*This Kim Chilberg story previously appeared in the April 2004 issue of **The Pacific Northwesterner.***

Brigadier General Barbara Doornink

U.S. Army Brigadier General Barbara Doornink is a 1973 Washington State University political science graduate and commander of the Defense Distribution Center at New Cumberland, Pennsylvania. A Prosser, Washington, native, she attended WSU after graduating from Pullman High School. While at WSU, she was a member of Alpha Delta Pi sorority and served on the Panhellenic Council. A May Queen finalist, she was also active in intramural sports. While at WSU, she worked on a congressional campaign and as a state legislature intern. She was a member of Spurs, the sophomore women's service honorary and, as a senior, was president of Mortar Board, a scholastic and service honorary.[1]

General Doornink assumed command of the Defense Distribution Center in the summer of 1998. The center provides defense materiel for all branches of the U.S. Armed Forces, from supply facilities in this country and around the world. Previously, General Doornink served as vice director of Logistics and Security Assistance, where she spent six months as deputy commanding general for Stabilization Force Support Command, in Zagreb, Croatia. Before this assignment, she was chief of Joint Logistics Operations in the U.S.-European Command Headquarters in Stuttgart, Germany.

General Doornink's initial Army assignment was as a platoon leader for the 104th Transportation Company at Fort Devens, Massachusetts. The general's military background has included assignments or commands at the U.S. Military Academy (West Point); teaching in the Department of Military Instruction in Seoul, Korea; at Fort Eustis, Virginia; at Fort Lewis, Washington; in Kaiserslautern, Germany; and at Fort Bragg, North Carolina. She earned a master's in information systems management from the University of Southern California and is a graduate of the Transportation Officer Basic and Advanced Courses, the Combined Arms and Services Staff School, the Command and General Staff College, and the Industrial College of the Armed Forces.[2]

General Doornink has earned many honors and citations during her illustrious career, including the Defense Superior Service Medal, the Legion of Merit, the Defense Meritorious Service Medal, five Meritorious Service Medals, two Army Commendation Medals, three Army Achievement Medals, the Parachutist Badge, and the British Parachutist Badge. On Saturday, May 6, 2000, General Doornink was the featured speaker for the WSU commencement in Pullman. During that ceremony, she was awarded the WSU Alumni Achievement Award.

First Lieutenant Eric D. Hedeen
Electronic Warfare Officer
B-52 Crew Member
Killed in Action – Operation Desert Storm

Eric Douglas Hedeen was born December 1, 1963 in Malaga, Washington, near Wenatchee. His parents were Mrs. and Mrs. Gerald R. Hedeen. Eric graduated from Wenatchee High School in June 1982 and enrolled at Washington State University that fall. He majored in architecture and pledged Phi Gamma Delta fraternity. Eric graduated with two degrees in May 1987 – a bachelor of science in architectural studies, cum laude, and a Bachelor of Architecture, cum laude – as well as a commission in the Air Force.[1]

After being employed in the architectural field in Wenatchee, Lieutenant Hedeen went on active Air Force duty on August 22, 1988. After his initial training in electronic warfare, he joined the 340th Bombardment Squadron, 97th Bombardment Wing in Arkansas. His unit was then deployed for action in the Persian Gulf War.[2]

On February 2, 1991, when returning from a mission, his B-52 bomber lost hydraulic power, and the crew had to bail out. Lieutenant Hedeen ejected, seat and all, but his seat failed to dislodge, causing his parachute to stream (not open) and he was killed on impact.

For his service, Lieutenant Hedeen was awarded the Meritorious Service Medal, Air Force Training Ribbon, and the National Defense Service Medal. The citation for his Meritorious Service Medal read:

First Lieutenant Eric D. Hedeen distinguished himself in the performance of outstanding service to the United States as Electronic Warfare Officer, B-52G, 340th Bombardment Squadron, 97th Bombardment Wing, Eaker Air Force Base, Arkansas, from 20 December 1989 to February 1991. During this period, both at Eaker and while deployed in support of United Nations Desert Storm Operations, the outstanding professional skill, motivation, and ceaseless efforts of Lieutenant Hedeen resulted in significant contributions to the effectiveness

and success of Air Force combat operations against Iraq and occupied Kuwait. His expertise and skill in electronic warfare and electronic countermeasures enabled the crew to successfully evade all enemy air defense systems, strike their assigned targets and escape enemy territory. The singularly distinctive accomplishments of Lieutenant Hedeen in the dedication of his service to his country reflect great credit upon himself and the United States Air Force. [3]

The Desert Storm hero was buried in the Evergreen Cemetery in Wenatchee, Washington. In 1991, the City of Wenatchee honored Hedeen by naming a downtown park/plaza in his honor. The memorial plaque read:

Dedicated in memory of Lt. Eric Hedeen
Co-designer of this plaza – and to all
the troops serving in Desert Storm.
*Duty * Honor * Country*

Rear Admiral Robert W. Higgins, M.D.
U.S. Navy Deputy Surgeon General
Served in the Navy and the Marines –
Vietnam and Desert Storm

Navy Rear Admiral Robert W. Higgins. *(Photo courtesy the United States Navy.)*

Robert Walter "Bob" Higgins was born November 9, 1934 in Uniontown, Washington. He graduated from Pullman High School in 1952 and entered Washington State College that fall, where he joined Phi Gamma Delta fraternity. He worked his way through college, graduating with a B.S. degree in pharmacy in 1957.[1] He worked as a pharmacist for several years, both in Wenatchee and in the family business in Pullman. In 1961, Bob was accepted into the University of Washington Medical School. Again working his way through medical school, this time as a pharmacist in Seattle, he received his M.D. degree in 1965, and completed his postgraduate training at Los Angeles County Harbor General Hospital in Torrance, California. He joined the Navy with the rank of lieutenant junior grade (JG) and was immediately sent to Vietnam where he served as a medical officer aboard the USS *Tutuila*.

Bob's first Vietnam assignment was serving as the only surgeon on board, operating on and patching up wounded Green Berets who were in combat in the Mekong Delta. At one point during the heavy fighting, he operated for 36 hours straight.[2] He was assisted by a staff that included eight corpsmen, a dentist and two dental technicians.

In 1967, after his tour of duty in Vietnam, Dr. Higgins returned to the States to enter private practice in Wenatchee, Washington, but remained active in the Naval Reserve. Returning to active naval duty with a regular commission in 1972, he initiated a Navy Family Practice Training Program, which he supervised for six years. By 1986, he was the commanding officer of two naval hospitals and 18 military clinics in three states. The next year, he was promoted to rear admiral, and became the senior medical officer of the Marine Corps. Admiral Doctor Higgins retired from active duty in 1993, the recipient of six citations and commendations, including the Secretary of the Navy Commendation for Achievement, and the Distinguished Service Medal, the highest peacetime medal awarded by the military. His Navy Commendation for Achievement citation read:

For outstanding achievement in the superior per-formance of his duties while serving the friendly foreign forces engaged in armed conflict against the Communist insurgent forces in the Republic of Vietnam from November 1966 to April 1967. Lieutenant Higgins, who was assigned as Medical Officer on board U.S.S. Tutuila (ARG 4), voluntarily participated in 15 Medical Civil Action Programs conducted in the Third Coastal Zone of the Republic of Vietnam. In Vietnamese Navy junk bases, hamlets, and villages, he provided medical treatment to many hundreds of Vietnamese. Lieutenant Higgins consistently took advantage of every opportunity to teach personal hygiene, sanitation and public health

measures to the villagers, their leaders and Vietnamese Navy corpsmen. On one occasion, Lieutenant Higgins treated over 70 villagers at a remote village in an area controlled by the Viet Cong, where danger of enemy attack was imminent. Through his efforts, a large number of former insurgents have returned to the allegiance of the Republic of Vietnam's government. Lieutenant Higgins' initiative and medical services were in keeping with the highest tradition of the United States Naval Service.[3]

The Distinguished Service Medal citation, signed by the Secretary of the Navy, read:

For exceptionally meritorious service to the Government of the United States in a duty of great responsibility as the Deputy Director of Naval Medicine, as the Deputy Surgeon General of the Navy on the Staff of the Chief of Naval Operations, as the Chief, Navy Medical Corps from August 1989 through August 1993. Rear Admiral Higgins' brilliant leadership and outstanding managerial skills were key elements in maintaining a level of superiority with respect to the Fleet and Fleet Marine Force especially during a period marked by decreasing defense spending. He served as the highly respected personal advisor to the Navy and Department of Defense health care senior leadership. Under Rear Admiral Higgins' stewardship, Navy Medicine instituted major programs and underwent significant changes which positively impacted the delivery of comprehensive and high quality health care services to our sailors, Marines, and their families worldwide. His unequaled ability to grasp complex medical issues, keen insight into the intricacies of the political-military arena, and his careful scrutiny of all viable alternatives resulted in the best possible balance between executable Department of the Navy medical programs in support of real world war fighting requirements, and led Navy Medicine to fully meet all requirements for medical support dictated by real world contingency operations like Operations DESERT SHIELD and DESERT STORM. Rear Admiral Higgins' exceptional integrity, relentless quest for quality, and singular devotion to duty reflected great credit upon himself and were in keeping with the highest traditions of the United States Naval Service.[4]

In 1988, Admiral Doctor Higgins was honored by his alma mater with the Alumni Achievement Award. Following retirement from active duty, he served nine years as regional vice president, president-elect, and president of the World Organization of National Colleges and Academies of Family Practice (WONCA), the "United Nations of Medicine." Higgins and his late wife Barbara have two sons and one daughter.

Captain R. Dale Storr*
Jet Fighter Pilot and Iraq Prisoner of War
Operation Desert Storm

Richard "Dale" Storr was born March 18, 1961 to Mr. and Mrs. Richard C. Storr. Dale's father was a career Air Force B-52 pilot, flying out of Fairchild Air Force Base near Spokane, Washington. Dale graduated from Spokane's Shadle Park High School in June 1979 and enrolled at WSU that September. His older brother, David, and younger brother, Doug, also attended WSU. Dale lived in Rogers Hall his first two years and later lived off campus. He majored in mechanical engineering and was a four-year Air Force ROTC cadet. During his junior year, he received flying lessons at the Pullman-Moscow Airport and soloed in a Cessna 152. He graduated cum laude with a bachelor of science degree in mechanical engineering in June 1983 and a commission as a second lieutenant.[1]

In February 1984, Storr reported for pilot training at Vance Air Force Base in Enid, Oklahoma. He graduated from pilot training the following January and became a T-38 flight instructor/pilot. In March 1989, he was reassigned to England Air Force Base in Louisiana, and was stationed there when Iraq invaded Kuwait in August 1990. Captain Storr's squadron was immediately deployed, along with six other squadrons to an airfield in Saudi Arabia to fly A-10s. The A-10 is heavily armed (bombs and cannons) ground-attack aircraft nicknamed the "Warthog." Storr

Captain R. Dale Storr. *(Photo courtesy Dale Storr.)*

initially flew as a wingman, then as a flight commander. He flew multiple missions during Desert Shield, then 18 during Desert Storm.[2]

On his 18th mission, Captain Storr's plane received a devastating blow just as he was pulling out from a strafing pass. His ship was so badly damaged that he had no control of the aircraft. His bailout and capture are best told in his own words:

My bullets were hitting the truck park and the trucks were on fire and exploding. I pulled off and that's when something hit the bottom of my A-10. It felt like a 50,000 pound sledge hammer hitting my plane . . . My plane was still flying, nothing had fallen off, I wasn't on fire, my engines were still turning, I still had hydraulics, so I didn't think I was in much trouble . . . but I had no control of the aircraft . . . there was nothing I could do, my plane was doing barrel rolls toward the ground . . . My wingman said "Storrman eject, eject, eject" . . . I hung in a little bit longer, then looked up and saw that even if the plane started flying again, I was in such a steep dive there was no way I could recover. I just got real lucky and ejected . . . As soon as I got out into the air stream I tried looking back to see if the chute opened, I couldn't see it, but I could hear it. I was so close to the ground I said to myself, "I have waited too long, and I am going to die." Two seconds later the chute was open . . . The very next thing I heard was a huge explosion right under me.

It was my airplane, and a huge fire ball was coming right at me. I thought, "Oh my God, my chute saved me, now I am going to die in the fireball." I started grabbing on the risers trying to get the parachute to drift away but the fire ball was coming too fast. I said to myself, "I am going to die in the fireball or my chute will burn and I will drop to my death, I'm a goner." So I closed my eyes and went in . . . It was searing hot just like an oven, and I thought "here I burn to death." Then I felt a rush of cold air and looked down and I could see the ground . . . and I prayed, "Oh my God, I'm going to make it, I can't believe I lived through that." The next thing I saw was an Iraqi truck coming to get me." [3]

Captain Storr spent the next 33 days in various Iraqi prisons blindfolded with his hands handcuffed behind his back. He was brutally beaten and tortured, his eardrum and nose broken, a shoulder dislocated, and he suffered cuts and bruises over most of his body. Toward the end of his captivity, his prison in Baghdad was bombed by American planes, and he narrowly escaped death. After 33 days in prison, he and his fellow POWs were cleaned up and turned over to the Red Cross, then flown out to friendly soil. He spent several days aboard a hospital ship and a week in a hospital at Andrews Air Force Base near Washington, D.C.

Captain Storr was awarded the Purple Heart, Air Medal, Aerial Achievement Medal with three Oak Leaf Clusters, the Air Force Commendation Medal, the Air Force Achievement Medal, and the Prisoner of War Medal. The citation for the Air Medal read:

Captain Richard D. Storr distinguished himself by meritorious achievement while participating in aerial flight as an A-10 Fighter Pilot, 76th Tactical Fighter Squadron, 23rd Tactical Fighter Wing (Provisional), Kingdom of Saudi Arabia, from 17 January 1991 to 25 January 1991. During this period, Captain Storr flew 18 combat missions over Iraq and Kuwait. These missions encompassed the widest variety of both day and night missions during Operation DESERT STORM. He was involved in the battlefield interdiction of enemy troops, armor, and artillery concentrations, armed reconnaissance of enemy supply routes and lines of communication, search for and destruction of enemy short range ballistic missiles, suppression or destruction of enemy surface-to-air missile systems, offensive counter-air missions against enemy airfields, and close air support of advancing Coalition ground forces. While over hostile territory, antiaircraft artillery fire and surface-to-air missile launches were often encountered. The superior airmanship and courage exhibited by Captain Storr on each of these missions, under extremely hazardous conditions, directly contributed to successful air and land campaigns. The professional skill and airmanship displayed by Captain Storr reflect great credit upon himself and the United States Air Force. [4]

According to another record:

His superior professional qualities allowed him to withstand 33 days of the most brutal conditions as a POW, and even when threatened with death he never revealed the location, numbers or tactics of A-10s operating in Desert Storm.[5]

Captain Storr left active duty in May 1992 but remains in the Reserves. He became a 737 pilot for American Airlines and later United Airlines. He is an Air Force National Guard KC-135 tanker pilot, flying out of Fairchild AFB near Spokane. He has flown with his Guard unit, providing combat support, refueling aircraft over Bosnia, Kosovo and the no-fly zone over Iraq. Dale Storr currently holds the rank of lieutenant colonel.

*This Dale Storr story previously appeared in the April 2004 issue of **The Pacific Northwesterner.***

APPENDIX I

WSU Veterans Who Contributed Oral Histories or Written Memoirs for This Book.
(All are on file in the Archives Section of the Washington State University Libraries.)

Achre, I. Katherine, October 2000

Adams, Harold B., January 2002*

Brain, George B., September 1997

Brunstad, Arthur, March 2001*

Buckley, Archie (papers concerning), September 2000*

Bustad, Leo K., September 1997*

Carey, Robert H., January 1998*

Chilberg, Kim Michelle, November 1998

Clark, Asa V., Jr., May 2001*

Clark, Girard, February 2001

Cox, Edna L., November 1997*

DeRuwe, Milan, October 2002

Fabian, John M., October 1999

Goldsworthy, Harry E., July 1997

Goldsworthy, Robert F., March 1997

Greening, C. Ross, (papers concerning), May 2001*

Hall, Carl W., (papers concerning), May 2001

Higgins, Robert W., July 1997

Holsclaw, Jack D., February 1998*

Long, Russell A., May 2001*

Johnson, Randall A., March 1997

Jones, Dennis B., November 2002

Miller, Robert L., September 2003

Munro, Douglas A., (papers concerning), July 2001*

Oman, Glenn E., October 2000*

Patterson, Eugene G. "Pat", September 1996*

Rants, Hanford F., (papers concerning) November 2002*

Smith, Keith A., April 1997

Storr, R. Dale, October 2002

Wills, John H., July 2000

Wise, Kenneth C., November 2002

*Deceased

APPENDIX II

The Mary B. Packingham Story

Mary B. Packingham
College Nurse and Red Cross Volunteer
WSC Heroine

Mary B. Packingham, WSU nurse and World War I heroine.
(Photo of painting by Randall A. Johnson.)

While serving as the WSC college nurse, Mary B. Packingham volunteered to became a Red Cross nurse to care for our wounded and dying soldiers in France during World War I. Waiting for shipment overseas, she served her patients, her state and her nation in the finest tradition of her calling.

Along with the entire country, she was dedicated to winning World War I. The college had accepted responsibility for training, housing, and caring for cadets in the newly organized Student Army Training Corps (SATC). The SATC was the forerunner of what is now called the Reserve Officers Training Corps (ROTC). The War Department planned to send 600 young men, in units of 300, to WSC for training. The first unit was barely accommodated when, in October 1918, another 600 unexpectedly arrived.[1] Here were 900 young men to be trained, housed and fed, in addition to several hundred other WSC students who were SATC cadets. Every residence hall was full, as were fraternity houses, the gymnasium, and hallways of several classroom buildings.

The men arriving in October brought with them numerous cases of the Spanish influenza. There were about 1,100 men housed in various shelters on campus and, by November, 825 of them had been stricken with the flu. The WSC campus was quarantined and all departments shut down. Short of medical facilities, WSC officials converted several churches, the college gymnasium, and a fraternity house into hospitals. In these makeshift facilities, college nurse Mary B. Packingham became the "Florence Nightingale" of the campus.

A characteristic of this virulent disease was that it almost immediately rendered its victims helpless, usually unable to even get out of bed. One can only imagine the burden of total care that was placed on the few doctors and nurses who were available. Now over 80 years later, we have only sketchy listings of those brave providers of medical services. In the case of Miss Packingham, however, we are able to assemble the fragments of a record that should not be forgotten. Those who knew her wrote of their admiration for her and what she accomplished. A single rather blurred and faded photograph of her has been found.

Professor William Landeen of the WSC History Department said in his book *E. O. Holland and the State College*, published in 1958, that the college nurse "lost her life in the line of duty."[2] Mary died on October 29, 1918, one day after her 38th birthday and 13 days before World War I ended. The November 1, 1918 edition of the *Pullman Herald* provided more extensive details. The story was also covered in the *Spokane Chronicle* and read:

The name of Miss Mary B. Packingham, registered nurse, located at Pullman for several years past, was Tuesday added to the long list of influenza victims. Miss Packingham having passed away at the Alpha Tau Omega (A.T.O.) fraternity house hospital early Tuesday morning. The death of Miss Packingham, according to physicians and others in touch with the situation, was the indirect result of overexertion and heroic self-sacrifice on her part in assisting in combating the epidemic, which within a few days enveloped the entire city. Miss Packingham is known to have worked thirty-six hours at one time without rest, organizing the A.T.O. and church hospitals and at the same time serving as head nurse at the A.T.O. house. With acute conditions accompanying the inability to secure an adequate staff of nurses at the outset of the epidemic, Miss Packingham labored faithfully to the limit of her endurance. When she was herself attacked with influenza, her bodily strength was not sufficient to stand the strain, and pneumonia speedily developed, claiming her life within a few days.

Miss Packingham had followed her profession in Pullman for about twelve years, being for several years associated with the Pullman hospital. She had recently enlisted in the overseas service and was awaiting her call to military duty when the epidemic, which resulted in her sudden demise, made its appearance among the soldiers at the State College.

In the hundreds of local homes where Miss Packingham served as a nurse in cases of illness, she was beloved and honored and her sudden death caused a pall of sorrow to envelop the entire community. Determined to do her full part in the great struggle for liberty, she enlisted for overseas nursing duties, but made the supreme sacrifice in the fight against the influenza epidemic before receiving her call. She has died the death of a hero and her name should be enrolled with those of the soldier dead on the parchment of honor and self-sacrifice.[3]

The Spanish Influence pandemic was one of the worst human catastrophes on record, with at least 21,600,000 deaths worldwide.[4] An estimated 850,000 deaths occurred in the United States.[5] However, due to the lack of accurate worldwide reporting, the death count may have been much higher. For example, Dr. F. M. Burnet, a physician that helped isolate the cause of influenza, suggested that the deaths during the pandemic numbered between 50 and 100 million.[6]

In Pullman, the crisis peaked in early November 1918, and ended as quickly as it began. Altogether, 47 deaths occurred, including 31 of the soldiers dispatched to Pullman by the War Department and ten Washington State College SATC cadets. Six civilians, including Nurse Packingham, also died. The low death rate in the Pullman outbreak is indicative of the supreme efforts of Nurse Packingham and her volunteer staff, and is extremely surprising when one considers that in 1918, there were no penicillin, antibiotics, or sulfa drugs. Moreover, oxygen was not yet available for those with respiratory problems, and treatment was limited to bed rest, drinking fluids, mustard plasters on the chest, and an occasional kettle of steam for inhaling. Aspirin and sponge baths were used to help lower temperatures. The WSC death rate was about five percent of the 825 who became ill with the disease.[7]

APPENDIX III

The Honor Roll of Washington State University Alumni War Dead

WORLD WAR I

The following names are those of Washington State College (WSC) students killed or who died of disease, primarily of the dreaded Spanish influenza, while serving their country during World War I. All but two of the 44 names appear on the World War I Honor Roll plaque, which was recently relocated from the main entrance of Bryan Hall to the WSU Veterans Memorial site in the center of campus. The names of Harold Heathman and Nurse Mary B. Packingham were added following research conducted for this book.

Amos, William H. – Army Engineers
Son of Mr. and Mrs. A. J. Amos. Received training at Washington Barracks, Washington, D.C. Died from influenza in New York, New York. November 1918.

Burbank, Richard – Army Infantry
Son of Mr. and Mrs. D. B. Burbank of Edmonds, Washington. Entered service October 1918. Received training in SATC*, Washington State College. Died from influenza at Pullman, November 1918.

Chesser, Ansel H. – Army Infantry
Son of Mr. and Mrs. G. C. Chesser of Stevenson, Washington. Entered service October 1918. Received training in 2nd Training Detachment, Washington State College. Died from influenza en route to an eastern camp, November 1918.

Cockerline, Conrad C. – Army, 28th Infantry
Son of Mr. and Mrs. M. J. Cockerline of Estacada, Oregon. Received training at Fort Lewis, Washington. Wounded at battle of Soissons, France, July 21, 1918. Killed in action by machine gun bullet at Argonne Woods, October 4, 1918.

Coulter, Harry H. – Army Infantry
Son of Mr. and Mrs. P. F. Coulter of Olympia, Washington. Entered service October 1918. Received training in SATC, Washington State College. Died from influenza at Pullman, October 1918.

Day, Lee A. – Navy
Son of Mr. and Mrs. H. J. Day of Pullman, Washington. Received

---

*Student Army Training Corps

training at Columbia University, New York. Lost his life by gas poisoning on October 26, 1918, while serving as Chief Machinist's Mate on U.S. Submarine Chaser 98 on patrol duty along English Channel.

Dosh, Percy – Army Infantry
Son of Mr. and Mrs. Charles Dosh of Palouse, Washington. Entered service October 1918. Received training in SATC, Washington State College. Died from influenza at Pullman, November 1918.

Dunham, Carl C. (Pvt.) – Army, 28th Infantry
Son of Mr. and Mrs. S. W. Dunham of Adna, Washington. Received training at Camp Mills, N.Y., and in France. Died from influenza at Pullman, November 1918.

Foss, Oswald J. (Sgt.) – Army, Medical Dept.
Son of Mr. and Mrs. K. B. Skibness of Spokane, Washington. Received training at Base Hospital, Camp Kearny, California. Died from influenza at San Diego, November 1918.

Gloman, Louis B. (2nd Lt.) – Q.M.C. Motor Supply Train
Son of Mr. and Mrs. K. S. Gloman of Bellingham, Washington. Received training at Presidio of San Francisco. Died from influenza en route to Camp Merritt, New Jersey, December 1917.

Graham, Thomas J. (Pvt.) – 361st Infantry
Son of Mrs. Marion Graham of Gould City, Washington. Received training at Fort Lewis, Washington. Killed in Action in France, October 10, 1918.

Halsey, Archie M. – Army, 9th Infantry
Son of Mr. and Mrs. W. C. Halsey of Asotin, Washington. Wounded in action in July 1918. Killed in Action, November 9, 1918.

Hamelius, Frank (Sgt.) – Army, 361st Infantry
Son of Mr. and Mrs. Math Hamelius of Pullman. Received training at Fort Lewis, Washington. Killed in Action in France, September 28, 1918.

Healy, Nicholas – Air Service
Son of Mr. and Mrs. N. C. Healy of Seattle. Killed in airplane accident, May 1918.

Heathman, Harold E. – Army Infantry
Son of Mr. and Mrs. James Heathman of Almira, Washington. Entered service in October 1918. Received training in the SATC, Washington State College. Died from influenza at the hospital in Davenport, Washington, November 1918.

Holmes, Clarence F. (1st Lt.) – Engineers
Son of Mr. and Mrs. A. J. Holmes of Spokane, Washington. Entered service April 27, 1918. Received training at Camp Lee, Virginia, and in France. Was with Flash Sound Rangers in St. Mihiel campaign and received injury that resulted in death. Died May 24, 1919 in Spokane.

Jans, William N.
Son of Mr. and Mrs. Carl Jans of Edwall, Washington. Received training at Fort Worden, Washington. Died from influenza at Fort Worden, November 1918.

Jinnett, Emil Dale (H. A. 1st Cl.) – Navy
Son of Mr. and Mrs. A. C. Jinnett of Pullman. Entered service March 18, 1918. Received training at Bremerton, Washington. Discharged June 18, 1919, totally disabled. Died from effects of pneumonia at Portland, Oregon, January 6, 1920.

Juvenal, Richard – Army Infantry
Son of Mr. and Mrs. J. T. Juvenal of Kahlotus, Washington. Entered service October 1918. Received training in SATC, Washington State College. Died from influenza at Pullman, November 1918.

Knight, Leslie M. – SATC
Son of Mr. and Mrs. A. J. Knight of Tacoma, Washington. Entered service October 1918. Received training in SATC, Stanford University. Died at Tacoma, March 31, 1919.

Leidl, Louis (2nd Lt.) – 7th Engineers
Son of Mr. and Mrs. Wendelin Leidl of Glenwood, Washington. Entered service August 1917. Received training at American University, Washington, D.C., and in France. Killed at battle of Cunel during the Meuse-Argonne Offensive, October 14, 1918. Went on the attack the morning of October 14, and was last seen going through the streets of Cunel under heavy machine gun and shellfire. Body was found November 16, 1918 across the Meuse River from Cunel, in the line of advance.

Leonard, Elmer O. – Army Infantry
Son of Mr. and Mrs. F. Leonard of Castle Rock, Washington. Received training at Fort Lewis, Washington. Wounded in action October 7, 1918. Died October 17, 1918.

Lewis, Lee C. (Capt.) – Army Infantry
Son of Mr. and Mrs. F. W. Lewis of Tumwater, Washington. Entered service August 30, 1917. Received training at Ft. Leavenworth, Kansas, stationed at Camp Greene, North Carolina. Went to the front July 25, into battle July 27, wounded at battle of Sergy, July 19,1917. Was taken to Evacuation Hospital No. 6 near Chateau-Thierry, where he died July 30, 1918.

Livingston, Ivan D. (Cadet) – Air Service
Son of Mr. G. F. Livingston of Toroda, Washington. Killed in airplane accident at Foggia, Italy, May 8, 1918.

McAlister, Alexander
Died in Scotland from exposure received at sinking of the USS *Tuscania.*

McCormack, Leo
Son of Mr. and Mrs. P. A. McCormack of Republic, Washington. Killed in Action in France.

Mason, Willis E. – Army
Son of Mr. and Mrs. J. R. Mason of Yakima, Washington. Entered service October 6, 1917. Received training at Fort Lewis, Washington, and Edgewood Arsenal, Maryland. Burned by mustard gas escaping from a burst valve. Died from the effects October 6, 1918.

Maynard, Boyd C. (1st Lt.) – Marines
Son of Mr. and Mrs. C. E. Maynard of Colton, Washington. Received training at Quantico, Virginia. Wounded in action April 1, 1918. Killed in Action near Chateau-Thierry, June 7, 1918. Was posthumously awarded the Croix de Guerre and cited for bravery by the French Government.

Mutty, Louis – Navy, Aviation Section
Son of Mr. and Mrs. Peter Mutty of Port Townsend, Washington. Received training at Seattle, San Diego and Cambridge, Massachusetts. Killed in airplane accident, July 9, 1918.

Neilly, James L. – Air Force
From Sprague, Washington. Died from pneumonia at Waco, Texas.

Newland, Charles J. (Lt.) – Infantry
Son of Mr. and Mrs. A. S. Newland of Ritzville, Washington. Killed in Action in France, September 27, 1918.

Nolan, William – Army Infantry
From Pullman. Entered service October 1918. Received training in SATC, Washington State College. Died from influenza at Pullman, November 1918.

Norvell, Theodore R. – Army Infantry
Son of Mr. and Mrs. J. S. Norvell of Helix, Oregon. Entered service October 1918. Received training in SATC, Washington State College. Died from influenza at Pullman, October 1918.

Packingham, Mary – WSC nurse
Heroine to countless solders and student cadets at WSC, died October 29, 1918 and was laid to rest in her home town, Strandville, Illinois.

Palmer, Leon – Air Service
Son of Mr. and Mrs. O. K. Palmer of Chehalis, Washington. Received training at Berkeley, California. Died from influenza at Berkeley, November 1, 1918.

Price, Ivan L. – Marines
Son of Mr. and Mrs. C. A. Price of Long Beach, California. Received training at San Diego (Marine Barracks). Killed in Action, November 3, 1918, on third day of Meuse-Argonne Offensive.

Shaw, Roy L.
Son of Mrs. Mary C. Baker of Baker, Oregon. Died from influenza November 1918.

Sieveke, Lawrence C. – Army Infantry
Son of Mr. and Mrs. Lewis Sieveke of Latah, Washington. Entered service October 1918. Received training in SATC, Washington State College. Died from influenza at Pullman, October 1918.

Turner, Henry E. (1st Lt.) – Air Service
Son of Mr. and Mrs. H. E. Turner of Seattle. Entered service June 1917. Received training at Berkeley, California, stationed at Bordeaux, France. Killed in air fight on Argonne front, October 23, 1918.

Van Voris, Howard H. (2nd Lt.) – Army
Son of Mrs. A. L. Yates of Stites, Idaho. Received training at Fort Lewis, Washington. Killed in Action at Meulebeke, Belgium, October 31, 1918. Posthumous award of medal given for exceptional bravery.

Weeks, Vern D. – Signal Corps
Son of Mr. and Mrs. J. H. Weeks of Carter, Montana. Entered service October 4, 1917. Received training at Fort Lewis, Washington. Engagements: Wounded by mustard gas in Argonne Forest on October 1, 1918. On Lorraine front, Cantigny front, took part in action at St. Mihiel, Soissons, Marne, Argonne, Meuse-Argonne Offensive. Died from exposure at Le Mans, France, February 5, 1919.

Wheeler, Logan (Cpl.) – Army Infantry
Son of Mr. and Mrs. F. H. Wheeler of Yakima, Washington. Received training at Fort Lewis, Washington. Killed in Action in France.

Witt, George Douglas (Ph. M.) – Marines
Son of Mrs. G. M. Witt of Harrington, Washington. Received training at San Francisco. Died in France on October 26, 1918 from wounds received October 6 while giving medical aid to wounded Marines in assault near St. Etienne-a-Arnes. Posthumously awarded Distinguished Service Cross and cited for extraordinary heroism.

Wivel, Fred B. – Army Infantry
Son of Mr. and Mrs. Charles H. Wivel of Shelton, Washington. Received training at Camp Mills, New York, and in France. Died of pneumonia in April 1919.

Washington State University Veterans Memorial

The following names are those of WSC/WSU students, faculty and staff killed or missing in action in World War II, Korea, Vietnam and the 1991 Persian Gulf War. Their names are engraved on the brass center-core of the WSU Veterans Memorial, cast in 1993 and dedicated on the eleventh hour of the eleventh day of the eleventh month (Veterans Day) of that year. On Veterans Day 1997, 32 additional names were added to the memorial. On October 7, 2000, new upright name plaques were added and the memorial was finished and rededicated thanks to a major contribution from the Golden Grads, WSC class of 1949.

Please note, for the sake of consistency all references in this Honor Roll to the veterans' alma mater list WSU even though most attended WSC (the college was elevated to university status on July 1, 1959). Also, in some cases, records indicating date and circumstances of death were not available; only a notation of "deceased" was entered on the WSC/WSU transcript stored in the WSU Registrar's Office.

A section of the Washington State University Veterans Memorial. *(Photo courtesy **Lewiston Tribune**.)*

WORLD WAR II

Adams, Robert H. – Air Force
Born April 16, 1920. Attended high school in Pomeroy, Washington. Attended WSU 1939-1941. Pre-dental major. Enlisted January 19, 1942. Missing in Action, September 2, 1943.

Adams, William Howard – Army
Born March 13, 1924. Graduated from Rogers High School in Spokane, Washington. Attended WSU 1942-1943. Pharmacy major. Enlisted December 1, 1942. Killed in Action in Europe, January 28, 1945.

Adell, Robert F. – Air Corps
Born February 19, 1923. Attended Pasadena Junior College in California and attended WSU two months in 1943. Killed at Douglas, Arizona.

Allison, Edward Curlin – Navy
Attended Goldendale High School in Goldendale, Washington. Attended WSU 1931-1934. Pharmacy major. Discharged from the National Guard, February 4, 1933. Died of wounds received in action in the Pacific, January 1, 1945.

Anderson, Ernest Herbert – Air Corps
Born November 13, 1919. Attended North Central High School in Spokane, Washington. Attended WSU 1939-1941. General Studies major. Enlisted December 3, 1941. Killed in Action in Italy, March 19, 1944.

Balsiger, Arthur Edward – Army Infantry
Born October 2, 1923 in Portland, Oregon. Attended Columbia Union High School in Hunters, Washington. Attended WSU 1942-1943. Agriculture and Education majors. Enlisted March 1, 1943. Killed in Action on Mindanao, May 20, 1945.

Beauchamp, John W. – Army
Born December 28, 1915. Attended Kern County High School in Bakersfield, California. Transferred from Bakersfield Junior College to attend WSU 1935-1939, graduating June 5, 1939 with B.S. and D.V.M. degrees. Killed in air crash over Wales in 1944.

Beinke, Sidney Carl – Marines
Born May 22, 1917. Attended Cleveland High School in Seattle. Transferred from University of Washington and attended WSU 1935-1939, graduating June 3, 1940 with a B.S. in Botany. Enlisted December 17, 1942. Killed in Action in South Pacific, December 5, 1944.

Benjamin, William R. – Air Corps
Born August 26, 1924 in Puyallup, Washington. Graduated from Stadium High School in Tacoma, Washington. Attended WSU in 1942. Economics major. Killed on transport in Mediterranean.

Benner, Melvin Joe – Canadian Army
Born September 20, 1916. Attended high school in LaCrosse, Washington. Attended WSU 1936-1938. Agriculture major. Enlisted April 20, 1944. Killed in Action in England, April 20, 1944.

Bishop, Robert Patrick – Air Force
Born May 5, 1923. Graduated from Tekoa High School in Tekoa, Washington. Attended WSU 1940-1943. Speech major. Enlisted February 1943. Killed in bomber crash in California, July 2, 1944.

Bitar, Emil Saleem – Army Infantry
Born May 27, 1913. Graduated from Raymond High School in Raymond, Washington. Attended WSU 1931-1935, graduating June 10, 1935 with a B.A. in Political Science. Enlisted June 1941. Killed in Action, August 7, 1943.

Black, Donald Calvin – Army
Graduated from Wenatchee (Washington) High School. Attended WSU 1929-1932. Civil Engineering major. Discharged from National Guard, February 6, 1932.

Boalch, Rodney Theodore – Marines
Born July 12, 1922. Graduated from North Bend High School in North Bend, Washington. Attended WSU 1940-1943. Police Administration major. Killed in plane accident Dallas, Texas, June 1, 1945.

Bollinger, Ora R. – Army
WSU Army Specialized Training Program participant from Arges, Indiana. Killed in Action.

Bolong, Olimpio
Born June 8, 1908. Graduated from Lincoln High School in Tacoma, Washington. Transferred from University of Detroit, attended WSU 1927-1935, graduating June 10, 1935 with a B.S. in Mining with Honors.

Bornander, Edwin Alexis – Army
Born March 5, 1918. Graduated from Fife High School near Tacoma, Washington. Attended WSU 1937-1941, graduating June 9, 1941 with a B.S. in Agriculture with Honors. Enlisted June 9, 1942. Killed in Action in Italy, November 7, 1943.

Bryant, Floyd C.
No information available.

Buckley, Archie M. – Navy
Born July 16, 1906 in Colville, Washington. Graduated from Colville High School. Attended WSU 1926-1934. He graduated June 2, 1930 with a B.S. in Physical Education. Granted five-year normal diploma. Granted life diploma February 4, 1935. Killed in Action, February 1945.

Burgess, Harland F. – Army
Enlisted March 1923. Deceased; torpedoed on Japanese prison ship.

Burgess, Walter K.
Killed in South America, June 1941.

Burke, Ernest W. – Marines
Died November 12, 1944 in Naval Hospital in Washington, D.C.

Burnet, James Lee – Air Corps
Born October 17, 1920. Graduated from Walla Walla (Washington) High School. Attended WSU 1939-1941. Agriculture Business major. Killed in airplane crash near San Angelo, Texas, May 31, 1945.

Burr, David, Jr. – Air Corps
Born February 19, 1921. Graduated from Lake Washington High School in Kirkland, Washington. Attended WSU 1940-1941. Electrical Engineering major. Enlisted January 1943. Killed in airplane accident in Pasco, Washington, October 27, 1943.

Calder, Robert James – Air Corps
Born June 23, 1917. Graduated from Yakima (Washington) High School. Attended WSU 1938-1941, graduating February 9, 1942 with a B.S. degree. Agriculture major. Killed in Action in France, September 1944.

Callison, William K. – Air Corps
Born August 5, 1921. Graduated from Palouse (Washington) High School. Attended WSU 1939-1941. Physics major. Killed in France by antiaircraft fire, August 8, 1944.

Cammon, Roger David
Born August 7, 1915. Graduated from Lincoln High School in Tacoma, Washington. Attended WSU 1934-1938, graduating June 6, 1938 with a B.S. degree.

Camp, Leland R. – Army Infantry
Attended WSU 1941-1942. Physical Education major. Enlisted February 6, 1943. Killed in Italy, September 15, 1943.

Campbell, Robert L. – Army Infantry
Born March 4, 1923. Graduated from Spangle High School in Spangle, Washington. Transferred from Eastern Washington College of Education to attend WSU from 1940 to 1942. Prelaw major. Killed in Action in Italy, April 24, 1945.

Carr, Keith Holiday – Air Corps
Born March 9, 1922. Graduated from Bellingham (Washington) High School. Attended WSU 1940-1941. General Studies major. Killed in training bomber crash in 1943.

Carroll, Joe D. – Air Corps
Attended WSU 1939-1940. General Studies major. Missing over Germany, February 22, 1944.

Carstensen, Myron B. – Reserve Corps
Born December 26, 1920. Graduated from Almira High School in Almira, Washington. Attended WSU 1938-1940, attended Gonzaga University in Spokane and returned to WSU between 1942-1943 to graduate May 24, 1943 with a B.A. in Political Science. Killed in Action in South Pacific, July 1944.

Chambers, Gilbert B. – Army Infantry
Born May 23, 1918. Graduated from high school in Wilbur, Washington. Attended WSU 1935-1940, graduating June 3, 1940 with a B.A. in Business Administration. Enlisted August 15, 1941. Killed in Action in the Philippines, June 1942.

Chapin, Walter Francis – Air Corps
Born March 9, 1922. Graduated from high school in Post Falls, Idaho. Transferred from Whitworth College to attend WSU 1941-1943. Music and Education majors. Enlisted March 24, 1943. Killed in airplane crash in England, October 11, 1944.

Christian, L. Kenneth – Army Infantry
Born December 30, 1912. Graduated from Pullman High School. Attended WSU 1931-1937. Business Administration major. Killed in Action at Mindanao, July 27, 1943.

Clifton, Marvin Scott – Naval Air
Born February 15, 1921. Graduated from Pullman High School. Attended WSU 1938-1940. General Studies major. Enlisted 1941. Killed in plane crash in England, January 1944.

Clumper, Alfred Browne – Air Corps
Born July 16, 1915. Graduated from high school in Moxee City, Washington. Attended WSU 1934-1942, graduating May 24, 1943 with a B.S. degree. Enlisted December 7, 1942. Killed in Action over Germany *(The Spokesman-Review*, October 24, 1944).

Cole, Harry Lewis, Jr. – Air Corps
Born August 22, 1920. Graduated from Pullman High School. Attended WSU 1938-1941. Business Administration major. Killed in Action in South Pacific, June 17, 1944.

Colley, Jess Lloyd – Army Infantry
Born March 1, 1917. Graduated from high school in Kahlotus, Washington. Attended WSU 1935-1937. Business Administration major. Killed in Action on Guadalcanal, January 12, 1943.

Conger, Allen Charles
Born February 28, 1920. Graduated from Bridgeport High School in Bridgeport, Washington. Attended WSU 1937-1941, graduating May 9, 1941 with a B.S. in Electrical Engineering.

Cook, Milton LeRoy – Navy
Born October 15, 1918. Graduated from Clarkston High School in Clarkston, Washington. Attended WSU 1938-1942, graduating June 1, 1942 with a B.S. in Chemistry. Enlisted October 17, 1942. Killed in plane crash in Texas, May 30, 1943.

Corbett, Horace Sumner, Jr. – Air Force
Born July 24, 1918. Hometown Lafayette, California. Transferred from University of California to attend WSU from 1940 to 1941. General Studies major. Killed during early raids over Germany.

Cozens, Richard B. – Air Corps
Attended WSU 1941-1943. Forestry major. Enlisted September 25, 1942. Killed in bomber crash in Texas in 1944.

Cullinane, David Edward – Armored Force
Born November 4, 1918. Graduated from Seattle Preparatory High School. Attended WSU 1936-1937. Business Administration major. Deceased December 23, 1944 from injuries received when the vehicle in which he was riding overturned near Jarney, France. He was a member of the 735th Tank Battalion, fighting in the midst of the Battle of the Bulge.

Dahlke, William Martin – Army
Born August 19, 1916. Graduated from high school in Waterville, Washington. Attended WSU 1933-1937, graduating June 14, 1937 with a B.A. in Economics. Varsity basketball player under WSU Coach Jack Friel. He was killed in 1945 near Ormont, Germany, while serving as a captain with the 347th Infantry. Awarded the Bronze Star posthumously.

Damascus, Gust John
Born September 30, 1921. Graduated from North Central High School in Spokane, Washington. Attended WSU 1939-1943, graduating May 24, 1943 with a B.S. in Civil Engineering with High Honors. Killed in Action in France, August 22, 1944.

Daniel, Stephen Forest – Army
Born June 7, 1922. WSC Army Specialized Training Program participant from Independence, Missouri. Killed in Action.

Daniels, Clair Livingston – Air Corps
Born May 23, 1924 in Spokane, Washington. Graduated from Lewis and Clark High School in Spokane. Attended WSU 1941-1943. Enlisted March 1, 1943. Killed in Action over Italy, May 31, 1944.

Davidson, Edgar
Attended WSU 1941 during summer school. Missing in Action in Italy, 1944.

Davison, George Arthur, Jr. – Army
Born December 23, 1922. Graduated from Twin Falls High School in Idaho. Attended WSU 1940-1944. ASTP instruction began November 2, 1943 with termination March 4, 1944. Business Administration major. Enlisted June 7, 1943. Killed in Action in European Theatre, March 18, 1945.

Day, Robert William – Army Engineers
Born September 20, 1914. Graduated from high school in Deer Park, Washington. Attended WSU 1932-1936, graduating June 5, 1939 with a B.S. in Agricultural Engineering. Discharged from National Guard, June 8, 1934. Enlisted April 24, 1942. Missing August 1944.

DeVoe, Lewis Earl – Air Corps
Born October 5, 1919. Graduated from North Central High School in Spokane, Washington. Attended WSU 1938-1940. Pre-dental major. Enlisted August 19, 1942. Killed in Action, June 1943.

Dhondt, Marion Emil – Air Corps
Born March 22, 1923 in Spokane, Washington. Graduated from John Rogers High School in Spokane. Attended WSU 1941-1942. Mechanical Engineering major. Enlisted February 1, 1943. Killed in air crash in Delaware, July 1944.

Dickerson, Walter F. – National Guard
Born December 8, 1919. Graduated from high school in Walla Walla, Washington. Attended WSU 1936-1937. Business Administration major. Enlisted August 1940. Killed in accident during maneuvers at Fort Lewis, Washington, December 5, 1940.

Dickson, Marvin R. – Air Corps
Enlisted July 1942. Killed in plane crash at Randolph Field, Texas, 1943.

Dixon, Robert Miller – Air Corps
Born July 28, 1921. Graduated from Latah High School in Latah, Washington. Attended WSU 1938-1942. Agriculture major. Killed in bombing raid over Germany, October 4, 1944 (radio gunner).

Dragnich, George N. – Air Corps
Born August 27, 1920. Graduated from Republic High School in Republic, Washington. Attended WSU 1940-1943. Industrial Arts and Education major. Enlisted February 28, 1943.

Drumhiller, Robert H.
Born September 27, 1921 in Granite, Idaho. Graduated from Yakima High School in Yakima, Washington. Attended WSU 1941-1942. Business Administration major. Missing in Europe.

Dunford, Ernest J.
Born April 9, 1915. Graduated from high school in Ellensburg, Washington. Attended WSU 1934-1938, graduating June 6, 1938 with a B.S. in Agriculture. Discharged from National Guard, January 30, 1936. Deceased June 1941.

Duprey, Rene John – Royal Canadian Air Force
Born January 15, 1920. Graduated from high school in Blaine, Washington. Attended WSU 1937-1940. Electrical Engineering major.

Eaton, Merle S. – Air Corps
Born August 11, 1921. Graduated from high school in Waitsburg, Washington. Attended WSU in 1940. Mechanical Engineering major. Enlisted September 1942. Deceased 1945.

Edes, Alfred Wayne – Infantry
Born February 16, 1916. Graduated from high school in Entiat, Washington. Attended WSU 1934-1940, graduating June 9, 1941 with a B.S. in Hotel Management. Enlisted July 22, 1941.

Eichenberger, Edward – Air Corps
From Walla Walla, Washington. Attended WSU in late 1930s. Enlisted September 1940. Killed in Action.

Ellsworth, Leon Wheeler – Marines
Born May 24, 1923 in Ellensburg, Washington. Graduated from Thorp High School in Thorp, Washington. Attended WSU in 1941. General Studies major. Killed on Iwo Jima, March 21, 1945.

Ennis, Robert Edward – Army
Born October 13, 1915. Graduated from Fergus County High School in Lewistown, Montana. Attended WSU 1934-1939. General Studies major. Died a prisoner of Japanese in 1942.

Erickson, Carl J. – Air Corps
Enlisted May 5, 1942.

Erickson, Gunner William – Navy
Born December 21, 1918. Graduated from Lewis and Clark High School in Spokane, Washington. Attended WSU 1938-1942, graduating June 1, 1942 with a B.S. in Electrical Engineering. Enlisted July 18, 1942. Died of pneumonia in Seattle, February 1944.

Erickson, Harvey R.
Killed on Okinawa, 1945.

Erickson, Roland V. – Army Air Corps
From Clarkston, Washington. Attended WSU late 1930s, early 1940s. Killed at Colorado Springs, 1943.

Fanazick, Joseph W. – Air Corps
Enlisted 1940. Killed in plane crash in California, 1942.

Felch, George A. – Army
Enlisted July 28, 1941. Killed in Action, Italian front, 1945.

Ferguson, Allen J. – Army
Enlisted September 1, 1941.

Ferguson, Ben Francis
Born December 9, 1916. Graduated from Sedro Woolley High School in Sedro Woolley, Washington. Attended WSU 1935-1939, graduating June 5, 1939 with a B.S. in Physical Education.

Finley, Leslie Hodges – Army
Born December 9, 1912. Graduated from Lewis and Clark High School in Spokane, Washington. Attended WSU 1937-1938. Pharmacy major. Enlisted February 1941. Died at Cabanatuan prison in the Phillipines, July 26, 1942.

Fisk, Jack Young – Air Corps
Born January 13, 1918. Graduated from high achool in Wapato, Washington. Attended WSU 1937-1938. Business Administration major. Enlisted April 1941. Killed in plane crash, Great Falls, Montana, September 2, 1943.

Foley, William Thomas – Army
Born July 2, 1915. Graduated from Rogers High School in Spokane, Washington. Attended WSU 1934-1938, graduating June 6, 1938 with a B.A. degree. Enlisted October 11, 1941. Killed in Australia, 1942.

Ford, Robert Mitchel – Army
Born July 25, 1920. Graduated from Clarkston High School in Clarkston, Washington. Attended WSU 1938-1939. English major. Killed on Okinawa, May 27, 1945.

Forsman, Robert Eugene – Naval Aviation
Born November 19, 1920. Graduated from Bremerton High School in Bremerton, Washington. Transferred from College of Puget Sound to attend WSU 1940-1942. Physical Education major. Enlisted August 18, 1942. Killed in plane crash in Pasco, Washington, May 23, 1943.

Fortier, Malcolm V. – Army
From Spokane, Washington. Attended WSU 1911-1914. Served in World War I and World War II. Reported Missing in Action in the Philippines, June 7, 1942. Died in Japanese prison camp.

French, Kenneth Pierce – Army
Born April 23, 1920. Graduated from Pullman High School. Attended WSU 1938-1939. General Studies major. Killed in Action in battle of Mindanao, July 27, 1943.

Froemke, Donald Harvey – Field Artillery
Born October 15, 1912. Graduated from Yakima (Washington) High School. Transferred from Yakima Valley Junior College to attend WSU 1935-1939, graduating June 6, 1939 with a B.S. degree. Enlisted March 6, 1941. Killed in Action in Holland, October 5, 1944.

Fryslie, John Vincent – Army
Born February 28, 1916. Graduated from high school in Buckley, Washington. Transferred from North Dakota Agricultural College to attend WSU 1936-1937 and 1940. Agriculture major. Killed overseas December 1, 1943.

Fuller, James Albert – Air Corps
Born May 14, 1923 in Seattle. Graduated from Bremerton High School in Bremerton, Washington. Attended WSU 1941-1943. Mining major. Enlisted December 1942.

Gamble, James Thomas – Navy
Born September 13, 1923 in Spokane, Washington. Graduated from Lewis and Clark High School in Spokane. Attended WSU 1942-1943. Agriculture major. Enlisted March 15, 1942. Killed in Action in South Pacific, March 1945.

Garrison, Robert Lloyd – Air Corps
Born March 2, 1921 in Castle Rock, Washington. Graduated from Castle Rock High School. Transferred from Lower Columbia Junior College in Longview, Washington, to attend WSU 1946-1947. Mechanical Engineering major. Enlisted March 13, 1942.

Gass, Virgil J. – Army
From Pullman, Washington. Killed in Action.

Gay, Charles William – Submarine
Born February 4, 1924 in Worland, Wyoming. Graduated from Washakie High School in Washakie, Wyoming. Attended WSU fall semester 1942. Agriculture major. Missing in Action.

Gay, John Elwood (Major) – Air Corps
Born March 22, 1915. Graduated from Lewis and Clark High School in Spokane, Washington. Transferred from Whitworth College to attend WSU 1937-1939, graduating June 5, 1939 with a B.A. in Business Administration. Enlisted September 1940. Died on Okinawa, July 1945.

Gilbert, Calvin L.
Born October 18, 1907. Graduated from Lincoln High School in Kansas City, Missouri. Attended WSU fall semester 1936. Veterinary Medicine major.

Gilbert, Henry George – Air Corps

Born September 23, 1919. Graduated from Lowell High School in Lowell, Wyoming. Transferred from New Mexico State College to attend WSU 1938-1940. General Studies major. Killed in Action in Rangoon, Burma, December 23, 1941.

Gilden, Robert O. – Army
From Anacortes, Washington. Killed in Action.

Gilding, Robert
Reported Missing in Action.

Gillingham, Bernard Paul – Air Corps
Born May 19, 1914. Graduated from John Rogers High School in Spokane, Washington. Attended WSU 1937-1941. Agriculture major. Enlisted April 1941. Killed in accident in Australia, April 16, 1942.

Gould, Jack Pickard – Air Corps
Born August 13, 1917. Graduated from high school in LaCrosse, Washington. Attended WSU 1936-1937. General Studies major. Enlisted Ocotber 1941. Killed in the Philippines in 1942.

Graves, Richard Dorsey – Air Corps
Born October 13, 1916. Graduated from high school in Puyallup, Washington. Attended WSU 1934-1939, graduating June 5, 1939 with a B.S. in Metallurgy with Honors. Enlisted December 30, 1940. Killed in service.

Graybill, Edward Curtis – Air Force
Born August 8, 1924 in Roseburg, Oregon. Grandson of Edward S. Curtis, who was famous for his photography of Native Americans in the early 1900s. Graduated from Lewis and Clark High School in Spokane, Washington. Attended WSU 1942-1943. Mechanical Engineering major. Enlisted February 28, 1943. Killed in France.

Greene, George Rodrick – Air Corps
Born June 24, 1920 in Sunnyside, Washington. Graduated from Deer Park High School in Deer Park, Washington. Attended WSU fall semester 1941. Mechanical Engineering major. Killed in Pacific, February 17, 1945.

Greening, Charles Ross – Army Air Force (pilot)
Born November 12, 1914 in Tacoma, Washington. Attended WSU 1932-1936, graduating in June 1936 with a B.A. in Fine Arts. Shot down over Mt. Vesuvius in Italy. Spent remainder of war in Italian and German prisoner of war camps. He died in 1957 of prolonged illness brought on by his POW experience.

Gronemeier, Paul E. – Signal Corps
Enlisted November 21, 1942. Stricken with polio. Died August 1946.

Guenther, Warren William – Army
Born May 30, 1920 in Coulee City, Washington. Graduated from Walla Walla (Washington) High School. Attended WSU fall semester 1941. Business Administration major. Killed in Europe.

Guthridge, Walter Joseph
Born March 19, 1916. Graduated from St. Vincent Academy in Walla Walla, Washington. Attended WSU 1936-1940, graduating June 3, 1940 with a B.A. in Business Administration with Honors.

Hair, Gene W.
Killed in Action, June 1944.

Haldeman, Vance Farrell – Navy
Born April 4, 1919. Graduated from Franklin High School in Los Angeles. Attended WSU 1938-1942, graduating June 1, 1942 with a B.S. degree.

Hardt, Richard Arthur
Born September 17, 1912. Graduated from Ridgefield High School in Ridgefield, Washington. Attended WSU 1936-1939, graduating June 5, 1939 with a B.S. degree.

Hempstead, Don Carlos, Jr. – Marines
Born August 28, 1920. Graduated from Lewis and Clark High School in Spokane, Washington. Attended WSU 1940-1941. Electrical Engineering major. Enlisted February 3, 1942. Died on Guam, July 26, 1944.

Hokenstad, Warren Raymond – Naval Reserve
Born December 26, 1917. Graduated from Snohomish High

School in Snohomish, Washington. Transferred from Pacific Lutheran College to attend WSU in 1937-1940, graduating June 3 1940, with a B.S. in Agricultural Business. Enlisted June 25, 1942. Died in Navy blimp crash in October 1943.

Holech, Harry J. – Army Civil Engineers
Born March 26 1916. Graduated from high school in Raymond, Washington. Attended WSU 1936-1940, graduating June 3, 1940 with a B.S. degree. Killed in Action in France, July 7, 1944.

Holsten, Claude – Navy
From Spokane, Washington.

Houlehan, Patrick P. – Army Infantry
Born August 3, 1915 in Middleshara, Kentucky. Earned B.S. from University of Alaska. Attended WSU 1942-1943. Geology postgraduate. Killed in Normandy, June 13, 1944.

Hronek, William H., Jr. – Marines
Killed in plane accident South Pacific, January 14, 1943.

Hughes, Billy Dean – Army Air Corps
Born March 2, 1920. Graduated from North Central High School in Spokane, Washington. Attended WSU 1938-1941. Speech major. Killed in plane crash in South Pacific, April 29, 1942.

Hughes, Harrison Sterling – Air Force
Born March 9, 1914. Graduated from Riverview High School

in Hover, Washington. Attended WSU 1934-1940. Mechanical Engineering major. Discharged from National Guard, March 12, 1940. Died on prisoner of war ship sunk in Philippines.

Hull, Thurston Charles – Army Air Corps
Born May 8, 1923 in Colfax, Washington. Graduated from Colfax High School. Attended WSU fall semester 1941. Mechanical Engineering major. Enlisted June 8, 1942. Killed in Action in Romanian oil fields, August 1, 1943.

Hurley, John J. – Army Infantry
From San Francisco. Attended WSU in early 1940s. Killed in Action in Italy, January 1944.

Imhoff, Robert Coleman – Army Air Corps
Born September 29, 1923 in Spokane, Washington. Graduated from Lewis and Clark High School in Spokane. Transferred from Gonzaga University to attend WSU from 1942-1943. Business Administration major. Enlisted March 10, 1943. Killed in Action over Europe, September 27, 1944.

Jett, William H. – Navy
Born September 23, 1920. Graduated from Wenatchee High School in Wenatchee, Washington. Attended WSU 1938-1939. Mechanical Engineering major. Enlisted August 3, 1942. Killed in Action on Peleliu, Palau Island, November 4, 1944.

Jones, Marion Elmer – Air Corps
Born October 3, 1914. Graduated from high school in Wilbur, Washington. Transferred from Cheney State Normal and Eastern Washington College of Education to attend WSU in 1934-1939 graduating June 5, 1939 with a B.S. degree. Enlisted June 19, 1942. Killed in plane crash in Arizona, February 1, 1944.

Judge, Jim Ralph – Air Corps
Born April 18, 1911. Graduated from high school in Missoula, Montana. Transferred from Montana State and Montana State Normal to attend WSU in 1936-1937. History major. Enlisted November 27, 1940. Died in Japanese prison camp, June 11, 1943.

Julian, Lewis – Army Infantry
No other information available.

Karnath, Lyle G
Born September 21, ?? (either 1914 or 1915). Graduated from high school in Camas, Washington. Attended WSU 1935-1937. Physical Education major. Killed in Action in Europe, October 1, 1943.

Kehoe, Robert James – Army Air Corps
Born August 10, 1921. Graduated from high school in California. Attended WSU 1938-1939. Veterinary Medicine major. Enlisted July 21, 1943. Lost over Hanover, Germany, April 4, 1945.

Kelleher, Chester Piere – Army Air Corps
Born April 12, 1921 in Cleveland, Ohio. Graduated from Alameda (California) High School. Attended WSU fall semester 1941. Veterinary Medicine major. Deceased February 7, 1942 auto accident.

Kelleher, Jack Joseph – Army Infantry
Born October 12, 1921. Graduated from High School in Ellensburg, Washington. Attended WSU 1939-1942. Business Administration major. Enlisted August 14, 1942. Died September 23, 1944 of wounds received in France.

Kelly, Joseph M.
No information available

Kennedy, James Delbert – Army Infantry
Born January 30, 1923 in Salem, Oregon. Graduated from Snoqualmie (Washington) High School. Attended WSU 1941-1943. General Studies major. Enlisted September 11, 1943. Died January 1945 of wounds received in Ulan Action.

Kerns, Ralph – Paratroopers
Born July 24, 1919. Graduated from Garfield High School in Garfield, Washington. Attended WSU 1939-1942. Mining major. Killed in Action in Sicily, July 24, 1943.

Kerr, Lee Donald
Born August 14, 1920. Graduated from Pullman High School.

Attended WSU 1938-1940. Business Administration major. Killed in plane crash in Canada, October 20, 1942.

Kilgore, James M. – Army
From Yakima, Washington. Died in hospital of wounds, April 4, 1945.

King, Warren Leery
Born July 28, 1920. Graduated from Sequim High School in Sequim, Washington. Attended WSU 1938-1943. Agriculture and Education majors. Killed in plane accident, January 1, 1945.

Kingman, Dale Newton – Navy
Born July 19, 1920. Graduated from Chelan High School in Chelan,Washington. Attended WSU 1938-1941. General Studies major. Killed in Pacific Theatre.

Kirkham, Charlie Noble – Navy
Born October 16, 1922 in Alpha, Saskatchewan, Canada. Graduated from Sunnyside High School in Sunnyside, Washington. Attended WSU 1941-1942. Mechanical Engineering major. Killed in Pacific Theatre in 1945.

Kirtland, Orville Austin – Army Air Corps
Born June 22, 1919. Graduated from Pullman High School. Attended WSU 1937-1940. Prelaw major. Enlisted March 14, 1941. Killed in Action in Australia, September 1942.

Kizer, Ralph Lloyd – Air Corps
Born March 13, 1919. Killed in plane crash in Lemmon, South Dakota, October 21, 1944.

Klemgard, Jim Edgar – Navy
Born October 10, 1923. Graduated from Pullman High School. Attended WSU fall semester 1940. Pre-medicine major. Killed in plane crash at Klamath Falls, Oregon, June 13, 1944.

Krantz, Robert Arthur
Born October 19, 1914. Graduated from Redlands High School in Redlands, California. Transferred from San Fernando Junior College to attend WSU in 1937-1940. Business Administration major. Died in the Philippines, April 13, 1942.

Kraus, Raymond Carl – Marines
Born September 13, 1918. Graduated from Valley High School in Menlo, Washington. Attended WSU 1936-1940, graduating February 10, 1941 with a B.S. degree. Killed in Action on Saipan, July 1944.

Lagounaris, Denny Frank
Born February 23, 1924 in Tacoma, Washington. Graduated from Lincoln High School in Tacoma. Attended WSU fall semester 1942. Business Administration major. Killed during Battle of the Bulge.

Lane, Horace Bartlett – Army Air Force
Born November 25, 1922. Graduated from Olympia High School in Olympia, Washington. Attended WSU 1940-1941. Chemical Engineering major. Enlisted December 1942. Lost over Europe, March 3, 1945.

LaSalle, Willard Dale – Navy
Born October 27, 1918. Graduated from high school in Dixie, Washington. Attended WSU fall semester 1937. Forestry Agriculture major. Killed in Action on Pearl Harbor, December 7, 1941.

Lasswell, Ben Erwin, Jr. – Army
Born February 24, 1924 in Spokane, Washington. Graduated from West Valley High School in Millwood, Washington. Attended WSU 1942-1943. Mechanical Engineering major. Killed in Action in France, December 1, 1944.

Levine, Edward M., Jr. – Army Engineers
Enlisted March 31, 1941. Killed in West Africa, June 15, 1945.

Lewellen (Norbeck), Jeanne M.
See Norbeck.

Lewis, Thomas H. – Army Infantry
Born August 4, 1912. Graduated from high school in Kahlotus, Washington. Attended WSU 1930-1931 and 1936-1940, graduating June 3, 1940 with a B.S. degree. Reported killed but found in German prison camp.

Loomis, Everett W. – Army
Born November 29, 1920. Graduated from Bellingham High School in Bellingham, Washington. Transferred from Western Washington College of Education to attend WSU in 1939-1942. Agriculture major. Killed in Action, 1945.

Love, Loren E. – Marine Corps
Enlisted July 1, 1942. Died of wounds received on Saipan, August 1944.

Ludwig, Robert Eugene – Army Infantry
Born May 8, 1921. Graduated from high school in Mason City, Washington. Attended WSU fall semester 1940. Agriculture major. Killed in Action in France, November 15, 1944.

Lull, Robert Herman – Army Air Corps
Born June 10, 1924 in Portland, Oregon. Graduated from Nespelem High School in Washington. Attended WSU 1942-1943. Physics major. Enlisted March 3, 1943. Killed in European Theatre, February 1, 1945.

Magnuson, Gus Allen, Jr. – Army
Born May 27, 1921. Graduated from Reardan High School in Reardan, Washington. Attended WSU 1939-1943, graduating May 24, 1943 with a B.S. in Psychology with High Honors. Died at Camp Roberts, California, of polio, October 30, 1943.

Markshausen, Robert T. – Navy
From Kelso, Washington. Attended WSU in early 1940s. Killed in Action.

Martyr, Carlton Lewis – Medical Corps
Born January 31, 1920. Graduated from Sacramento High School in California. Transferred from Sacramento Junior College to attend WSU in 1939-1940. Pre-dental major. Enlisted September 11, 1942. Killed in civilian car crash while in training.

Mathiesen, Glen E. – Army
From Colfax, Washington. Attended WSU in early 1940s. Died in Holland as result of wounds, December 4, 1944.

Matzger, Charles William – Army Air Corps
Born January 1, 1923 in Colfax, Washington. Graduated from Colfax High School. Attended WSU 1941-1943. Civil Engineering major. Enlisted December 14, 1942. Killed in plane crash in Italy

McAllister, Donald Frank – Air Corps
Born October 10, 1920. Graduated from Lewis and Clark High School in Spokane, Washington. Attended WSU 1940-1941. Home Economics major. Killed in plane crash in California, November 29, 1942.

McCalder, Robert W. – Army Infantry
From Pullman, Washington. Attended WSU fall 1934. Enlisted September 16, 1940. Died of battle wounds on Luzon, April 20, 1945.

McCanse, William Warren – Army Infantry
Born July 2, 1922. Graduated from Pomeroy (Washington) High School. Attended WSU 1940-1944. Army Specialized Training Program instruction began November 2, 1943. Agriculture and Education majors. Killed in Action in Pacific Theatre.

McClellan, Joseph Lewis – Army
Born June 25, 1917. Graduated high school in Billings, Montana. Attended WSU 1936-1940, graduating June 3, 1940 with a B.A. degree.

McNabb, Robert Emmett
Born December 24, 1912. Graduated from high school in Chehalis, Washington. Attended WSU 1936-1939. Mechanical Engineering major.

McNeil, William H. – Aviation Ground Force
Died in Japanese prison camp in July 1943.

Mickelson, Clayton Johnston Hileman – Veterans Corps
Born August 16, 1911. Graduated from Lincoln High School in Portland, Oregon. Transferred from Glendale Junior College in California to attend WSU 1935-1939, graduating June 14, 1939 with a B.S. degree and Doctor of Veterinary Medicine. Died in a prison camp in 1945.

Miles, Clifford Orin – Army Engineers
Born April 30, 1911. Attended WSU 1931-1937, graduating June 14, 1937 with a B.S. in Civil Engineering. Enlisted September 3, 1940. Killed in Sicily, August 1943.

Miller, Glen W. – Air Corps
Killed in plane crash in California, August 1943.

Miller, Louis Ivan – Air Corps
Born September 13, 1918. Graduated from Centralia High School in Centralia, Washington. Transferred from Central Washington College of Education to attend WSU in 1937-1941. Music and Education majors. Enlisted November 7, 1941. Killed in Action at the Battle of Bismark Sea, March 1943.

Miller, J. Reginald
Born May 10, 1915. Graduated from high school in Hollywood, California. Attended WSU 1933-1938, graduating June 6, 1938 with a B.S. degree.

Miller, Richard Conrad
Born July 7, 1920. Graduated from Jefferson High School in Portland, Oregon. Attended WSU 1938-1939. Prelaw major. Killed in Action.

Mohr, Gerald Eugene – Army Infantry
Born May 26, 1922. Graduated from Colfax (Washington) High School. Attended WSU 1939-1943, graduating May 24, 1943

with a B.A. in Music with Honors. Died at Camp Wheeler, Georgia, of heart attack, July 3, 1944.

Mollett, Harold B.
No information available

Moore, John Wesley – Air Corps Medical Corps
Killed in bomber crash in New Guinea, March 20, 1944.

Moran, Frank Robbins – Paratroopers
Born May 28, 1921. Graduated from Roosevelt High School in Seattle. Attended WSU fall semester 1939. Business Administration major. Killed in Action in France, June 12, 1944.

Morgan, Don K.
Born February 20, 1924 in Elma, Washington. Graduated from Elma High School. Attended WSU 1946-1947.

Morgan, Donald Quenton – Army Air Corps
Born February 26, 1921 in Innisfail, Alta. Graduated from North Central High School in Spokane, Washington. Attended WSU spring semester 1942. Police Administration major. Enlisted June 10, 1942.

Morgan, Donald R. – Veteran Corps
Enlisted April 22, 1940.

Mottet, Harold Oscar – Army
Died of polio on Leyte, December 19, 1944.

Munn, Robert S. – Army Reserve Corps
From Tacoma, Washington. Killed in Action in Italy, April 14, 1945.

Munro, Douglas A. – Coast Guard
Cle Elum, Washington. Enlisted September 17, 1939. Service in the South Pacific. Killed in Action, September 27, 1942. Received the Congressional Medal of Honor.

Munson, Raymond G. – Air Corps
Killed over Italy, March 22, 1943.

Myers, Edward James – Army Infantry
Born October 30, 1921. Graduated from Puyallup High School in Puyallup, Washington. Attended WSU 1940-1944. Army Specialized Training Program instruction began November 2, 1943. Agriculture major. Killed in Action in Europe in early 1945.

Nabby, Thomas L. – Army
Born January 4, 1925 in Milwaukee, Wisconsin. Attended WSU 1943-44 as member of the Army Specialized Training Program. Killed in Action.

Nardi, Elmer J. – Army Air Corps
Enlisted February 22, 1942. Killed in Action.

Needham, Robert Forest – Army Tank Company
Born October 8, 1916. Graduated from high school in Hanford, Washington. Attended WSU 1935-1939, graduating February 5, 1940 with a B.A. in Business Administration. Killed in Action in the Philippines, January 1942.

Nellor, Robert Henry – Army Air Corps
Born October 7, 1920. Graduated from high school in The Dalles, Oregon. Attended WSU during 1941. Enlisted December 29, 1941.

Nolan, Robert Willard – Marines
Born November 1, 1919. Graduated from high school in Cowiche, Washington. Attended WSU 1937-1941, graduating February 4, 1942 with a B.S. in Agricultural Business. Killed during invasion of Guam, July 21, 1944.

Norbeck (Lewellen), Jeanne M. – Army Air Force
Employed by the Army Air Force as a test pilot. Killed in plane crash, October 16, 1944.

Oliver, David U.
No information available.

Oliver, Karl Allen – Naval Aviation
Born February 12, 1916. Graduated from high school in Hoquiam, Washington. Attended WSU 1934-1938, graduating June 6, 1938 with a B.A. in Economics. Naval Air Force. Killed in plane crash January 23, 1942.

Palmer, Marvin B.
Killed in airplane accident in Asia, March 1, 1943.

Parkins, Harlow
Killed in Italy, April 1944.

Patten, Robert Alexander – Navy
Born April 3, 1920. Graduated from Olympia High School in Olympia, Washington. Attended WSU 1938-1942, graduating June 1, 1942 with a B.S. in Physics with Honors. Killed in Action, July 24, 1944.

Perry, Norris – Army Air Corps
Graduated from high school in Sedro Woolley, Washington. Attended WSU 1931-1935, graduating June 8, 1936 with a B.S. in Electrical Engineering. Discharged from National Guard, June 7, 1933. Died in Knoxville, Tennessee, November 1945.

Petaja, Wayne Richard – Army Specialized Training Program
Born February 9, 1921. Graduated from North Central High School in Spokane, Washington. Attended WSU 1939-1940. Mechanical Engineering major. Enlisted July 15, 1942. Died in Germany, June 4, 1945.

Pickard, James Arthur – Air Corps
Born July 18, 1919. Graduated from Walla Walla High School in Walla Walla, Washington. Attended WSU 1937-1940. Prelaw major. Died in plane crash in New Guinea, July 1943.

Plowman, Noel Elwin – Air Corps
Born September 4, 1922 in LaCrosse, Washington. Graduated from LaCrosse High School. Attended WSU 1941-1942. Agricultural Business major. Enlisted September 18, 1942. Reported Missing in Action, November 1944; later confirmed Killed in Action.

Porter, Grenville Neil – Army Infantry
Born February 15, 1915. Graduated from Lincoln High School in Tacoma, Washington. Attended WSU 1936-1941, graduating June 9, 1941 with a B.A. in Economics. Enlisted September 1, 1941.

Prater, Charles Lowell – Naval Aviation
Graduated June 3, 1940 with a B.S. in Agriculture. Enlisted August 15, 1940.

Protherough, Robert George – Marines
Born October 28, 1918. Graduated from West Valley High School in Millwood, Washington. Transferred from Spokane Junior College to attend WSU in 1939-1941. Speech major. Killed in plane crash in New Orleans, August 15, 1943.

Prouty, Gerrel A. – Naval Aviation
Born May 2, 1920. Graduated from Metaline Falls High School in Metaline Falls, Washington. Attended WSU 1939-1942. Speech major. Lost during reconnaissance flight in San Francisco area, October 29, 1943.

Rasque, George William – Naval Engineering Corps
Born May 30, 1914. Graduated from North Central High School in Spokane, Washington. Transferred from Cheney Normal to attend WSU in 1933-1937, graduating June 14, 1937 with a B.S. in Architectural Engineering. Discharged from National Guard, June 10, 1935. Killed in Action on Okinawa in 1945.

Reymore, George William – Marines
Born September 10, 1924 in Cheyenne, Wyoming. Graduated from high school in Kennewick, Washington. Attended WSU 1942-1943. Agriculture major. Enlisted March 18, 1943. Killed in Action on Guam (*The Spokesman-Review,* August 30, 1944).

Richey, James A. – Army Infantry
Killed in Action in Africa, May 6, 1943.

Riemland, Jack Berton – Air Corps
Born February 29, 1920. Graduated from Sultan Union High School in Sultan, Washington. Attended WSU 1940-1941. Agriculture major. Killed in crash in Ohio in 1944.

Ritchie, William Howard
Graduated from South High School in Salt Lake City, Utah. Attended WSU from 1936-1938. Business Administration major.

Roberts, William John – Army Air Corps
From Pasco, Washington. Killed in Corsican Campaign, February 1944.

Rock, Harold Ralph – Army Infantry
Born January 23, 1919. Graduated from Colfax High School. Attended WSU 1937-1941, graduating June 9, 1941 with a B.A. in Political Science with Honors. Killed in plane crash over Germany, June 5, 1945.

Roeder, John Otto
Born June 22, 1924 in Tacoma, Washington. Killed in air accident in Texas in 1944.

Rumburg, Ira Christian – Army
Born August 13, 1915. Graduated from West Valley High School in Millwood, Washington. Attended WSU 1934-1938, graduating June 6, 1938 with a B.A. degree. Lost in sinking of troop transport crossing English Channel, December 25, 1944.

Sax, Paul Joseph – Marine Air Corps
Born January 26, 1920. Graduated from high school in Colville, Washington. Attended WSU 1937-1941, graduating June 9, 1941 with a B.A. in Political Science. Killed in South Pacific, October 5, 1943.

Schildroth, William H. – Army
WSU faculty member and Army ROTC instructor in early 1940s. Killed in Action in France.

Schmella, Marvin John
Born July 7, 1914. Graduated from high school in Toppenish,

Washington. Attended WSU 1933-1937. Metallurgy major. Killed on African front early 1943.

Schmitz, Rudolph Edward – Army
Born August 16, 1924 in Glendale, California. Enrolled WSU in 1943-44 as member of the Army Specialized Training Program. Killed in Action.

Scholz, Howard Allison – Marine Corps Reserve
Born August 8, 1921. Graduated from Colfax (Washington) High School. Attended WSU 1939-1943, graduating May 24, 1943 with a B.S. in Agriculture with Honors. Died of wounds received in South Pacific, September 14, 1944.

Sebastian, Maximo Paulino – Medical Corps
Born November 18, 1913. Graduated from high school in Isabella, Philippine Islands. Attended WSU 1935-1937. Education major. Killed by enemy aircraft bombing in the Philippines.

Seike, Toll – Army
Born October 8, 1923 in Seattle. Graduated from Highline High School in Seattle. Attended WSU 1942-1943. Business Administration major. Killed in France, October 29, 1944. Awarded the Bronze Star for heroism.

Sellers, (Arthur) Lee Rue
Born December 24, 1917 in Taylorville, Illinois. Attended WSU fall semester 1942. Electrical Engineering major.

Selph, Nathan James – Navy
Born October 29, 1920. Graduated from high school in Kahlotus, Washington. Attended WSU fall semester 1939. Enlisted January 24, 1944. Died August 9, 1944 following appendectomy after long Navy duty in Central Pacific and Saipan.

Simmons, Howard Elliot, Jr. – Army
Born December 27, 1920. Graduated from Puyallup High School in Puyallup, Washington. Attended WSU 1939-1943, graduating May 24, 1943 with a B.S. in Agriculture. Killed in France, December 1944.

Smith, Josephine M. – Women's Army Auxiliary Corps
Home Economics instructor. Died of infection at Camp Buttner, North Carolina, May 4, 1944.

Smith, Robert A.
No information available.

Snyder, Jack – Army
Born September 30, 1924 in Phoenix, Arizona. Attended WSU 1943-44 as member of the Army Specialized Training Program. Killed in Action.

Somers, Wilber Earl – Air Corps
Born August 23, 1918. Graduated from North Central High School in Spokane, Washington. Attended WSU 1937-1941. General Studies major. Died February 22, 1944 of battle wounds

received in Italy.

Sorrells, Dallas H.
Born May 19, 1919. Graduated from Pullman High School. Attended WSU 1939-1942. Sociology major. Killed in Action on Okinawa, July 1945.

Stambaugh, Millard Dean – Army Infantry
Born January 25, 1920. Graduated from Creston High School in Creston, Washington. Attended WSU 1940-1941. General Studies major. Enlisted April 27, 1942. Killed in Action in Italy, April 19, 1944.

Stoddard, Robert Earl – Army Infantry
Born December 29, 1924 in Spokane, Washington. Graduated from West Valley High School in Millwood, Washington. Attended WSU 1942-1943. Mechanical Engineering major. Enlisted October 14, 1944. Killed in Action on Luzon, June 10, 1945.

Stone, Eagle Andrew
Born May 3, 1919. Graduated from high school in Lake Oswego, Oregon. Attended WSU 1937-1942, graduating June 9, 1942 with a B.A. in Economics. Died January 1946.

Stoops, Charles Everett – Army
Born September 29, 1924 in Winchester, Indiana. Attended WSU in 1943-1944 as member of the Specialized Army Training Program. Seriously wounded clearing a minefield near Budesheim,

Germany. Died shortly afterward in an Army field hospital.

Story, Ernest C. – Army Engineers
Born March 28, 1915. Graduated from Kennewick High School in Kennewick, Washington. Attended WSU 1935-1937. Civil Engineering major. Enlisted September 1, 1942. Died in Bideford, England, November 4, 1943.

Streeter, Jack S. – Navy
Enlisted February 3, 1942.

Stringer, Robert Lee – Air Corps Reserves
Born June 27, 1924 in Colfax, Washington. Graduated from Palouse High School in Palouse, Washington. Attended WSU fall semester 1942. Agriculture major. Killed in Italy, February 7, 1945.

Tagged, Elson Cameron, Jr. – Army Infantry
Born July 16, 1920. Graduated from high school in Oregon. Attended WSU 1938-1943, graduating May 24, 1943 with a B.A. in Economics. Enlisted April 23, 1943. Killed in Action on Okinawa, April 8, 1945.

Terry, Lyman B. – Army
Born January 19, 1912. Earned his B.A. from De Pauw University in Greencastle, Indiana. Attended WSU 1940-1942, graduating June 1, 1942 with an M.A. in Foreign Language. Killed in Action, December 3, 1943.

Thurston, Robert Munroe – Air Corps
Born October 25, 1924 in Spokane, Washington. Graduated from Fairfield (Washington) High School. Attended WSU fall semester 1942. Mechanical Engineering major. Enlisted February 5, 1943. Missing in Action in Africa, April 1944.

Tipler, Jack E. – Army Air Corps
Enlisted March 31, 1943. Killed in plane crash in Kansas, June 15, 1944.

Transeth, Willard Alfred – Army Air Corps
Born August 13, 1921. Graduated from high school in Walla Walla, Washington. Attended WSU 1939-1942. Pre-medicine major. Killed in plane crash in England, April 26, 1944.

Truesdell, Floyd Harold – Air Corps
Born August 16, 1919. Graduated from high school in Anchorage, Alaska. Attended WSU 1939-1940. Mechanical Engineering major. Pilot of a flying fortress. Killed in Action, August 31, 1943.

Volz, Raymond Justin – Army
Born April 2, 1924 in Cincinnati, Ohio. Attended WSU 1943-1944 as member of the Specialized Army Training Program. Killed in Action.

Waldner, Frank Andrew – Army
Born January 17, 1919. Graduated from Lincoln High School in Tacoma, Washington. Attended WSU 1938-1942, graduating January 29, 1943 with a B.S. degree. Killed in Action in France, January 23, 1945.

Wappenstein, William A. – Army Infantry
Prisoner of War from Bataan. Died in Japanese prison, April 6, 1942.

Welchko, Cecil Richard
Born March 2, 1915. Graduated from high school in Bonners Ferry, Idaho. Attended WSU 1935-1939. Business Administration major. Lost life on Japanese prison ship when it was bombed in December 1944.

Wells, Harry Earl – Air Corps
Born March 10, 1918. Graduated from Valley High School in Menlo, Washington. Attended WSU 1936-1940. Mechanical Engineering major. Killed in plane crash in Oklahoma, April 14, 1942.

West, (Dr.) Jesse H. – Army
Died of wounds received in France.

Wheeler, Charles R.
Born December 14, 1909. Graduated from Queen Anne High School in Seattle. Attended WSU 1929-1936, graduating June 8, 1936 with a B.A. in Education.

Whittemore, Harold Eugene – Marines
Enlisted October 12, 1942. Died of wounds received in South Pacific, September 1944.

Wollenberg, Fredrick Richard
Born October 17, 1916. Graduated from high school in Edwall, Washington. Attended WSU 1934-1938, graduating with a B.S. in Mechanical Engineering. Missing in Action in South Pacific, December 1942.

Woodruff, David Pearson – Army
Born December 17, 1922. Graduated from high school in Trout Lake, Washington. Attended WSU 1942-1943. Agriculture major. Enlisted March 3, 1943.

Yeilding, Arthur Talles – Army Air Corps
Born October 23, 1918. Graduated from Benson Polytechnical High School in Portland, Oregon. Attended WSU 1938-1939. Chemistry major. Enlisted June 25, 1941. Killed in Action over Cape Gazelle, Southwest Pacific, January 23, 1944.

Young, Orman W., Jr. – Army Air Corps
Born April 3, 1921 in Spokane, Washington. Graduated from Lewis and Clark High School in Spokane. Attended WSU 1941-1942. Police Science major. Enlisted February 11, 1943. Killed in air crash.

Zoradi, Stephen W. – Army

Born March 31, 1923 in Mina, Nevada. Attended WSU 1943-1944 as member of the Specialized Army Training Program. Killed in Action on the outskirts of Schleusingen, Germany. His platoon moved to clear a road block, came under heavy enemy fire and was forced to withdraw. T/5 Zoradi provided covering machine-gun fire even after being mortally wounded. His brave actions reduced the number of casualties that otherwise would have occurred. Awarded the Silver Star posthumously.

KOREA

Allen, Ace
Graduated from Jefferson High School in Tampa, Florida. Attended WSU 1946-1950, graduating May 28, 1950 with a B.S. in Business Administration. Killed in Action in Korea, August 9, 1950.

Carey, Edwin Austin
Born July 16, 1926 in Fond du Lac, Wisconsin. Attended Bellermine High School in Tacoma, Washington. Attended WSU 1946-1947.

Hunt, Robert Griffith
Born September 9, 1923 in Walla Walla, Washington. Attended Moses Lake (Washington) High School. Attended WSU 1946-1950, graduating May 28, 1950 with a B.S. in Agriculture.

Jacobs, Edward James, Jr.
Born July 13, 1928 in Mt. Vernon, Washington. Graduated 1946 from Mt. Vernon Union High School. Transferred from Skagit Valley Junior College and attended WSU 1949-1951.

Kangas, Wilbert E. H.
No information available.

McKay, Connie Clyde
Born October 1, 1929 in Oberlin, Kansas. Graduated from high school 1947 in Omak, Washington. Attended WSU 1947-1951, graduating June 3, 1951 with a B.A. in Speech.

Pratt, Parker Hinate
Born July 31, 1918. Attended high school in Blaine, Washington. Attended WSU 1937-1938. General Studies major.

Price, Robert Guy
Born December 19, 1923 in Bellingham, Washington. Attended high school at Quillayute High School in Forks, Washington. Attended WSU 1942-1943. Agriculture-Forestry major.

Putnam, James E.
Born February 5, 1926 in Wheatland, Wyoming. Graduated 1943 from Aberdeen High School. Attended WSU 1948-1950. General Studies and Agriculture majors.

Rist, Alfred Lawrence – Air Force
Born November 28, 1926 in Spokane, Washington. Graduated from Lewis and Clark High School in Spokane. Attended WSU 1946-1950, graduating May 28, 1950 with a B.S. degree. General Studies major. Killed in Action, June 10, 1952. Following his death, Rist's parents donated a memorial fireplace in his honor in Spokane's Manito Park.

Sexon, Jack Raymond
Born March 27, 1928 in Spokane, Washington. Graduated from Orville High School in Orville, Washington. Attended WSU 1946-1950, graduating May 28, 1950 with a B.A. in Business Administration. Killed in Korea, October 12, 1952.

Taylor, David Scott – Marine Corps
Born September 19, 1920. Attended high school at Walla Walla (Washington) High School. Attended WSU 1940-1943. Business Administration major. Killed in Action in Korea, August 1950.

VIETNAM

Clowe, Robert Earl
Born October 9, 1944 in Seattle. Graduated 1962 from Mossyrock High School in Mossyrock, Washington. Transferred from Centralia College and attended WSU 1964-1966, graduating August 5, 1966 with a B.A. in Agriculture.

Dennison, Terry Arden
Born January 20, 1934 in Cosmopolis, Washington. Graduated 1952 from Weatherwax High School in Aberdeen, Washington. Transferred from Grays Harbor Junior College in Aberdeen and attended WSU 1955-1956. Hotel Administration major.

Denny, Jerry David
Born March 3, 1943 in Omaha, Nebraska. Graduated 1961 from Lewis and Clark in Spokane, Washington. Attended WSU 1961-1965, graduating May 30, 1965 with a B.S. in Chemistry.

Fabian, William Hilric – Air Force
Born April 20, 1940 in Houston, Texas (brother of astronaut John Fabian). Graduated 1958 from Pullman High School. Attended WSU 1958-1962, graduating June 3, 1962 with a B.S. in Police Science and Administration with Honors. Killed in Action in Vietnam, November 14, 1968.

Fors, Gary Henry
Born April 29, 1941 in Puyallup. Washington. Graduated 1959 from Puyallup High School. Attended WSU 1959-1963, graduating June 2, 1963 with a B.A. in Business Administration. Missing in Action.

Franck, Ralph Henry, Jr.
Attended WSU fall semester 1965.

Fry, James Ray
Born April 7, 1948 in Mineral Wells, Texas. Graduated 1966 from Artesia High School in Artesia, California. Attended WSU fall semester 1966.

Gerth, Peter Hudson
Born August 29, 1947 in Yakima, Washington. Graduated 1965 from Eisenhower High School in Yakima. Attended WSU 1965-1967. Zoology major.

Harris, William Lee
Born May 17, 1942 in Tonga, Oklahoma. Graduated 1960 from Kent-Meridian High School in Kent, Washington. Attended WSU 1962-1964. General Studies major.

Henrickson, Keith R.
No information available.

Hostikka, Richard A.
Born January 24, 1942 in Yacolt, Washington. Graduated 1959 from Battle Ground High School in Battle Ground, Washington. Transferred from Clark College in Vancouver, Washington, and attended WSU 1962-1964. Physical Education major.

Houck, Stephen C.
Born March 21, 1947 in Seattle. Graduated 1965 from Bainbridge Island High School, Bainbridge Island, Washington. Attended WSU 1965-1966.

Hyatt, George Jackson
Born October 6, 1946 in Ft. Meade, Maryland. Graduated 1964 from Lakes High School in Tacoma, Washington. Attended WSU 1964-1965.

Lang, Timothy Michael – Army
Born August 1, 1937 in Yakima, Washington. Graduated 1955 from Gonzaga Preparatory High School in Spokane, Washington. Attended WSU 1956-1960, graduating May 29, 1960 with a B.A. in Geography. Helicopter pilot shot down and killed in Vietnam.

Logan, Jacob Drummand
Born October 24, 1940 in Oak Park, Illinois. Graduated 1958 from West Seattle High School. Attended WSU 1958-1962, graduating June 3, 1962 with a B.A. in Business Administration.

Masterson, Michael J.
No information available.

McHugo, Donald Lyle
Born March 6, 1935 in Spokane, Washington. Graduated 1952 from Central Valley High School in Greenacres, Washington. Attended WSU 1952-1953. Business Administration major.

Murdock, Michael G.
Born August 5, 1946 in Denver. Graduated 1964 from Freeman High School in Freeman, Washington. Attended WSU 1964-1965.

Nelson, David L.
Born November 10, 1943 in Seattle. Graduated 1962 from Queen Anne High School in Seattle. Attended WSU 1962-1963. Business Administration major.

Nelson, Lewis Charles
Born December 31, 1943 in Seattle. Graduated 1962 from Chief Sealth High School in Seattle. Attended WSU 1962-1966. General Studies major.

Neth, Danny Alvin
Born June 6, 1938 in Osage City, Kansas. Graduated 1957 from Columbia High School in Richland, Washington. Transferred from Yakima Valley Junior College and Central Washington College to attend WSU during spring semester 1960. Physical Education major.

Pearson, Robert Harvey
Born August 20, 1942 in Everett, Washington. Graduated 1960 from Marysville High School in Marysville, Washington. Attended WSU 1960-1964, graduating May 31, 1964 with a B.A. in Political Science.

Powers, John Robert
Born February 17, 1947 in Portland, Oregon. Graduated 1965 from Rainier Beach High School in Seattle. Attended WSU 1965-1966.

Prentice, Kenneth M.

Born May 26, 1946 in Greenville, Ohio. Graduated 1964 from Curtis High School in Tacoma, Washington. Attended WSU in 1964-1965.

Ray, Ronald Edwin

Born March 15, 1942 in Oakland, California. Graduated 1960 from Central Valley High School in Veradale, Washington. Attended WSU 1960-1965. Prelaw major.

Shriner, Thomas John

Born May 7, 1945 in Colville, Washington. Graduated 1963 from Kettle Falls High School in Kettle Falls, Washington. Attended WSU 1963-1968, graduating June 9, 1968 with a B.S. in Mining Engineering.

Shultz, David Joel

Born January 2, 1947 in Red Bank, New Jersey. Graduated 1965 from West Seattle High School. Attended WSU 1965-1967.

Starkel, Max Paul

Born September 25, 1934 in Lewistown, Montana. Graduated 1952 from Puyallup (Washington) High School. Attended WSU 1952-1958, graduating June 1, 1958 with a B.S. in Chemistry.

Steinbrunner, Donald Thomas

Born April 5, 1932 in Bellingham, Washington. Graduated 1949 from Mt. Baker High School in Deming, Washington. Attended WSU 1949-1953, graduating February 4, 1954 with a B.S. in Physical Education.

Sullivan, John Anthony

Born April 7, 1948 in Bremen, Germany. Graduated 1966 from Seattle Preparatory High School. Attended WSU 1966-1967.

Trimble, Larry Allen

Born March 6, 1947 in Colfax, Washington. Graduated 1965 from Oakesdale High School. Attended WSU 1965-1969, graduating June 8, 1969 with a B.A. in Business Administration.

Weber, Wiltse Lee

Born December 20, 1943 in Tacoma, Washington. Graduated 1962 from Curtis High School in Tacoma. Transferred from Western Baptist Bible College and Olympic College in Bremerton, Washington, to attend WSU 1966-1968, graduating with a B.S. in Police Science June 9, 1968.

Weightman, Gregg E.

Born October 4, 1947 in Spokane, Washington. Graduated 1965 from Tekoa High School in Tekoa, Washington. Transferred from Spokane Junior College and attended WSU 1966-1968.

Worthington, Richard C.

Born March 19, 1946 in Seattle. Graduated 1964 from Bothell High School in Bothell, Washington. Attended WSU 1964-1966. Fine Arts major.

Wright, Robert F.

Born June 8, 1944 in Bremerton, Washington. Graduated 1962 from West Bremerton High School. Transferred from Olympic College in Bremerton to attend WSU spring semester 1964. Business Administration major.

Zacher, Lyle David.

Attended WSU fall semester 1963.

1991 PERSIAN GULF WAR

Hedeen, Eric D. – Air Force

Born December 1, 1963. Graduated 1982 from Wenatchee High School in Wenatchee, Washington. Attended WSU 1982-1987, graduating May 9, 1987 with a B.S. in Architectural Studies, Cum Laude, and Bachelor of Architecture, Cum Laude. Killed in Action in the Persian Gulf War, February 2, 1991.

ENDNOTES

Foreword

1. Brokaw, Tom *The Greatest Generation Speaks: Letters and Reflections.* New York: Random House, 1999, p. 49.

2. Morrill Act, *United States Statutes at Large*, Vol. 12, Chapter 80, Sec. 4, p. 504.

3. For information on compulsory military training and the ROTC at WSC/ WSU see George A. Frykman's *Creating the People's University, 1890-1990.* Pullman: Washington State University Press, 1990, especially pages 181-183; and William L. Stimson's *Going to Washington State: A Century of Student Life.* Pullman: Washington State University Press, 1989. Murrow's time as a WSC student is vividly portrayed in Joseph R. Persico's *Edward R. Murrow: An American Original.* New York: McGraw-Hill, 1988, chapters 4 and 5.

World War II Case Studies

Ida Katherine Achre (Chew)

1. Records on file in the Office of the Registrar, Washington State University.

2. Records reviewed at the National Personnel Records Center (Military Records) in St. Louis.

3. Personal oral history interview with the author, October 24, 2000 and on file with the Archives Section of the WSU Libraries.

Dale W. Aldrich

1. Records on file in Office of the Registrar, Washington State University.

2. Hipperson, Carol Edgemon. *The Belly Gunner.* Brookfield: Twenty-First Century Books, p. 15.

3. Ibid, p. 26.

4. Ibid, pp. 31-32.

5. Ibid, p. 34.

6. Portions of the remaining "Dale Aldrich Story" excerpted, with permission, from the book *The Belly Gunner* referenced above, pp. 51-122.

7. Records reviewed at the National Personnel Records Center (Military Records) St. Louis.

Elizabeth L. Anderson

1. Records on file in the Office of the Registrar, Washington State University.

2. *Tacoma News Tribune*, November 21, 1943.

Emil S. Bitar

1. Records on file in the Office of the Registrar, Washington State University.

2. *The Spokesman-Review*, November 11, 1943.

3. Records reviewed at the National Personnel Records Center, (Military Records), St. Louis.

Robert V. Bowler

1. Records on file in the Office of the Registrar, Washington State University.

2. Excerpted from records reviewed at the National Personnel Records Center (Military Records) in St. Louis.

3. Ibid.

George B. Brain

1. Records reviewed at the National Personnel Records Center (Military Records), in St. Louis.

2. Private records of Lt. George Brain, dated March 3, 1945.

3. Records reviewed at the National Personnel Records Center (Military Records) in St. Louis.

Arthur Brunstad

1. *Memoirs of a Norwegian Emigrant* by Arthur Brunstad, unpublished.

2. Records on file in Office of the Registrar, Washington State University.

3. Army records reviewed at the National Personnel Records Center (Military Records) in St. Louis.

Archie M. Buckley

1. Military records reviewed at the National Personnel Records Center (Military Records) in St. Louis.

2. Ibid.

3. Fry, Richard B. *The Crimson and the Gray: 100 Years with the WSU Cougars*. Pullman: Washington State University Press, 1989.

4. The *Chinook* yearbook, 31st edition, published by the Associated Students of Washington State College, 1930.

5. Personal interview with Colonel Robert Carey (Ret.), June 19, 2000 (also see Col. Robert Carey's story in this book).

Leo K. Bustad

1. Records on file in Office of the Registrar, Washington State University.

2. Chant, Christopher. *Gurkha: The Illustrated History of an Elite Fighting Force*. New York: Blandford Press, 1985.

3. Excerpted from Capt. Leo K. Bustad's military records stored in the National Personnel Records Center (Military Records) in St. Louis.

4. Excerpted from a personal oral history interview with the author, September 13, 1996 and on file with the Archives Section of the Washington State University Libraries.

5. Bustad, Leo K. *Compassion: Our Last Great Hope*. Renton, Washington: Delta Society, 1990, page xxii.

6. Personal oral history interview with the author, September 13, 1996, and on file with the Archives Section of the WSU Libraries.

7. Data from the citation honoring Dr. Leo K. Bustad with the WSU Regents Distinguished Alumnus Award in 1987.

Robert H. Carey

1. General Orders Number 307, Headquarters Ninth Air Force, December 31, 1944.

2. Records on file in Office of the Registrar, Washington State University.

3. *Spokane Pilot*, an oral history interview on March 28, 1996 with Colonel Robert H. Carey, United States Air Force, Retired. Conducted by Randall Johnson and filed with the Eastern Washington State Historical Society and the Archives Section of the Washington State University Libraries.

James R. Carter

1. Records on file in the Office of the Registrar, Washington State University. Letter to the author from the Records Procedures Branch, Directorate of Customer Assistance, Department of the Air Force, Headquarters Air Force Personnel Center, Randolph AFB Texas, January 20, 1997.

2. Letters to the author, etc.

3. *The Pullman Herald*, February 11, 1944.

4. *Spokane Daily Chronicle*, September 15, 1944.

5. *Spokane Daily Chronicle*, February 5, 1945.

6. *The Spokesman-Review*, February 10, 1945.

Asa "Ace" V. Clark Jr.

1. The 1938-1941 *Chinook* college yearbooks, published by the Associated Students of Washington State College.

2. Records on file in Office of the Registrar, Washington State University.

3. Personal oral history interview with the author, May 18, 2001, and on file with the Archives Section of the Washington State University Libraries.

4. Ibid.

5. *Spokane Daily Chronicle*, September 9, 1944.

D. Girard Clark

1. Records on file in the Office of the Registrar, Washington State University.

2. Personal oral history interview with the author, February 22, 2001, and on file with the Archives Section of the Washington State University Libraries.

Alfred "Bud" Coppers

1. Records on file in the Office of the Registrar, Washington State University.

2. Coppers, A. B. *The Untold Story*, unpublished mimeograph on file with the Archives Section of the Washington State University Libraries.

3. Ibid.

4. Army records reviewed at the National Personnel Records Center (Military Records) in St. Louis.

5. Personal oral history interview with the author, July 21, 2003, and on file with the Archives Section of the Washington State University Libraries.

Edna L. Cox

1. Records on file in the Office of the Registrar, Washington State University.

2. The *Chinook*, published by the Associated Students of Washington State College, 1931.

3. Personal oral history interview with the author, November 2, 1997. Transcription of the interview now on file with the Archives Section of the Washington State University Libraries.

4. *Seattle Post Intelligencer*, July 17, 1942.

David G. Davis

1. Records on file in the Office of the Registrar, Washington State University.

2. Records reviewed at the National Personnel Records Center (Military Records) in St. Louis.

3. News release from Headquarters, Ninth Air Force, European Theatre of Operations, Public Relations Office, August 20, 1944.

4. Records reviewed at the National Personnel Records Center (Military Records), St. Louis.

5. *Wenatchee World*, November 21, 1996.

Leon W. Ellsworth

1. Records on file in the Office of the Registrar, Washington State University.

2. *The Spokesman-Review*, April 17, 1945

3. Records received from the Department of the Navy, Bureau of Naval Personnel, Washington, D.C.

Harry E. Goldsworthy

1. Goldsworthy Family Memoirs, unpublished, provided to the author by Harry E. Goldsworthy.

2. Records on file in the Office of the Registrar, Washington State University.

3. Excerpted from personal oral history interview with the author, July 11, 1997, and on file with the Archives Section of the WSU Libraries.

4. Ibid.

5. Records reviewed at the National Personnel Records Center (Military Records) in St. Louis.

Robert F. Goldsworthy

1. Personal oral history interview with the author, December 11, 1996, in Spokane, Washington.

2. Goldsworthy, Robert F. *Our Last Mission*, unpublished WWII Memoirs,

1948, on file with the Archives Section of the Washington State University Libraries.

3. Ibid.

4. Ibid.

5. Ibid.

6. Records reviewed at the National Personnel Records Center (Military Records) in St. Louis.

7. Ibid.

8. *The Spokesman-Review*, October 11, 1997.

C. Ross Greening

1. The *Chinook* yearbook, 37th edition, published by the Associated Students of Washington State College, 1936.

2. Details gleaned from Colonel Greening's memoirs and corroborated by many sources, including Ted W. Lawson's book *Thirty Seconds Over Tokyo*, New York: Random House, 1943.

Carl W. Hall

1. Hall, Carl W. *99th Infantry Division, the Checkerboard Division: Infantry S-2 at the Front in WWII*, unpublished.

2. Ambrose, Stephen E. *Citizen Soldiers*, New York: Simon & Schuster, 1977.

3. Records reviewed at the National Personnel Records Center (Military Records) in St. Louis.

4. Records on file in the President's Office, Washington State University.

Jack D. Holsclaw

1. Records on file in the Office of the Registrar, Washington State University.

2. News release published in the *Portland Oregonian*, July 22, 1944. (A similar story appeared in *The Spokesman-Review*.)

3. Military records reviewed at the National Personnel Records Center (Military Records) in St. Louis.

4. Personal oral history interview with the author, February 10, 1998, in the Saddlebrook Resort Community, near Tucson, Arizona, and on file in the Archives Section of the Washington State University Libraries.

5. *Liberty Magazine*, March 10, 1945, pp. 13-14.

6. Cooper, C. and Cooper, A. *Tuskegee's Heroes*. Osceola, Wisconsin: Motorbooks International, 1996, p. 111.

Randall A. Johnson

1. Records on file in the Office of the Registrar, Washington State University.

2. Personal oral history interview with the author, March 17, 1997, and on file with the Archives Section of the Washington State University Libraries.

3. Ibid.

Robert L. Loeffelbein

1. Records on file in the Office of the Registrar, Washington State University.

2. Loeffelbein, Robert L. "I Was There," a young sailor's log of the occupation of Japan.

Russell A. Long

1. Records in the Office of the Registrar, Washington State University.

2. Records reviewed at the National Personnel Records Center (Military Records), St. Louis.

3. Long, Russell A. "Memories and Stories," unpublished memoirs, on file with the Archives Section of the WSU Libraries.

4. Records reviewed at the National Personnel Records Center (Military Records), St. Louis.

Naomi M. McCracken

1. Data reviewed at the National Personal Records Center (Military Records) in St. Louis.

2. Ibid.

3. Personal correspondence and interview with Colonel McCracken, 1997.

4. The 1977-1984 *Chinook* college yearbooks, published by the Associated Students of Washington State University.

Loren G. McCollom

1. Records on file in the Office of the Registrar, Washington State University.

2. This citation and others that follow received from the Records Procedures Branch, Directorate of Customer Assistance, Department of the Air Force, Randolph Air Force Base, Texas, under the Privacy Act of 1974.

3. Greening, C. Ross. *Not As Briefed: From the Doolittle Raid to a German Stalag*. Pullman, Washington State University Press, 2001, p. 180.

4. *Seattle Post-Intelligencer*, May 29, 1945.

Clayton H. Mickelsen

1. Records on file in the Office of the Registrar, Washington State University.

2. *Life Magazine*, March 2, 1942, p. 51.

3. Whitman, John W. "The Last U.S. Horse Cavalry Charge." *Military History Magazine*, June 1995, p. 42.

4. Arburua, Joseph M. "Narrative of the Veterinary Profession in California." San Francisco: California Veterinary Medical Association, 1966, pp. 337-339.

5. Ibid.

Robert L. Miller

1. Records on file in the Office of the Registrar, Washington State University.

2. Excerpted from personal oral history interview with the author, October 24, 2003, and on file with the Archives Section of the WSU Libraries.

Douglas A. Munro

1. Excerpted from the September 1992 issue of the *Coast Guard Commandant's Bulletin*, pp. 22-25.

2. Transcripts of Douglas A. Munro's permanent academic records received from the Registrars of Cle Elum High School and Central Washington University.

3. *NKC Tribune*, Cle Elum, Washington, May 16, 1996.

4. Douglas A. Munro's service record, provided by the U.S. Coast Guard historian.

5. *The Spokesman-Review*, October 4, 1942, and *The Stars and Stripes*, September 25-October 1, 1995.

6. Guadalcanal story condensed, with permission, from "Semper Paratus: Douglas Munro" by Coast Guard historian, Dr. Robert M. Browning Jr., published in *Naval History*, Winter 1992, and the *Coast Guard Commandant's Bulletin*, September 1992.

7. From a personal letter to Doug Munro's parents from Lieutenant Commander D. H. Dexter, U.S. Coast Guard, dated October 2, 1942 in Guadalcanal, in the British Solomon Islands.

8. Coombs, Janice. "The Death of Doug Munro," published in the June 15, 1943 issue of *The Shield*, Vol. 2, No. 12.

Edith F. Munro

1. Kruska, E. J. "A Veterans' Day Salute to a World War II SPAR – Edith Fairey Munro." *The Coast Guard Reservist*, November 1994, pp. 14-15.

Jeanne Lewellen Norbeck

1. Keil, Sally VanWagenen. *Those Wonderful Women in Their Flying Machines: The Unknown Heroines of World War II*. New York: Rawson, Wade Publishers, Inc., 1979, p. 4.

2. Holm, Jeanne. *Women In The Military: An Unfinished Revolution*. Novato, California: Presidio Press, 1982, p. 315.

3. Keil, Sally VanWagenen. *Those Wonderful Women in Their Flying Machines: The Unknown Heroines of World War II*. New York: Rawson, Wade Publishers, Inc., 1979, p. 5.

4. Records on file in the Office of the Registrar, Washington State University.

5. Seymour, Dawn, et. al. *Women Air Force Service Pilots, WWII: In Memoriam*. Denton: Texas Women's University Press, 1996, p. 26.

6. Pateman, Lt. Col. Yvonne C. *Women Who Dared: American Female Test Pilots, Flight-Test Engineers, and Astronauts, 1912-1996*. New York: Norstahr Publishing, 1997, pp. 42-46.

7. Granger, Byrd H. *On Final Approach*. Scottsdale: Falconer Publishing Co., 1991, p. 425.

Glenn E. Oman

1. Records on file in the Office of the Registrar, Washington State University.

2. All military information from a personal oral history interview with the author, October 20, 2000, and on file in the Archives Section of the WSU Libraries.

Eugene "Pat" Patterson

1. Records on file in the Office of the Registrar, Washington State University.

2. Records reviewed at the National Personnel Records Center (Military Records) in St. Louis.

3. Personal oral history interview with the author, September 13, 1996, and on file with the Archives Section of the WSU Libraries.

Scotty Rohwer

1. Records on file in the Office of the Registrar, Washington State University.

2. *Spokane Daily Chronicle*, January 27, 1945.

3. Hengen, Nona. *Palouse Pilot*. Spangle, Washington: Palouse Press, 1994.

Ira Christian Rumburg

1. Stimson, William L. *Going to Washington State: A Century of Student Life*. Pullman, Washington: Washington State University Press, 1989.

2. The *Chinook*, published by the Associated Students of Washington State College, 1938.

3. Army records reviewed at the National Personnel Records Center, St. Louis.

4. Personal letter from Chief of Staff John Keating to Mrs. Naomi Rumburg, January 27, 1945.

5. Personal letter from Captain Robert D. Campbell to Dr. J. Fred Bohler, August 9, 1945.

6. Personal letter from Mrs. L. A. Rumburg to Dr. E. O. Holland, President of Washington State College, May 15, 1945.

Jerry M. Sage

1. Sage, Colonel Jerry. *SAGE*. Wayne, Pennsylvania: Miles Standish Press, 1985.

2. *The Seattle Times*, May 27, 1987.

3. Records in the Office of the Registrar, Washington State University.

4. Stimson, William L. *Going to Washington State: A Century of Student Life*. Pullman, Washington. Washington State University Press, 1989 pp. 97-107.

5. Ibid.

6. The remainder of this Sage saga is excerpted from Sage's book, *SAGE*, published in 1985 by the Miles Standish Press.

Howard A. Scholz

1. *The Seattle Times*, October 30, 1944.

Toll Seike

1. Private correspondence from Benjamin Seike (Toll's brother), June 17, 1997.

2. Hirabayashi, Gordon. "Growing Up American in Washington" *Washington Comes of Age: The State in the National Experience*. Pullman: Washington State University Press, 1992 pp. 22-23.

3. Tanaka, Chester. *Go for Broke: A Pictorial History of the Japanese American 100th Infantry Battalion and the 442nd Regimental Combat Team*. San Francisco: Presidio, 1982.

4. Fukuhara, Francis M. *Uncommon American Patriots*. Published by the Nisei Veterans Committee, Seattle, Washington, 1991.

Smawley Brothers

1. Records on file in the Office of the Registrar, Washington State University.

2. *WSU Week*, a weekly newspaper published by Washington State University, April 28, 2000.

3. Bjorge, Gary J. *Merrill's Marauders: Combined Operation in Northern Burma in 1944*. Combat Studies Institute, Fort Leavenworth, 1996.

4. *Merrill's Marauders, February–May 1944*. Center of Military History, United States Army. Washington, D.C., 1990.

Allan H. Smith

1. Washington State University News Bureau files.

2. Robert Ackerman, WSU Department of Anthropology, 1999.

Shirley K. Stewart

1. Records on file in the Office of the Registrar, Washington State University.

2. *Lewis County Senior Center* magazine, April 2001.

3. Personal correspondence, March 15, 2001.

Glenn Terrell

1. Personal correspondence between the author and Glenn Terrell, confirmed though military records.

2. Ambrose, Steven E. *The Good Fight: How World War II Was Won*. New York: Simon & Schuster, 2001, p. 48.

3. Bowden, Mark. *Our Finest Day – D-Day: June 6, 1944*. San Francisco: Chronicle Books LLC, 2002, p. 22.

4. *WSU Hilltopics*, June 1985.

5. Ibid.

Jerry Williams

1. Personal interview with Mrs. Jerry Williams, July 10, 2001.

2. Records reviewed at the National Personnel Records Center (Military Records) in St. Louis.

3. The 1947-1950 *Chinook* yearbooks, published by the Associated Students of Washington State College.

4. Fry, Richard B. *The Crimson and The Gray: 100 Years With the WSU Cougars*. Pullman: WSU Press, 1989, p. 188.

5. *The Spokesman-Review*, January 1, 1998.

6. Ibid.

7. Personal interview with Mrs. Jerry Williams, July 10, 2001.

John H. Wills

1. Records on file in the Office of the Registrar, Washington State University.

2. Excerpted from a personal oral history interview with the author, July 19, 2000 and on file with the Archives Section of the Washington State University Libraries.

3. "Iran in Wartime." *The National Geographic Magazine*, Volume. LXXXVIII No. 4, October 1945.

Going To The Front With Class

1. Ambrose, Stephen E. *Citizen Soldiers*, New York: Simon & Schuster, 1997.

2. Ibid.

3. Glotzbach, Bob. *Fortunate Soldiers: Or Soldiers of Fortune*. Glen Ellen, California: Regeneration Resources, 1997.

4. Personal correspondence from Edward A. Bergh, National President, 11th Armored Division Association, and chair of the ASTP reunion held at WSU on Veterans Day 1997. During the campus ceremony the nine KIAs were honored with their names engraved on the WSU Veterans Memorial. January 9, 1997; March 9, 1998; October 31, 1998; January 7, 1999; May 8, 1999.

5. Personal correspondence dated March 29, 2001 from William "Bill" Bakamis, member of the Junior ROTC Class of 1943.

6. Records reviewed at the National Personnel Records Center (Military Records) in St. Louis.

World War II & Korean War Case Studies

Ace Allen

1. Records on file in the Office of the Registrar, Washington State University.

2. *Pullman Herald*, September 9, 1950.

3. Letter from Secretary of the Army to Mrs. Allen, September 25, 1950 provided to the author by the National Personnel Records Center in St. Louis.

4. *Spokane Daily Chronicle*, September 7, 1950.

James B. Baker

1. Records on file in the Office of the Registrar, Washington State University.

2. *Powwow*, July 1952, and Army form DA 639–Recommendation For Award–Heroism, dated March 12, 1952.

3. Personal correspondence with James Baker, June 5, 2001.

Dale C. Gough

1. Records on file in the Office of the Registrar, Washington State University.

2. Records reviewed at the Department of the Navy, Bureau of Naval Personnel, Washington, D. C.

3. *Pullman Herald*, September 7, 1953.

John F. Kinney

1. Records on file in the Office of the Registrar, Washington State University.

2. Reprinted, with permission, from: Kinney, John F. *Wake Island Pilot*. Washington: Brassey's, 1995.

3. Ibid.

4. Ibid.

5. *Spokane Daily Chronicle*, May 19, 1942.

6. *WSU Hilltopics*. Washington State University, October/November 1986.

7. Reprinted, with permission, from: Kinney, John F. *Wake Island Pilot*. Washington: Brassey's, 1995.

8. Ibid.

9. Records reviewed at the National Personnel Records Center (Military Records) in St. Louis.

Leo R. Pierson

1. Records on file in the Office of the Registrar, Washington State University.

2. Records received from the Department of the Navy, Bureau of Naval Personnel, Washington, D.C.

3. Ibid.

4. *Spokane Daily Chronicle*, May 24, 1953.

Dallas P. Sartz

1. Records reviewed at the National Personnel Records Center (Military Records) in St. Louis.

2. Ibid.

3. Records obtained from the WSU News Bureau.

Korean War and Vietnam War Case Studies

Donald L. Bauer

1. Records on file in the Office of the Registrar, Washington State University.

2. *The Spokesman-Review*, May 17, 1953.

3. Personal correspondence with the author and Lt. Col. Bauer, June 11, 1998.

Keith A. Smith

1. Personal oral history interview with the author, April 16, 1997, and on file with the Archives Section of the WSU Libraries.

2. Records on file in the Office of the Registrar, Washington State University.

3. Records provided to the author by the U.S. Marine Corps.

Vietnam Case Studies

Harold B. Adams

1. Records on file in the Office of the Registrar, Washington State University.

2. Biography provided by the United States Air Force, Secretary of the Air Force, Office of Public Affairs, Washington, D.C.

3. Fredriksen, John C. *Warbirds: An Illustrated Guide to U.S. Military Aircraft, 1915-2000*. Santa Barbara: ABC-CLIO, 1999, and Green, William and Swanborough, Gordon. Observer's Directory of Military Aircraft. New York: Arco Publishing, Inc., 1982.

4. This and subsequent medal citations reviewed at the National Personnel Records Center (Military Records) in St. Louis.

5. Ibid.

John M. Fabian

1. Records on file in the Office of the Registrar, Washington State University.

2. Records reviewed at the National Personnel Records Center (Military Records) in St. Louis.

3. Excepted from a personal oral history interview with the author, October 23, 1999, and on file with the Archives Section of the Washington State University Libraries.

4. Ibid.

5. Ibid.

Felix M. Fabian Jr.

1. Records on file in the Office of the Registrar, Washington State University.

2. Records reviewed at the National Personnel Records Center (Military Records) in St. Louis.

3. Personal oral history interview of Colonel John M. Fabian with the author, October 23, 1999, and on file with the Archives Section of the Washington State University Libraries.

William H. Fabian

1. Records on file in the Office of the Registrar, Washington State University.

2. Records reviewed at the National Personnel Records Center (Military Records) in St. Louis.

3. Ibid.

James P. Fleming

1. Records on file in the Office of the Registrar, Washington State University.

2. Department of the Air Force: USAF Civil Air Patrol Northeast Liaison Region, McGuire AFB, New Jersey, August 1, 1990.

3. *Medal of Honor Recipients 1863-1973: In the Name of the Congress of the United States.* Printed for the use of the Committee on Veterans' Affairs. U.S. Government Printing Office, Washington, D.C., 1973.

David A. Guzman

1. Personal interview with the author, April 2002.

2. Medal citations listed from records received from the National Personnel Records Center (Military Records), St. Louis.

Milton Hunter

1. Records on file in the Office of the Registrar, Washington State University.

2. Biography provided by the U.S. Army Corps of Engineers, South Pacific Division, San Francisco.

3. *Hilltopics*, April/May 1991. Office of News and Information Services, WSU news release, August 16, 1991.

4. Record obtained from the WSU News Bureau.

Dennis B. Jones

1. Records on file in the Office of the Registrar, Washington State University.

2. Personal oral history interview with the author, September 25, 2002, and on file with the Archives Section of the WSU Libraries.

3. Record provided by USAF Records Procedures Branch, Directorate of Customer Assistance, Randolph AFB, Texas.

4. Personal oral history interview with the author, September 25, 2002, and on file with the Archives Section of the WSU Libraries.

Robert D. Russ

1. Records on file in the Office of the Registrar, Washington State University.

2. Biography, United States Air Force, supplied by the Secretary of the Air Force, Office of Public Affairs, Washington, D.C.

3. All citations from records supplied by the Department of the Air Force, Records Procedures Branch, Directorate of Customer Assistance.

Operations Just Cause (Panama) and Desert Storm Case Studies

Kim Michelle Chilberg

1. Army records reviewed at the National Personnel Records Center (Military Records), St. Louis.

2. Personal oral history interview with the author, November 13, 1998, Fort Ord, California, and on file with the Archives Section of the WSU Libraries.

Barbara Doornink

1. The 1970-1973 *Chinook* yearbooks, published by the Associated Students of Washington State University.

2. Biography of Brigadier General Barbara Doornink provided by the U.S. Army.

Eric D. Hedeen

1. Records on file in the Office of the Registrar, Washington State University.

2. Records received from the Department of the Air Force, Headquarters Air Force Personnel Center, Randolph Air Force Base, Texas.

3. Ibid.

Robert W. Higgins

1. Records on file in the Office of the Registrar, Washington State University.

2. Personal oral history interview with the author, July 21, 1997, and on file with the Archives Section of the WSU Libraries.

3. Records reviewed at the National Personnel Records Center (Military Records) in St. Louis.

4. Ibid.

R. Dale Storr

1. Records on file in the Office of the Registrar, Washington State University.

2. Personal oral history interview with the author, October 4, 2002, and on file with the Archives Section of the WSU Libraries.

3. Ibid.

4. Records provided by the Department of the Air Force, Records Procedures Branch, Directorate of Customer Assistance, Headquarters Air Force Personnel Center, Randolph Air Force Base, Texas.

5. Record received from the Department of the Air Force, Headquarters, Air Reserve Personnel Center, Denver, June 1, 1998.

Appendix II

Mary B. Packingham

1. Landeen, William M. *E. O. Holland and the State College of Washington 1916-1944*. Published by Washington State College, 1958, pp. 116-118. In his book, Landeen apparently misspelled the name, calling the college nurse Mary Buckingham. The correct identity was substantiated in the articles and obituaries in the two newspapers cited, as well as the Whitman and Garfield County Directories, 1916-17 and 1917-18 issues, published by R. L. Polk and Company of Seattle.

2. Ibid, p. 117.

3. *Pullman Herald*, November 1, 1918 (WSU Archives).

4. Jordan, Edwin O. *Epidemic Influenza: A Survey*. Chicago: American Medical Association, 1927, p. 214.

5. *The New Encyclopedia Britannica*. Chicago, Volume 26, 1991.

6. Burnet, F. M. "Portraits of Viruses: Influenza A" in *Intervirology 11*, 1979, p. 203.

7. Bryan, E. A. *Historical Sketch of the State College of Washington, 1890-1925*. Inland-American Printing Co., Spokane, Washington, 1928, p. 438.

RELATED READINGS

• Warren, James R. *The War Years: A Chronicle of Washington State in World War II*, Seattle: University of Washington Press, 2001. In *The War Years,* James Warren (WSC '49) chronicles the role of the state of Washington in World War II. His book documents the heroism and gallantry of all of the Medal of Honor recipients from the state, as well as a comprehensive list of Washington State's WWII war dead. Warren served with the 42nd Rainbow Division in the ETO. He was wounded and captured by the Germans during the Battle of the Bulge. The American 69th Division freed him from prison on April 25, 1945. After the war, he enrolled at Washington State College and earned a bachelor's degree with honors in 1949. He served as a radio news announcer while working on advanced degrees at the University of Washington. In 1969, Dr. Warren was named the first president of Edmonds Community College.

• Greening, C. Ross *Not As Briefed: From the Doolittle Raid to a German Stalag,* Pullman: Washington State University Press, 2001. *Not As Briefed* are the memoirs of Colonel C. Ross Greening (WSC '36) published 44 years after his death. They chronicle his role on the famous 1942 "Doolittle Raid" on Tokyo and his experiences as a bomber pilot over North Africa, Sicily, and Italy. Shot down over Mt. Vesuvius, Greening was wounded, captured, and spent the rest of the war in various POW Camps. Greening was a consummate artist, and his book is illustrated with more than a hundred of his color paintings, drawings, and photographs.

• Kinney, John F. *Wake Island Pilot: A World War II Memoir*, Washington, D. C.: Brassey's, 1995. In *Wake Island Pilot*, Marine Brigadier General John F. Kinney (WSC '36) details the defense of and ultimate surrender of Wake Island, his capture by the Japanese, and his experiences as a POW for three and a half years in various enemy prison camps. He finally escaped and, with the help of friendly Chinese, made it back to freedom. He remained in the service and had a storied career in the Marines.

• Sage, Jerry *SAGE,* Wayne, Pennsylvania: Miles Standish Press, 1985. In this book, Colonel Jerry Sage (WSC '38) recounts his experiences as the OSS guerilla leader and saboteur who fought behind the lines against the Nazis in WWII. After his capture, his many and persistent attempts to escape landed him in solitary confinement so often that he was nicknamed "The Cooler King." His many escape attempts were featured in the popular WWII movie *The Great Escape*.

• Hengen, Nona *Palouse Pilot*, Spangle, Washington: Palouse Press, 1994. *Palouse Pilot* follows the combat career of Scotty Rohwer (WSC '41), a farm boy from Spangle, Washington, and a B-25 bomber pilot in World War II. His 67 missions involved attacking retreating Germans in northern Italy, and supporting the Allied landings in southern France.

• Ladd, Dean *Faithful Warriors: The Second Marine Division in the Pacific War*, Spokane: Teen-Aid Inc., 1993. This is a riveting account by Lieutenant Colonel Dean Ladd (WSC '48), a Marine Infantry officer who saw extensive combat in the Pacific at Guadalcanal, Tarawa, Saipan, and Tinian. He was wounded three times, the most seriously during the landing on Tarawa.

• Lewis, Flora *One of Our H-Bombs Is Missing*, New York: McGraw-Hill, 1967. On Monday, January 17, 1966, two U.S. military planes – a B-52 bomber and a KC-135 tanker – collided six miles above Palomares, Spain. They exploded, showering the earth and sea with debris, including four H-bombs. Three were recovered and one was lost. This book details the clean up on land and the hunt below the sea for the missing bomb. General Delmar E. Wilson (WSC '36) supervised the search that eventually snagged and recovered the bomb in the depths of the ocean.

• Rants, Hanford *My Memories of WWII*, Unpublished mimeograph, on file in the Archives Section of the WSU Libraries. In *My Memories of WWII*, Sergeant Hanford Rants (WSC '49) documents his 251 days and nights in combat on New Guinea and the Philippines. Rants served with the 34th

Regiment of the 24th Infantry Division, the same outfit that this author served with in Korea.

• Pateman, Yvonne C. ***Women Who Dared: American Female Test Pilots, Flight-test Engineers, and Astronauts, 1912-1996***, New York: Norstahr Publishing, 1997. This book by Lieutenant Colonel Yvonne Pateman records the history of American female test pilots, flight-test engineers, and astronauts from 1912-1996. The book contains the story of Jeanne Lewellen Norbeck (WSC '32).

• Hipperson, Carol E. ***The Belly Gunner***, Brookfield, Connecticut: Twenty First Century Books, 2001. This book traces the life of a young lad from Coulee City, Washington, from training in the states to an airbase in England, where he was assigned as a belly gunner in a B-17 bomber. Shot down and captured on January 22, 1943, Sgt. Dale Aldrich (WSC '41) spent the rest of the war as a prisoner in Stalag 17, a notorious camp. Many of the prison camp escapades he witnessed were made famous in a Hollywood movie titled *Stalag 17*.

• Wise, Kenneth C. ***Course of the "Hutch"***, unpublished mimeo-graph on file in the Archives Section of the WSU Libraries. *Course of the "Hutch"* by Coast Guard Lieutenant (J. G.) Kenneth Wise (WSC '42) is a 17-month log tracing the 74,000-mile journey of the USS *Hutchinson* from April 29, 1944 to October 2, 1945. The *Hutchinson* supported troop landings in New Guinea and Leyte, the Philippines.

• Elliott, Lawrence. **"1000 Men and a Baby,"** *Reader's Digest*, December 1994, pp. 49-54. "A Christmas Child." *American Legion Magazine*, December 1991, pp. 24-44. The early life of a WSU graduate was showcased in two national magazine articles and one made-for-TV movie. It all started in July 1953 in Korea as peace talks were just beginning. Some soldiers found a young infant abandoned in a trash pile near Inchon, Korea. The baby was thin, weak, and starving. His legs were burned and a rash covered most of his body. A call went out for help and was answered by a young Navy doctor from Spokane, Washington, Dr. Hugh C. Keenan. The baby survived and prospered because of the care of the doctor and the 1,000 or more seamen aboard ship. Dr. Keenan received clearance to adopt the baby, and was eventually helped through the passport and visa red tape with the assistance of then Vice President Richard Nixon. The young lad, now named Daniel Edward Keenan, was delivered into the arms of his new mother in Spokane, while the new father remained on duty on a hospital ship offshore in Korea. Young Daniel grew up in a loving family in Spokane and graduated from Gonzaga High School in 1971. He enrolled at WSU that fall as a communications major. He graduated in February 1977 and became a journalist, first with the *Grant County Journal* in Ephrata, Washington, and later in Spokane. Dan Keenan is not a veteran himself, but the military implications of his unique and heartwarming story make his story essential reading for all.

• ***Honor By Listening*** and ***Honor By Listening: The Next Stories 2000***, Two-volume booklet available through Eastmont High School, Wenatchee, Washington, and on file in the Archives Section of the WSU Libraries. These two volumes of transcribed interviews with military veterans also complement this study. Students from Eastmont High School in Wenatchee, Washington, compiled and printed transcripts of more than 90 interviews of veterans of World War II, Korea, and Vietnam. The interviewing project was done under the direction of Gene Sharratt (WSU '83), superintendent of the North Central Educational Service District in Wenatchee.

• DeRuwe, Milan. ***Who Were Milan and Bernie: The Journals of Milan DeRuwe, 1944-1946***, Mimeograph, 2001, on file in the Archives Section of the WSU Libraries. World War II Infantryman Milan F. DeRuwe (WSC '47) published an interesting journal detailing his military experiences starting July 18, 1944 through various ETO campaigns, the Battle of the Bulge, his stay in several military hospitals, and VE-Day. His journal ends with his Army discharge, marriage in August 1946, and return to WSC.

Index
(See Also Photo Index on Page viii)